Praise for *Shattered*

"From sunshine and roses to the darkest shadows in the grip of a madman, Debbie Puglisi Sharp tells her story of victory over horror and captivity. I read this with absolute concentration where no sound or duty dared interrupt. It is a classic in the true crime genre, but it is more than that—it hands a portion of power and belief in herself to every woman who reads it. I recommend it wholeheartedly!"

—Ann Rule

"This is true crime from the point of view of the victim, and reading it is an unforgettably intense experience."

—*Booklist*

"Riveting and disturbing."

—*Kirkus Reviews*

SHATTERED

Reclaiming a Life Torn Apart by Violence

Debra Puglisi Sharp
with Marjorie Preston

ATRIA BOOKS

New York London Toronto Sydney

ATRIA BOOKS
1230 Avenue of the Americas
New York, NY 10020

ISBN: 0-7432-2916-9
0-7434-4456-6 (Pbk)

First Atria Books trade paperback edition August 2004

10 9 8 7 6 5 4 3

ATRIA BOOKS is a trademark of Simon & Schuster, Inc.

For information regarding special discounts for bulk purchases,
please contact Simon & Schuster Special Sales at 1-800-456-6798
or business@simonandschuster.com

Manufactured in the United States of America

In memory of Nino,
the silent victim,
and Dr. Constance Dancu,
who gave me the courage to live as a survivor

Acknowledgments

It is my prayer that this account inspires crime victims to draw on their strength and move on, as I have done.

Love and thanks to my heroes, Melissa and Michael. They are survivors and continue to be my reason to live. My sincere gratitude to Jeremy Okrasinski and his family, who cared for Melissa when I could not.

"New Beginnings" is inscribed on our wedding rings. Bill Sharp and I love and support each other through good times and bad. Thank you, Bill, for just being you. Thanks also to my stepdaughter, Dorian, and her husband, Bill, who have supported Melissa, Michael, and me through the tough times.

No words can express my gratitude to each and every member of my family. Much love to Dad, my stepmothers Barb and Sue, my sisters Darlene and Jane, my brothers Robert and Gary, my sisters- and brothers-in-law, my nieces and nephews, my aunts and uncles.

I owe my life to 911 Enhancement, and I appreciate all the health professionals and law enforcement personnel who rushed to my aid. They are too numerous to mention.

I am indebted to the community for the Anthony Puglisi

Memorial Fund, the benefit held to help fund the continuing education of my children, and the financial aid provided through the Violent Crimes Compensation Board. I could not have made it without the assistance of my attorney, Bruce Hudson, and my financial adviser, Jeff Ickes.

The hundreds of cards and letters of love and support I received in the wake of the crime were deeply appreciated.

I would like to thank Judge Norman A. Barron, Detective Domenick Gregory, and the prosecutors Jim Ropp and Mark Conner for their endless hours of help in and out of the courtroom.

My thoughts and prayers continue for Donald Flagg's other victim, the woman identified in this book as Patricia Mann. He cannot hurt you anymore.

In the absence of Dr. Dancu, I was privileged to have ongoing mental health counseling with Dr. Sandra Duemmler and Dr. Jeffrey Faude. Their patience, understanding, and compassion were instrumental in my healing process.

I am blessed with many, many friends. Though I am not able to personally thank so many wonderful people in one small passage, please know who you are and how profoundly proud I am to be your friend.

I could not have told my story without my loyal writing partner, Marjorie Preston; our agent, Philip Spitzer; our editors Kim Meisner and Brenda Copeland; and publicist Louise Braverman. Thanks also to Valorie Jarrell, Donna Keegan, and Frank Garrity for their help.

In closing, I have one final message. Yes, Gene, I will always love roses!

Debra Puglisi Sharp

To Garland, my daughter, for whom I lived, and Quincy, my friend, who lived for me.

Marjorie Preston

April is the
cruellest month . . .
—*T. S. Eliot*

Preface

I WALK FROM the darkness of the garage into the darkness of his home, where shades and curtains are drawn, making it seem like night has fallen in the middle of the day.

I'm just blind without my glasses. I see nothing but shapes: shapes of furniture, shapes of things on the wall, a moving shape along a baseboard that is a cat. So he has cats, too.

His shape, broad and dark, is close behind.

I'm raw inside, and pain prods at my temple like a knifepoint. When he tugs at the quilt I go weak, knowing he'll discover that I've undone the cord. This makes him very unhappy, as I guessed it would. I suppose he decides I must atone. He pushes me to the floor, turns me over, yanks at my sweatpants, and rapes me again, the other way.

I know some people do this, but I've never. It hurts beyond hurting, which seems to make it even better for him; he puffs with excitement, till his hot breath wets my neck.

"Are you going to kill me?"

"Shut up."

He forces my jaw open, pressing the corners of my mouth until it snaps wide like a hinge. Just before he thrusts in the washcloth, I take a deep breath, as if I am going underwater. He must have planned this, I think, because everything is ready; now he is winding duct tape around my head, once, then twice, so I'll stay shut up.

When he blindfolds me, I think, absurdly, Well, that's silly. I'm just blind without my glasses.

He pulls the cord tight around my wrists, and my ankles, too, yanking hard so it digs into the flesh. Then he pushes me down a narrow hallway, cursing at me when I bump into the wall.

I hear the sound of an opening door, and he forces me to my knees, then my belly. I feel his boot on my back.

The tile is cold against my face. A bathroom. Even in this peculiar setting, with everything all nuts, my mind continues to click along, gathering information. I note this detail and that detail—the texture of the floor tiles and the rug, the sound of water rushing through the pipes. I log them, almost dispassionately.

I wonder what next.

Thankfully, nothing; he's going to leave me alone for a little while. But before he closes the door, he tosses a blanket over me. It makes it a lot harder to breathe under here.

Somewhere out there a phone rings, and after a few rings the machine clicks on. "Don?" A woman's voice. "Are you coming in to work tonight?" He doesn't pick up.

For brief intervals, no more than moments at a time, I am elsewhere. I'm in my garden, worrying the rosebushes, sifting the soil in my bare hands, wondering about pH and acidity, wondering if the poor things will survive my bumbling. I don't want them to die.

I'm not sleeping or passed out; if anything, I'm hyperaware, more alive than I've ever been. I feel the thinness of my skin and the way my bones fit together. In my veins I can hear the sound of my blood, and it sounds like the water running through those pipes, whooshing along.

I feel so breakable.

I want to scream, because I know there is someone else out there. Life is going on outside this house, and I can't believe I can't go out into it. Then I do hear screaming, screaming out loud, but it's him, the man in the next room. He fires a gun, and at the sound of the gunshot I shake so hard my body jerks up off the floor. He fires again, and something made of glass breaks.

Mom, I say inside, pleading, thinking I will be with her soon. *Mom.* Make it go easy for me. Make it not hurt.

SHATTERED

Prologue

WHY I SAVED the tape I can't begin to say, so I decide it must
have saved itself for me.

As I scoured the house for a blank audiocassette, I found it—
unmarked, tossed in an old shopping bag from some long-ago
Christmas. It's part of the limitless stuff you take when you move
from one house to another, stuff that may end up lost or discarded or simply relegated to a cardboard box in a dusty corner,
under tons of other stuff.

The tape player is on a low shelf under the TV. I pop in the
tape and push play, and the gooseflesh rises up on my arms. It's
Nino. He's talking on what must be an old answering machine
tape from years ago—way back in 1993, maybe '94. Amazing
that this is still around.

My breath stops in my throat. I sink to my knees, then sit
cross-legged on the floor by the tape player. I put my head down
and listen hard, feeling the vibrations of the words as they come
out of the speaker. When I turn up the volume, it's like he's
speaking right into my ear.

Nino.

As far as I can tell, it's a business call. That's how I date it—

1993. It must have been recorded then, because shortly afterward Nino switched from bulk paper sales to a career in funeral planning.

He speaks down low—or maybe it's the tape quality—so I can't hear a lot of the words. There's something in there about C-fold towels and rolls of waxed paper and paper bags by the gross and how he can get a better discount for quantity.

Back then he worked for Advance Paper and Chemical of Wilmington, and he sold all these janitorial products to big industrial firms as well as to small companies and mom-and-pops. He was good at it, made a good living for the time, and it was all due to his gregarious nature. Nino had an innate friendliness that just drew people to him and him to them. He was a natural salesman who leaned hard on his Italianness and that kind of blunt, humor-filled haggling to get people's respect and trust. It worked.

Of course, like most Italians, he especially loved selling to places where he could grab a bite to eat: restaurants, pizza places, sub shops. Those were his favorite stops, and he'd gladly find an excuse to linger for a while during the workday at some little roadside deli and order the biggest, sloppiest sub going, with lots of provolone and prosciutto and peppers and oil. Sometimes he'd take one wrapped for the road and share it with me when he got home. The man loved to eat: meat and potatoes, fried baloney sandwiches, and heaps and heaps of pasta.

It was an old joke between us. Nino had the vanity of a man who had always been attractive. In middle age, he watched with dismay as his waistline slowly expanded, but he could never curb that big appetite. And me, no matter what or how much I ate, I could never get up past 118 pounds.

Whatever he's talking about on the scratchy old tape—the this-and-that of business or a detail about a pending deal—the thrill for me is simply hearing his voice, a voice I haven't heard in more than a thousand days.

■ ■ ■

THERE WAS A TIME I would have been unnerved by this sudden encounter with my late husband. I might have felt angry or desolate. I might have fallen back into the dark, closed-in place I went to when he first died. Today, I'm amazed to realize that this feels only good: a moment of reunion, warm, like an unexpected clasp of hands. I catch a glimpse of myself in the glass door of the stereo cabinet, and I'm smiling.

I can't talk back to him, can't ask him the questions I've yearned to ask or tell him the things I think he'd like to know about our lives since he left us. I think he knows anyway. Somehow, putting one foot determinedly in front of the other, we've all of us—me and the kids—come through it. We've all learned how to be glad again, unself-consciously glad, and our thoughts of him are mostly good.

Hi, Nino, I tell him in my mind. I've been thinking about you so much. You are so welcome here.

On the tape, too, is a message from my mom.

"Hi, Debbie," she says. Her voice, always matter-of-fact, sounds softer, like it's wrapped in gauze. "I just wanted to wish you a happy Nurses Day. . . ."

I want to catch every sound, every pause and intake of breath. Unbelievable. How long has it been?

"Happy Nurses Day."

That was so like Mom, to notice a made-up holiday on the calendar and call just to acknowledge it. She was unerringly thoughtful. Not effusive and never sentimental, just thoughtful and nice.

Natalie Matilda Purse (divorced from my dad, she took back her maiden name after Darlene, the youngest of us, turned twenty-one, and she always called herself "Gnat," like the little bug) was not one to spend hours on the phone. Once she said what needed to be said, it was, "Well, I've got to hang up now." And off she'd go back to her treasured solitude, with her cats and her teapot and her crossword puzzles.

But she never lost touch with her kids, with Robert or Gary, with Darlene or with me. In a day or two she'd find a reason to call again, and we'd exchange the few words that were necessary to stay close and caught up.

We've missed both of you, I think, hoping my thoughts carry across from the place I am to the place—if it is a place—they now occupy. Nino, Mom, we never imagined we could miss you as long and as hard as we have. Nor did we know that one day it would all be okay again. We never thought it could.

Well, Mom, it's okay. Really okay for the first time in a long while.

Nino, the twins are doing so much better. You'd be proud to see them as they evolve out of that college kid thing into accomplished, responsible adults: Melissa with a good job at a bank, happy and engaged (yes, to Jeremy—it's lasted), Michael working hard and studying and feeling a whole lot better.

They're healing up, too, from all that happened. I know it would be incredibly important to you to know that. We're through the worst of it, out of the keenest part of the sorrow and into the life that comes after.

NINO AND I WERE married almost twenty-five years and were in fact just days from our silver anniversary when he died. We'd planned no big party; that was out of the question with both the kids in college. And we'd reluctantly decided that the second honeymoon we planned years and years ago—a twenty-fifth anniversary trip to Hawaii—would have to wait till the next big milestone ("Maybe the thirtieth," said Nino).

I managed to be okay with the change in plans, and Nino did come up with a great consolation prize: a pair of antique diamond earrings. The fact that he bought them secondhand from a coworker dimmed their luster a little bit, but really, they were gorgeous.

But overall, and secretly, I was disappointed. I'm the kind of person who would have said, Ah, to hell with it, let's rent a hall and hire a great Italian caterer and invite all our friends from Maryland and Jersey and Delaware. Let's get a DJ and bring all

Nino's musician pals to play, too. Let's drink and dance, eat Chesapeake Bay crabs and baked ziti and roast beef sandwiches, and we'll worry about the cost later. You only live once.

I STILL MOURN HIM, Nino, my husband, Michael and Melissa's father. But now mourning has a kinder face, an almost companionable nature. The fact that I can love the sound of my late husband's voice, feeling comforted by it rather than saddened, means I've turned a corner in the long, lingering goodbye that is grieving.

Once it was almost impossible for me to believe that the acute, relentless yearning that was my grief for Nino would ever let up. Somehow it has, though. Time has blunted the most painful edges. I've started to experience my memories as friendly little prompts that remind me of all the things I loved about my husband, without making me ache in that bad old way.

I went through this first with Mom. She died way too soon, at sixty-five. It had taken us the better part of a lifetime to grow as close as we both wanted to be, to get past the mother-daughter turmoils and become dear friends. And just as I was starting to love that and count on it, she was gone. Heart failure. I was bereft. Our best conversation had just begun.

The hurt came in waves, as sharply physical as the pain of childbirth, with the same sort of ebb and flow. For a while, I'd be okay. She was gone, I was coping, like everybody eventually does. Then it would well up again, a sadness so big I'd want to physically outrun it.

It took months, maybe a year before it started to ease up. I came to think of the experience as sorrowing. Not a noun. A verb. Sorrowing. It was an active thing, a thing I had to do and work at. On rough days I'd feel like the sailor on choppy waters who has to just grip the sides and hold on. I'd literally tell myself, Debbie, come on. This thing has a curve. It goes up, it hurts, it hurts, then you cry, then you crash down, and then it's calm for a while. Ride it out, girl.

In time, as the waves started to recede, I started to remember Mom as she deserved to be remembered: not with pain but with gratitude. For her grace and loyalty, her intelligence and independence, her pungent honesty, and her quiet devotion to us.

This isn't anything you learn to do better the second time. With Nino's death in April 1998, grief came around again; again, it was unexpected. But this grief was all new; this was hurricanes and torrents that propelled Melissa and Michael and me to places I never imagined we'd have to go.

My husband, my friend, companion, lover, and partner of twenty-five years, was murdered, shot down by the man who came to our house looking for me.

Well, he was not looking specifically for me, Debbie, at least not until he saw me in my yard that spring day. He was looking for a woman, any woman or girl he deemed attractive. He was looking for someone to savage and rape and, if necessary, to kill.

You'd think such a crime would take great planning, great cunning and secretiveness. No. He just drove around until he found someone—me. He started with the neighborhoods near his home in Bear, Delaware, then wandered into Newark, about five miles away, then into Academy Hill, where we lived, then onto Arizona State Drive. Simple as one plus one. It wasn't a dark and stormy night; it was the middle of the afternoon, a bright, blue Monday in April.

That afternoon, I was in the side yard of our new home. I was busy planting a bank of rosebushes there, along the perimeter of our property.

It was my big landscaping project. If I got it right—doubtful to begin with—maybe our corner lot would start to rival some of the prettily landscaped and manicured yards throughout the rest of Academy Hill. I envisioned it as a fringe of gorgeous bursting color that Nino and I could see from our kitchen window. Not that I'd had much luck at this sort of thing. When we first moved in, just ten months before, an overgrown herb garden near the side door had defied my most valiant attempts to tame it. Finally, feeling utterly inept, I called on some friends from our old neighborhood just over the state line in Elkton, Maryland.

"They're taking over, like the Blob," I said. "Help!"

They did. Over one long autumn weekend, it took all six of us—Kathy and Barb, Dale and Sam, Dot and me—to wade through the intractable tangle of mint and basil and tarragon and thyme. We tied some off to stakes. We deadheaded some and pulled others out completely. We came out scratched up and dirty, but everyone went home with bundles of herbs to dry, and from then on I managed to keep the creeping foliage at bay.

Yard work was definitely not my forte. But I was game. I was willing to have another go at it. That Monday I threw on pink sweats and a gray hooded sweater and pulled on some work gloves. Then I headed outside into the nicest day of the year so far to plant my roses, pink and coral, bloodred and ivory.

FROM THE START we called it our dream house: the big Cape Cod on a corner lot in Newark, Delaware. With a cathedral ceiling in the foyer, five bedrooms, and (best of all) a deck with a hot tub, this was it: our reward for a lifetime of hopes, dreams, and economic conservatism. When we moved here from Elkton in July 1997, Nino and I knew we were staying put. We planned to stay here for the rest of our lives.

From the time we lived in our first tiny one-bedroom apartment, we had worked toward this. Even as newlyweds, we talked endlessly about what we wanted in what I thought of as our "someday" home: a refuge and a haven, in a quiet neighborhood where we'd be comfortable leaving the house open and the car door unlocked. We refined that vision for more than twenty years, and in 1997, when we started looking in earnest, we knew just what we were after.

"I want lots of light, plenty of windows," I said. "No faux paneling, no small rooms, nothing dark. Everything light and airy."

"We need more space, certainly," said Nino. "Enough room

for the kids to come home weekends and bring their friends. Oh, yeah," he added, as if it was an afterthought, "a place to park the boat."

Besides everything on our wish list, there were very practical reasons we needed to move back to Delaware. We both worked there, and it made sense to live closer to our jobs. But the big thing was Michael's choice of college, the University of Delaware. Out of state, we just about managed his tuition. In state, we got a financial break that made life a whole lot easier.

We found everything we needed—the location, the space, and a small-town, Mayberry feeling—in a development called Academy Hill.

Academy Hill is only about twelve miles from Wilmington, but it might as well be in another galaxy. One of many subdivisions in the area, it was designed to feel as removed as possible from the teeming cities and four-lanes and eight-lanes that crowd the area and link it to Philadelphia and New York, Baltimore and Washington.

The subdivisions have subdivision names: Arbour Park, Eagle Trace, Beaulieu. We looked at them all, but Academy Hill struck us as ideal, with spick-and-span homes of various models, and little of the cookie-cutter sameness of older communities. Here, behind carefully cultivated shrubbery, surrounded by insulation walls to blunt the roar of Interstate 95, Nino and I had found our version of the good life.

Of course, Academy Hill wasn't really Mayberry. It was a suburban approximation set along those four-lane and eight-lane crossroads. But for us, at this stage of our lives, it was the right choice. We'd worked hard for this: the breathing space, the peace and quiet, the elbow room. We may have stretched our finances a bit to bankroll the new life, but it was worth it. With lots of space inside and out, we kept spare rooms for Michael and Melissa, both away at college. I decorated to my heart's content, with my ever-propagating collection of Beanie Babies, my cats and cows, my angels, and *Gone With the Wind* plates.

I had always liked the country look, and I indulged myself,

especially in the kitchen, which was as bright and airy as any in a magazine. This home on Arizona State Drive was the model home for the community when it was under construction, so it had great window treatments (daffodil yellow in the breakfast nook) that we got to keep.

We made new friends easily. Though something of a home-body, Nino was still very social within the neighborhood. He made it a point to meet the people on our street, to the extent of going up and greeting perfect strangers. We were especially close to Gene and Karen Nygaard next door; we became comfortable enough to walk in and out of each other's homes, barely knocking, for a cup of coffee or whatnot.

Gene's an engineer, but he may have missed his real mission in life: he's great in the garden. His property always looked like a showplace—like something out of Martha Stewart, with jewel-like lawns and lush flowering trees. Sometimes I'd compare his place with ours and cringe. We practically had tumbleweeds blowing across the yard, and I'd think, Gee, he must hate living next door to us.

But Gene was sweet. When he saw our landscaping left something to be desired, he gave us an unofficial and belated house-warming gift: four rosebushes to plant out front.

"They don't get enough sun over here," he said, digging them out from a spot at the top of his driveway and placing them, one by one, in black plastic garbage bags. "But you've got light all day."

Later he wished he could take back that friendly gesture. It was a hard burden for him. But how could we assure him that nothing that happened that Monday was his fault?

He never said the words straight out. But I know Gene continued to torment himself. What if he hadn't given me the roses?

"WHAT IF?"

Whenever they arise—the what-ifs—I dodge them fast, before my mind has a chance to take them seriously.

Any circumstance, good or bad, can be endlessly decon-structed, reconstructed, rescripted. I could certainly do it with April 20, 1998.

What if, that day, I had gone shopping instead? I had a shop-ping list. I needed milk, juice, cereal.

What if Nino had decided to join me out in the garden after work instead of going inside for a snack? He was a maniacal mower: he trimmed that grass down so low that it never reached the quarter-inch mark. The yard was something we could have worked on together.

Or what if we had never moved to Academy Hill? There were literally dozens of beautiful communities in the same area, so why here, and why this house?

Or what if it had rained? What if?

I could go that road, easily, trying to mentally change and rearrange everything in forty-plus years of living that might have altered the events of one day. But do I want to do that? Would I really make changes in the whole of my life just to try to avoid a few minutes of it, the minutes it took for so much of my future to be determined?

If so, why not go back even further and ask, What if I had never met and married Nino? What if I had never found this great job in Delaware? What if I didn't like roses? But I did all these things. I couldn't help it, didn't *want* to help it. And I cer-tainly couldn't decide now to regret it.

When what-ifs come up, I do the mental equivalent of stick-ing my fingers in my ears and humming, loud. I refuse them, just block them out.

Some things you must accept, even things from which you naturally recoil, like the gross and evil things and people of life.

Some things, damn it, you must just accept.

AND WHAT IF I'd had a busy night the night before? I was a hospice nurse on overnight call. Sometimes during my shift I'd be on the run for sixteen hours nonstop, visiting patients at home, counseling their families, and monitoring their care before rushing off to the next stop, which could be two blocks down the street or an hour up north.

But it didn't happen that way. I had a quiet Sunday night with no calls. Otherwise, I would never have taken on what was for me a strenuous chore: working in the garden on Monday. I would have been too bushed.

And if I had not been in the garden, the cruiser—the man in the green Plymouth—would never have spotted me. He would have driven past the empty yard on the corner of Arizona State Drive, and some other woman or girl would have been the recipient of what turned out to be my fate. I would have remained unchosen.

Later on, I probably would have heard about a crime, a murder, a rape, and been horrified and alarmed and sorry for some other woman and her family. I would have wondered, Oh, my Lord, what if that had been me? and talked about it with people at the market or the post office. I would have shuddered at the thought that it could happen so close to my home. I would have sent up a little thank-you that nothing that shattering had ever happened to our family.

And my life—busy, happy, relatively uneventful, sometimes mundane—would have rolled out over the years, much as it had in the years before.

Of course, I don't go there, to "what if."

Except sometimes when I do.

USUALLY, AFTER MY shift ended at 8 A.M., I said good-bye to Nino then slept most of the morning away. Most days I managed to wake about one in the afternoon, just in time to make lunch and loll in front of the TV for one delicious lazy hour, usually to watch *All My Children*. Then, time to gear up for another night.

Nino always said that by late afternoon on these days, once I was thinking about and preparing for work, I became a different person. "Debbie," he'd observe, "I can always tell when you're going into work mode."

I could tell, too. It was a very conscious thing, but, by this point in my career, pretty automatic, too. It was important for me to center myself and marshal my energies for the night to come. I seldom knew how the night would play out, but I couldn't see patients with my energy flagging or half my heart in it. I had to be all there, every time. No one dies twice. I have a lot of professional pride about this. I couldn't allow myself to get it wrong, not even for one of my patients.

Dying is hard work. The job of a hospice nurse is to make the arduous physical transition a little easier, helping ease the pain so patients can deal with what dying's really about: taking leave of a world of people and things they love. It's our job to educate the dying person and his family about what's going on at every stage of the leave-taking: from month to month, and at the end, from moment to moment. So that they, not we, are in charge of how a death goes.

Being admitted into hospice, which is designed for those with a six-month life expectancy or less, is a great commitment for family members. For the patient plan to work, they must learn all they can about things like symptom management, the care of a bed-bound patient, how drugs work, and how to combat the nausea and vomiting that accompany some drugs. This is how it goes, and the workload can be hard and unpleasant.

But thanks to hospice care, families get to do this important event—death—together, actively. They're not helpless spectators in an antiseptic cubicle, at the whim of rotating strangers in white coats. Patients get to die at home, in their own beds, with kids and grandkids in attendance, surrounded by their own things: framed photos and cherished keepsakes and pets—it's funny how often they want their pets there.

Given the choice, people can transform dying into a luminous affair, even a celebration. I once attended the death of a woman whose family gathered at her bedside to sing her favorite hymns. "Amazing Grace." "Will the Circle Be Unbroken." With lamps lit and candles all around, they filled the room with an almost incandescent energy. Her death was as peaceful as any I have ever seen. None of this could happen in a hospital cubicle.

As a nurse, it wasn't my place to partake in the emotion of a death. The whole philosophy of hospice precludes it. My role was that of helper, a support—strictly supplemental. But like every hospice worker I've ever known, the time comes when you break the rules. The bonds develop, whether you want them to or not. Your heart and your humanity don't always observe the protocol.

Take Keith. At the outset, I would never have imagined that I could fall in love with this young man or his family. They were more distant than most, to the point of being aloof with me and the other nurses. Understandably, Dot and Charles were fiercely protective of their son's privacy and reluctant to let anyone observe their collective sorrow.

Keith had AIDS, at a time when AIDS was not just a death sentence but a moral and social scourge. He was just thirty-four. After the death of his partner, Keith moved back home to be with his mother and dad, and together they waited for the inevitable. Months passed before I could gain their confidence; they were reluctant to reveal themselves, even to Alex, one of our spiritual counselors. It was as if they thought that we, too, might tar their son with the stigma that often accompanied a diagnosis of AIDS—that we would make it our place to judge his lifestyle, his choices, and his fate.

But in time they eased up. They stepped out from behind their emotional armor. They began to look forward to our weekly visits, when Keith, with evident pride, always wore his AIDS ribbon. They knew we cared—how could we not? Keith couldn't help but respond to kindness, because in it he recognized himself. He was one of the gentlest, most caring people I have ever known. Once the barrier between us fell, it became impossible for me to stay with the company policy of professional detachment. Keith just melted my heart.

During the couple of hours a week I typically spent with him, Charles always set up a TV tray, and Dot always served home-made iced tea and cookies. In nice weather, we sat in the garden, where we chatted about anything at all: news, politics, entertainment, especially the movies. I had to admire Keith, who insisted on leading as normal a life as possible. In the direst circumstances, he went to the movies at least once a week with his father. For him, this was no small task. As the disease progressed, so did the wasting of his body. But his spirit was almighty. Even near the end, when what was left of him could have blown away on a breeze, Keith's vitality overwhelmed me. We'd hug, and I could feel the skeleton beneath his skin, the way his bones interlocked, even the protrusion of his joints. But boy, when Keith hugged me, I knew I was being hugged.

Keith fought hard to live. He was in the program a little more than two years. As he began his last decline, I stepped up my visits to twice a week, then three times. When the time came to prepare for his death, his parents requested that I be there, no matter who was on call. This, too, required some juggling. An important tenet of hospice nursing (besides not getting emotionally involved to begin with) is to let go, let the team take over when the shift is through. Share the burden. Break that rule and you'll burn out fast.

But for me, this was no longer the death of a patient. This had become a death in the family. When Dot and Charles called that May evening, I jumped in the car and hurried over. The three of us sat at Keith's bedside, hearing his faint final breaths and gently giving him permission to go. His favorite music played in the background. Then Keith, the patient I now called a friend, died with dignity in the room where he grew up.

WITH RARE EXCEPTIONS, I'm on call Sunday through Wednesday. The rest of the week is mine to do whatever I want. I'm on call three nights out of seven then I have four days off. Kind of a lopsided way to live, but I like the freedom, so the schedule suits me.

That Sunday night, my pager was silent. No one was dying or even required care, so I didn't have to go out. I even managed to sit down with Nino and Michael (visiting for the weekend from his dorm at the University of Delaware—with his laundry, of course) to watch a movie. We rented *Kiss the Girls,* with Morgan Freeman.

It didn't exactly make for restful sleep, this thriller about a serial murderer who targets women. It left me with a scary feeling. On the job I often visit the shabbier neighborhoods of Wilmington and Newark and Bear, which all have their problems with crime. And often as not, I'm out there in the overnight hours.

Nino usually came with me when the neighborhood was dicey, but this wasn't always possible or practical—he had to work, too—and like any woman, I occasionally wondered what I'd do if I were approached or harassed or, God forbid, mugged. From time to time I'd thought of taking martial arts training to help me feel more secure. I never got around to it.

I lay down about eleven and tossed a little, wishing I hadn't watched that damned movie. This wasn't like me. Usually I loved a good scare. Finally I dozed off and didn't get up till Nino did, a little after five in the morning.

1

MONDAYS ALWAYS SEEM more hectic than other weekdays. It shouldn't be true for Nino and me. His work schedule isn't your typical nine-to-five, nor is mine. But Mondays are Mondays are Mondays.

Though as routine as ever, this Monday is busy from the start. I've had a decent night's sleep—an extraordinary seven hours—so I'm up. But for some reason, I'm a little out of sorts. Nino's grumpy, but that's how he greets every day till he gets his quota of caffeine. I'm relieved when he heads out for his morning cup of coffee from the Wawa, a chain convenience store in our area. I used to make coffee at home, but home-brewed doesn't suit him—only Wawa's will do, and he stops there every morning for a big sixteen-ouncer, cream, and sugar, along with his daily pack of Winston Lights.

I feed our four cats, then feed Fish, a single massive grommie who reigns in solitude in his big tank. Fish belonged to my mom. I inherited him when she died, and since then we've developed a strange intraspecies relationship.

Nino and the kids don't believe me, but I'm convinced there's affection for me behind those big fish eyes; in fact, when I walk through the dining room, his eyes follow me everywhere with what seems like lively interest. This morning I pause by his tank, and as usual he lifts his big pink head for a pinch of food.

I have to smile.

"Hey, Fishie," I say this day. "Morning, buddy."

THE FIRST MINUTE I get, I pour a strong cup of tea and call Michael, bent on continuing a discussion that began over last night's dinner. Of course we end up bickering.

On Tuesday there's a school dinner, where our son is supposed to receive an academic award. But he's being typically balky. Modesty is a commendable trait, but Michael is almost too retiring; he never wants to flaunt his accomplishments before the world, even the little world of his classmates and teachers.

Michael has strong principles about this sort of thing. To him, there's no contest but the contest with himself. He shuns the idea of being judged "better" than someone else. It's a very pure way of thinking, noble even. I respect it. But Nino and I are proud parents, and we wish just once he would change his mind.

We talked about it at the table on Sunday, where he put forth his usual arguments: he didn't compete against other people, academically or in sports. All that mattered to him was doing his personal best, and he didn't know why this stuff was so important to us.

"Well, soon you'll be out there interviewing for jobs, Michael. It'll look so impressive if you've won all these awards. . . ."

"Mom," he said, with exaggerated patience, staring down at his meat loaf and peas, "if they want to know about me, they can just look at my GPA."

At that, Nino sighed—a big, deep sigh that meant he was starting to get ticked off. "Michael, please," he said, biting off the words. "It's one night of your life. Do it for your mother."

Good move, Nino—if at first you don't succeed, there's still the old guilt trip. I'd tried it myself, earlier in the day: "Michael, honey, come on. Just do it for your dad." Michael will not be persuaded.

Up till now, all his awards have ended up at the bottom of his bedroom closet, buried under a pile of track shoes. It's become a tug-of-war between us—I'll display the running trophies or plaques on the hearth, and when I'm not looking he'll turn them face down or lock them away altogether.

This morning around eleven I give it another shot—"Come on, honey"—and I hear him groan on the other end of the line.

"Mom, what's the big deal with this?"

"The big deal is it means a lot to your dad." I hear the edge creep into my voice; I'm getting impatient, too. "If it doesn't mean anything to you, do it to please him. How much effort does it take?"

From there it's all downhill. One or the other of us, I can't remember which, hangs up.

Stubborn kid. I stand with the receiver in my hand, fuming. Then I decide to shrug it off. No use fretting this into something bigger than it should be.

Stubborn kid. Stubborn parents.

I'll talk to him again later, when we've both cooled off.

NINO STOPS HOME for lunch, and I do the fried baloney thing.

Fried baloney is a kind of family joke, and the kids still snicker when their dad demands what is for him a childhood tradition: four thick slices hot off the grill, piled high on two pieces of bread with mustard. It's comfort food for Nino, just as tomato soup with grilled cheese (we called them "cheese-and-cook-it" sandwiches) put me right back in the kitchen of my girlhood home in Burlington, New Jersey.

After lunch he girds himself to make a phone call that could have an appreciable impact on our money situation. It's to Melissa's financial aid office, and he's calling to inquire about one of her loans.

By choice, Nino has always handled money management for our family, including those damned college loan applications. But he hates every contentious second of it. He constantly reminds me how frustrating it is to fill out the endless forms, year after year, trying to convince the ruling boards that we're not too well-off to qualify for aid and going into battle with the dense, multiple levels of bureaucracies that hold the keys to the kingdom.

Worst of all, he says, is doing this by phone, where he has to listen to prerecorded messages directing him to make one of a dozen menu choices then listen to Muzak for minutes at a time while praying for a live (and hopefully responsive) human being.

He's doing that now: waiting, his ear pressed to the receiver, growing more flushed with each passing minute. He shakes his head. "You know, Debbie, I don't know what you'd do if you had to handle this on your own."

It's not the first time he's expressed this sentiment. All our married life he's chafed about being the one who has to balance the checkbook and get everything paid on time. His refrain: "Debbie, I'm glad you don't have to deal with this. You'd never be able to figure it all out." According to Nino, I remain the tender, hapless little woman who can't cope with the important things of life, things like mortgages and tax returns and car repairs. Those are man's work.

Today, though, wrangling with the loan people, he's reached the end of his tether. When he crashes the phone down, I know it hasn't been a successful call.

He grabs his jacket and storms toward the door. "You know what?" he says. "I might as well just take my car and drive off the Delaware Memorial Bridge."

And he's gone.

TWO DOWN. Both Nino and Michael are mad.

Well, okay. Everybody's at cross-purposes today, but I don't have to let it wreck my own day. It's still early, and it's beautiful out: sunny and breezy, not too cold, perfectly April. I'm free until

4 P.M., when I call in for my assignment. I've got just enough time to accomplish something, so at about two in the afternoon, I lug the four rosebushes out to the side yard, where I've already dug four deep holes and filled them with the good organic soil recommended by Gene.

With trowel and spade in hand, I start to dig. I feel clumsy and inexpert. Homey, one of our four cats—the only outside one—curls beside me in a square of sunlight.

About 3 P.M., Nino comes home from work. He parks his Jeep in the driveway and ambles over. By now he seems okay. The lines have eased out of his forehead, and his shoulders are down, relaxed. Thank God.

I'm surprised he doesn't offer to join me; Nino loves yard work. The joke in our family is, "When Dad gets out the weed whacker, stand back." He couldn't be bothered with edging and raking, but if it involves a tool that makes noise, he's all for it. Gene Nygaard's always telling him he trims the grass too short: "Hey, you really need to bring the blade up on your mower." Nino just laughs and, heedless, roars on.

But today, he's not interested. Must be tired. "Better you than me," he says, then smiles at Homey. "Hey, looks like you've got a helper there."

"Yeah."

He heads inside, where he typically grabs a snack after work.

"Do me a favor, Nino," I call after him, "tell me when it's 3:45. I need to report in to work."

I labor on, packing loose earth around the balled roots of the rosebushes. After a while it seems like it must be getting close to four. But Nino hasn't called. As a nurse, I need to be on time; he knows that.

Maybe he's asleep, I think; he sometimes takes a nap after work. I brush the caked dirt from my knees and walk toward the open garage, where a staircase leads to the kitchen.

As I approach the house, Homey at my heels, I see kids scrambling from a school bus at the corner and construction workers swarming over a building site across the street.

Our neighbor Joe Strykalski is walking his dog.

Gene Nygaard waves from his front lawn, where he's on the cell phone with Karen. She's in North Dakota for the funeral of her father.

As I walk into the garage, I hear nothing but the distant buzz of a sod cutter somewhere out in the April afternoon. I open the door and walk into the kitchen.

IT'S SO FAST. A blow catches me from the left, my glasses fly off, and instantly I'm in a blurred world; my eyesight is so poor that without glasses or contacts I can scarcely count the fingers on my hand.

I fall forward through space, almost in slow motion, though the floor seems to rush up at me. I crack my head against the cat food bowl, and water splashes out, and blood splashes out.

My first reaction—a thought, not quite a thought—is confusion. What was that? What fell?

I fell. Through the distorted lens of my vision I see someone moving around me. I lift my head and stare up at the dark silhouette of a man. Tan jacket, baseball cap—I can't see much more. The sunshine in the kitchen creates a weird backlight, glowing from behind him so his big shape looks haloed.

"Where's your money?" he says. This is no voice I've ever heard; the sound of it is deep and quiet, but there's another quality in there, too, something like excitement. Like he's about to tell me a secret.

Fear doesn't happen yet; it's two beats away, or three. I'm stunned, still trying to decide and accept that someone is in the room with me, a stranger who has struck me. Why did he do that? Oh, yes. Money. Hurry. Give it to him.

"My purse. My wallet's in my purse. On the counter by the sink." I don't keep lots of cash on hand. For the first time in my life I'm hoping there's lots of it in there. I know my rings—my diamond anniversary ring and a diamond pinky ring—are there, too, along with my watch, where I took them off before gardening.

Take them.

I watch to see him move away. I wait, all my senses tuned up, for the sight and sound of him walking out of the room. But he doesn't go. Blood spreads across the floor, and my head hurts.

"Where's your husband?" he says.

"I don't know." It comes out a whisper.

NINO'S AN ORDERLY MAN, a creature of habit whose activities and location can almost always be charted by the calendar and the clock. When he comes home from work most afternoons, he has a snack, lies down for a half hour or so, then goes outside to walk and chat up the neighbors, pacing off the frustrations of his day.

If he went out today, he must have taken the front door leading out onto Oklahoma, the broad drive that leads from the street into our development. Otherwise we would have passed each other in the side yard.

THE BLOW WAS so strong that I'm senseless on the tile floor, with an odd buzzing inside my head. I feel stupid. I can't put thoughts together so they mean anything.

Something inside says, Move. Run. Do something. I can't. I'm just hunched into myself, arms up around my head where he struck me.

Just go away, I think, and in that instant I am gathered up in his arms.

The basement door opens. Somehow I'm on my feet again. He's prodding at the small of my back, propelling me down the narrow wooden stairs. I'm wobbly, but I manage to stumble down them without tripping.

I notice for the first time that my right hand, held tight against my stomach, is shaking. For a second this surprises me. Then I recognize in a strangely detached way that I must be really scared.

This may be the first thing I clearly articulate in my mind: I must be really scared.

At the bottom of the stairs he gives a big shove. I land face first on the concrete floor, so hard that I wonder if I've broken my nose. Whatever fear that was kept at bay by that first stunned feeling now just opens up inside, blossoms, explodes, rushes to every part of me like electricity.

"Now," he says, with that same tense excited voice, "let's do this."

With rough hands he's pulling my sweatpants down, then my panties. Oh, Jesus. Jesus Christ. Not this.

My eyes are wide open and staring. Though very little light comes in—the basement windows are dusty and set up high—I can look from side to side and see things. The basement is heaped up with lots of old musical equipment, boxes of old tax records, boxes I marked "summer clothes" and "holiday decorations" and "Mom's dishes"—twenty-five years' worth of pack rat stuff. The dehumidifier whirs in a corner.

I get intermittent flashes of clarity, lucid thoughts spooling out in front of me like old home movies. We have been here so briefly—just one Halloween, one Thanksgiving, one Christmas. Improbably, I'm thinking of last Christmas, when, for the first time ever, Nino didn't argue when we got a real tree to fit the fourteen-foot foyer.

Most years he lobbied for an artificial tree ("So clean, so economical"), a notion I resisted with all my might. And on this at least, I always prevailed. No pipe cleaner Christmas tree in my house, no plastic greens and garland. I wanted that good sweet fresh tree smell all around, and though Nino grumbled, he let me have my way.

On that first Academy Hill Christmas, my sister Darlene and her husband, Bill, bought the tree at the local firehouse. When they lugged it in, we all just gaped. It was massive. We made hot cider and ate spice cookies and loaded that tree down with all the decorations we'd collected over the years. My mom's fragile glass ornaments hung alongside things the kids had made at school over the years, gingerbread men made of felt and Popsicle sticks and Elmer's glue. No tinsel, though. Not after the time one of our cats, Kiki, ate a few strands, then walked around the house with most of it hanging out the other end.

NOW HE IS BEGINNING. He is brutal. He's all over me from behind, making low noises as he does it. It goes fast, which is no mercy. I'm so tense I tighten up, and it hurts. When he's through, I'm wet from him and dirty and ashamed of my degradation.

I hear a sound like a little girl's, the kind of sound my Melissa used to make when she was small and scared of something in the night.

"Shut up, bitch," he says, so I know the sound must be coming from me. "Shut up."

Melissa was always afraid of storms, especially the sound of the wind and the sight of everything tossing all around. It made her feel the world was falling down around us. But I reveled in it—the rain, the wind, the lightning, and the majesty and energy of it all. And when she'd run to me, whimpering, I'd bundle her up on my lap and we'd watch together out the window. "See? It can't hurt you, honey. So hush."

"Shut up, bitch," he says.

BACK TO THE KITCHEN. We have moved there somehow, and now everything's going fast. The phone rings. Must be four o'clock. I get my daily work assignment at four precisely, no deviation, every single day I'm on call. If I don't call them, they call me. The phone stops, rings again, stops.

Back to the floor. I take another hard landing, smash my nose again, then he's got my arms pulled up behind me. He loops some kind of thin cord around my wrists, over and over. Then something falls over me. It's the flowered quilt from Nino's and my bedroom, which is on the first floor off the dining room.

I'm worried for my husband. I know Nino. If he walks in on this, he'll do anything to defend me and our home, and I don't know if he can win a fight with this man, who is bigger and probably a lot younger.

A part of me is willing him away. Another part is helplessly angry, wondering why he hasn't come to rescue me.

Nino, for God's sake, stay away.

Nino, for God's sake. Come home.

THE MAN WALKS away. Long minutes pass, ticking off on the kitchen clock. Five minutes. Ten. I listen for anything at all and hear nothing. My breath, which had been coming in short sharp bursts, starts to calm. It's over.

The littlest of our cats, who's old but so tiny and round he still looks like a kitten, comes sniffing around. Paddington sticks his nose under the quilt, and I'm comforted. He's there. The intruder is gone. And now the front door opens, and I know my husband's back.

Breathe.

But no. The tread of these steps is heavy and slow. Not like Nino's steps.

Kitchen drawers open and slam shut, one after the other. What's he looking for? He's going through the cutlery, it sounds like. There is clatter, and it sounds big and violent in my ears. What's he looking for?

When he lifts me, it's like he's carrying something disposable, not a person at all. He takes me into the foyer, and I can hear things from the outside—construction sounds, traffic—so I know our front door is open.

"Oh, no. No, no, Jesus. Don't do this."

"Shut the fuck up."

I'm on the floor, on my back this time, and there is a flash of brightness and I see the knife: long sleek blade, fat black handle.

He brandishes it so I can see—like he's going, Look at this!—then presses the sharp end to my neck, so hard I can feel the point of it piercing my skin.

"Do you want to just shut your fucking mouth?" Then I hear the rip of duct tape.

For nine years, I've worked with people on the cusp of death. Sometimes I'd wonder, couldn't help wondering, how I'd die. With a little prayer going up, I'd think, Please, nothing devastating, none of the cancers. It's so hard on everybody, especially if dying comes too early or lasts too long. I wanted that good death where you live out all your seasons, do most of the things you have planned, last long enough to hold the grandchildren and maybe even the great-grandchildren, then pass softly, like a sheaf of wheat falling before the wind. I have been so idealistic about this, and arrogant, too, thinking I could choose. I believed if I concentrated hard enough, I could create that graceful, good death for myself.

Now I know how the story really ends. I'm going to be murdered.

More than anything else, it's surprise I feel. I never thought of this.

But wait. I need time to prepare. Let me get used to this. Let me figure out a way to do it.

He carries me lightly, effortlessly. Three things are before me, like the snapshots that always crowded the front of our refrigerator, stuck on with smiley-face magnets and cow magnets: Melissa. Michael. Nino.

Still wrapped in my favorite quilt—it's brand new, I think, in that odd detached way, hoping it doesn't get damaged or dirty—I'm tossed into the back of his car. I hear every sound as a distinct thing, a warning bell, a death knell, and with every sound I am flooded with disbelief. The hatchback slams. The driver's side door opens and closes. The key turns in the ignition. The engine starts.

I have heard this many times on TV over the years: if you're being attacked, never let yourself be taken to a "secondary crime scene." I remember it now so distinctly, seeing the detective, J. J. Bittenbinder with the big mustache, talking about this on *Oprah*. "Do anything you can to keep from being taken from your own environment. Take any risk, do anything you can."

I'd shuddered to hear it, especially when he said it's better to struggle and run and be shot at than to be forced into a car and driven off.

The man eases his car from the front door into the street then pulls slowly away.

2

NIGHTMARE, please. Let this be one. But as my head slowly clears, I know this is a conscious, genuine, absolute thing. A thing that is happening. I try to gauge what is going on and where we are—me, and the man.

Oh, Jesus. Who is it, who is it, who is it, sweet Jesus?

He makes no stops, and few turns. He is not driving recklessly: no veering in and out of traffic. He is being very careful. He knows what he's doing. He doesn't want to draw any attention to himself.

Nightmare, please. Wake me up, for sweet Jesus' sake.

Huddled in the back of his car, I work the ropes that bind my wrists, frantically trying to pull free. If I can just get up, lift the felt top covering the hatchback and make someone see that I'm here, if I can just lift one hand and press it against the window, maybe someone will notice and call 911.

But in my struggle, I am jarring the felt top, bumping up against it, so it lifts and I can see the sunlit underside of leaves. All of a sudden he veers to the right, crunching gravel, and the car lurches to a halt.

He is there then, flinging the hatchback lid up, pounding on the felt cover to secure it. "Bitch!" he screams, and in the dimness of the car trunk I can see his eyes wide open and his mouth wide open. "Don't you hurt my car!"

I cower in the blackness. I can feel my pulse in my temples, in my ears, thudding in my chest and stomach.

Don't hit me again.

I burrow down into the well of the trunk, trying to stay out of his reach. But he doesn't lift the top. He just screams ("Don't you mess up my car!") then slams the hatchback, hard, furiously. In seconds, we're moving again, farther and farther from my home, and with every mile I know I am farther from safety.

Nino must have returned by now or awakened; he must be walking our rooms, calling for me. Oh, God, somebody, God help Nino find me fast, before it's too late. Our life together could end this very day.

WE MET AS KIDS, back in 1971—kids of twenty-one and twenty-four who believed we were all grown up. Me, I'd never traveled farther than Long Beach Island, our family's summer getaway at the Jersey Shore. Even downtown Wilmington—no more than six city blocks of office buildings and restaurants along with one theater—was dazzling in my eyes. So in 1971, an evening at the Anvil Inn—a tumbledown roadhouse in rural Chester County, Pennsylvania—seemed like a big night on the town.

We went in groups of girlfriends, at least those of us who weren't engaged or going steady. We all dressed in our "uniforms": low-slung bell-bottoms or miniskirts and halters, with the obligatory pale lipstick, black eyeliner, and dangly earrings. We wore our hair long and straight, parted down the middle like Peggy Lipton from *The Mod Squad*.

I'd dated my share of boys, had my fair share of high school beaus, even had one real "relationship," at least as I identified it then—that one I ended when the boy proved abusive. Then I met my first true love, Bill Sharp, and thought, This is my prince.

A funny, fast-talking, great-looking guy with a white Corvette (way better than a white horse), Bill was already in his twenties, which only added to his appeal. But it was the age difference that proved our undoing. When Bill wanted to hit the bars—and he *always* wanted to hit the bars—I was left behind. Then there were plenty of other girls out there, legal girls, vying for his attention. I was unwilling to join the throng.

Though I had a mad crush on Bill—the first grown-up I'd dated—I realized he couldn't go back to being the boy next door for my sake. But he was a good guy, perhaps the first to make me feel he really cared for and valued me. He was also the first man to tell me I was pretty (me with the owl-like glasses, me with no chest) and make me believe it. Despite the end of our romance, we stayed friends.

I did not know it for a quarter of a century, but it was Bill Sharp who played Cupid for me and another "older" man— Anthony Puglisi, known almost exclusively as Nino.

Nino was an aspiring musician and marketing major. To me, he was as handsome as a movie star: tall, attractive, and Mediterranean-looking, with dark hair and eyes and a strong, wonderful profile. He, too, was just out of a long-standing relationship.

That night at the Anvil, he was feeling footloose. As I later learned, he approached Bill and asked if he knew a girl "nice enough to take home to Mom."

Bill pointed me out, and Nino sauntered over to introduce himself. I gaped up at this big guy with long brown hair, decked out in tight jeans and a cream-colored pullover that was partly unzipped in front, showing lots of broad, hairy chest.

The attraction was mutual and immediate. Years later he'd tell the kids, "I went for your mom right away—I thought she was just gorgeous," and I'd laugh, wondering what he saw in a shy girl, skinny as Olive Oyl, hanging on the perimeter of the dime-sized dance floor.

We danced, fast then slow. That was the test—the slow dance—and Nino passed with flags flying. I liked the feeling of his arms. They were big and strong; they just wrapped me up. This, I knew, was a man who could protect me. I was also relieved to realize I could be attracted to someone other than Bill, who in my teenaged dreams had been the be-all and end-all, forever and ever. That old connection snapped like a string as I danced with this big, handsome Italian.

Over his shoulder I could see my girlfriends giggling and pointing as we twirled around and around the floor. When the night ended, I held my breath till Nino asked to see me again.

We fell hard and, in retrospect, much too fast, but that's the way kids did it back then. For a short time, I continued a long-distance relationship with a New York boy named Greg, but I soon knew Nino was the man I would marry. I started trying on his name and scribbled "Debbie Puglisi" on endless sheets of paper like a lovesick child.

One night Nino was with me when Greg happened to call. I fumbled with my words, trying to break the news that I had met someone new. Nino took over. He held out his hand, then took the receiver and coolly informed Greg that Debbie Engel was no longer available. I was thrilled.

The day after Valentine's Day 1972—less than four months after we met—he took me for a drive then offhandedly asked for something from the glove compartment. When I opened it, I found the tiny black velvet box. We were engaged.

A portrait of Nino and me from the early years still hangs over Melissa's bed, and it pretty much sums up the dynamic of our relationship at the time: he is gazing out, confident, smiling slightly, in his seventies bouffant and Edwardian suit. I stand in the crook of his arm, my head tucked into his chest, clearly smitten, and happy to be so.

WE FIRST LIVED in a tiny, one-bedroom apartment in Belle-fonte, Delaware, a few blocks from Nino's parents. It had one all-important asset: a detached garage we rented for seven dollars a month, where Nino kept our cars (his 1966 Pontiac Tempest, my 1969 Rally Sport Camaro). He made sure they were always in showroom condition and washed them, literally after every puddle.

Then there were the boats. In centuries past, Nino might have been a sea captain. From the start we were frugal about money, yet we always indulged Nino's love of powerboating. Before we married, he kept an old wooden bucket that, to him, might as well have been a cabin cruiser. Nino doted on that thing, waxing and buffing it till it gleamed. Weekends during the summer, he'd take it and me to Villas, New Jersey, where his folks had a summer cottage. Out we'd go into the ocean or the bay, where the rolling swells always made me feel half-sick.

I wasn't the ideal first mate, but Nino was a true mariner. On the water, as he manned the helm like some latter-day Ahab, tasting the salt air and calling out orders in incomprehensible nautical language, I clung to the sides like the landlubber I really was. Sometimes, if I accidentally referred to him as a sailor, he'd look at me like I was a moron. "Not a sailor, Debbie," he scolded. "Sailors sail. This is a powerboat." I must have thoroughly disappointed him.

Nino was a great surfer, too. And a great water-skier. He'd get out there and do those fancy tricks: one leg up, twisting around in midair, slaloming over ramps like some Olympic contender. I got a kick out of watching and envied his prowess.

But as a kid I'd learned to fear the water. More than once, playing in the surf off Long Beach Island, I was swept up in the strong current. The terror of being lifted off my feet and carried out toward the jetties was something I had never been able to shake. Years later, I was still chicken around the water. Much as I tried to argue myself out of it, much as I scolded myself for my irrationality, I feared deep water in a primal way that didn't respond to reason. Among our friends, I had the unfortunate reputation of being the only person who could go waterskiing and never get her hair wet. Because I never let my head go underwater.

. . .

ALL MY CHILDHOOD fears intersect here in the trunk of this car: fear of closed-in places and worse, fear of the water. As much as I try to redirect my thoughts, they stray there, as if I must rehearse this agony before the fact. The Delaware River runs right alongside I-95, and though I can see nothing, I know we're near the interstate—no matter where you are in Delaware, you're close to it.

He wouldn't do that, would he? He wouldn't do that.

I had just heard the news—heartbreaking, I'd said at the time—about the body of a missing woman, a carjack victim, who weeks after her abduction was finally found: still bound and gagged, washed up on the banks of the Delaware near Philadelphia.

The image is a torment. I imagine myself, tied up, unseeing, helpless, sinking beneath the oily green surface of the Delaware and lost forever to those I love. Oh, my God, my children. My husband. This is going to kill them.

OURS HAD ALWAYS been an uncommonly close family, and the mortar was the kids, who arrived in 1978. I was somewhat isolated as a young mom, but the twins were all the company I needed. I adored being a mother, all the more because getting pregnant hadn't been easy. After a few years of trying, I finally decided to take fertility treatments, and then it took only three months before I conceived.

Though I continued to work (I'd been a medical transcriptionist at the DuPont Institute for eight years and wanted to get ten years in), I soon realized I was missing the milestones in my babies' lives, all the firsts. I wanted to be at home.

Nino objected at first. We were in our first home by now, a little brick-front rancher in a tiny town called Bear, and he said we needed that extra paycheck to stay afloat. But he relented when he realized we were spending most of my earnings on baby-sitters. After that, I found a company that enabled me to do transcription at home.

The twins were premature (a little less than five pounds each), and their first months were one scare after another. Michael was colicky. Melissa had sleep apnea, and though she never needed a monitor, nights were a hold-your-breath time for me. I was already sleep-deprived, because I transcribed medical tapes from ten at night till one or two in the morning and the kids woke at six.

But by the time they were walking, all the health problems were a memory and the house was a happy chaos. I used one of my old steno books to keep a record of their infancy, and I was obsessive: every hiccup, every deviation in their sleep pattern, even every diaper change.

As toddlers, the twins had almost identical bathroom habits. I think they saved up their largest deposits for those Monday nights when Nino let me escape for a few hours. I would visit my friends Nancy and Becky for a quick game of Rummikub, and when I got home, usually about ten or eleven, Nino would be at his wits' end. He'd launch into a hapless, comic tirade about how much crap he had to clean up. And I'd scoop up my little ones— one squirmy pink body under each arm—and deposit them in a tub of soapy water.

It was a perfect time of life.

Well, nearly perfect. I was lonesome sometimes. In addition to his day job, Nino worked constantly as a musician. A natural instrumentalist and vocalist who always had a band (Nino and the Stairways, Encore), he played pickup in many other groups. Weddings, bar mitzvahs, country club soirees—there was always a night job, and on the weekends he sometimes worked two gigs a day, racing from an afternoon house party to a night job at a restaurant or bar.

The saxophone was his first instrument. Later he taught himself bass guitar. Good bass players were few and far between, and with that skill under his belt he could work as much as he wanted. And he sang like a dream.

Thankfully, unlike a lot of musicians, Nino seldom drank, and he always came home when the gig was over. But I still felt like a band widow. Through all the years of our marriage, I never planned on a big New Year's Eve celebration; Nino was always working. Though I sometimes went along, it was hard when the bell tolled midnight. As everyone around me kissed and hugged, my sweetheart was on the bandstand, playing "Auld Lang Syne." I always had to wait for my kiss.

Of course, there was one place we could still go to be together and alone: the boat. Gone were the days of the old wooden bucket. After we married he got a fifteen-foot fiberglass runabout that we kept on the Bohemia River in Cecil County, Maryland. Just below the Mason-Dixon line, Cecil County is so rural that parts of it still feel like the Deep South. The whole region—Cecil County and Kent County, the Bohemia and Elk and Sassafras Rivers—became our second home. We loved it so much that when the kids were young, we lived there for several happy years in a town called Galena.

Eventually we moved back to Delaware, but whenever we needed to reconnect or whenever we wanted to run away from home, Nino and I ran there, to rural Maryland and her beautiful rivers and our boat.

I'LL RUN. The next time he stops the car, I'll make a run for it, no matter what. That first stunned feeling has worn off; I'm ready to kick, I'll scream, do what I must, do what I fear. I'll fight like hell. I've managed to untie my wrists, and the duct tape across my mouth has started to come loose.

The car begins to slow. We are turning. We must be off the highway, but we're not going over the ground; wherever we are, it's still a road. The entire drive has taken no more than fifteen minutes.

I think, This is it. Get ready. We've arrived somewhere. God knows where.

But when the car rolls to a stop, I hear the unmistakable hum and crank of a garage door. As he gets out and lifts the hatch, I realize he has pulled into a darkened garage and closed the door.

The man, whoever he is, has taken me to his home.

3

"HOLY MARY, mother of God, pray for us sinners, now and at the hour of our death. . . ."

It's the prayer I learned when I converted to Catholicism, a condition of my marriage to Nino twenty-five years ago. Fragments of the words float through my consciousness as he hustles me from the garage into a house.

"Pray for us. . . ."

Blindfolded, I can't see the few steps that lead up into the house, and I trip on the trailing pink edges of the quilt. He grabs me from behind and pushes. He is angry, impatient. Then we're moving very quickly down a hallway. The man's fingers grip my upper arms, pressing into the flesh till I can feel the sharp edges of his fingernails.

Moments earlier, I'd had a plan: loosen the ties, then, when he stopped the car, go crazy. Scream. Anything, everything. Get someone to notice and help. In my panic, I still managed to remember one of the axioms I'd heard about how to get away from a bad situation, a bad person. Don't yell rape. People will be afraid to intervene when it's a rape. Yell fire instead.

For a second, I consider this: I've never screamed—really

screamed—in my whole life. No reason to. *Can* I scream loud? I don't know yet.

But that was before, when I had a plan. Now we're in his house, and there's no plan left.

Listening is all I can do. Sounds are all I have to try to determine what's going on here. A door opens and closes. Another door opens, but this one doesn't close. Now he pulls back the quilt, and I hear the sharp intake of his breath, followed by a choked-up-sounding string of obscenities. He seizes my hands and yanks them apart, and the loosened cord falls away. "Well," he says, "what do we have *here?*"

He wheels me around, so he is once again behind me. I stagger forward, and my knees hit some sort of obstacle. Then I fall face down on a mattress. We are in a bedroom.

I had a plan to get away. For this infraction, I am about to be punished.

He uses some kind of lubricant—K-Y jelly, I guess—and rapes me again, anally. I gasp, tighten, moan, cry, clutch the top of the mattress with my fingers. The first pressure becomes an intense pain. "No, no, don't, no." This time it's longer and rougher than the first rape in my basement, when he ejaculated almost immediately.

Yes, I do know how to scream, but it's the scream of a little thing, like a rabbit. Later I remember the sound and where I heard something like it: it was a TV documentary about greyhound racing. They used real rabbits, snapped into vicelike devices that were attached to a ring; the devices were mechanized to spin at high speeds along the ring, to goad the dogs into running. And the rabbits cried.

I cried, too, watching the show and never got that horrible, tiny rabbit scream out of my mind.

"Stop, please! I don't like this."

"Shut up," he hisses, but I can't, even when he grips my shoulders and pounds me, bodily, up and down on the mattress.

Doesn't anybody hear me?

Dimly, through a pain so fierce I feel I will split apart, I realize he is not just angry with me and not just paying me back for hoping I could run away. Despite all I've ever heard about rape (the mantra: it's a crime of violence, of domination, of power, not sex), this man is loving this. He is loving the sex. My pain is not just his pleasure. It is his joy.

After endless, relentless pounding, just as I think he's through, he's not completely. He turns me over. "Wheee. Looks like I've got a hairy one here." Then he does it again, vaginally.

HE IS FINISHED. He lifts his heavy body from mine. I brace myself. Is it time to die yet?

Lord, just welcome me. Mom, hold my hand through this. Don't let me be alone.

In some small, remote island of the mind that continues to function rationally, I'm astounded to know that I am already racing toward acceptance. From the utter normalcy, the complacency, of my life just an hour ago, when I hummed and planted roses in my brand-new garden plot, I've rushed to a place where I can actually consider and accept the unthinkable thing: my own death, here and now. At the whim of a stranger. Someone to whom I've done no harm and who can have no reason in this wide world to hate me. On a Monday (just another Monday), when nothing at all of great importance was supposed to happen.

I think of my last brief conversation with my husband: so banal, so bereft of meaning.

"Looks like you have a helper there."

"Be sure to call me at 3:45."

"Better you than me."

AFTER FORCING the washcloth into my open mouth, he wraps the whole lower part of my face in layers of duct tape.

I imagine him thinking, Now you'll shut up, bitch.

Using thick coils of rope—no more flimsy cord—he ties my wrists and ankles and pulls the ropes tight, so they dig in. It's like

being bitten into, except the teeth don't let go. He then links the
ropes with what I know is called a hog tie: a third rope that pulls
the limbs up in the back, in an antifetal position. It is hellishly
uncomfortable.

Now, bitch, you're not going anywhere.

He opens a door, heaves me up, and throws me onto the floor.
My face crunches on impact. A heavy blanket of some kind,
thick and woolen, falls down on me. Trussed up like an animal to
slaughter, I am pure sensation, quivering and alive, electric with
fear.

Time. What is that, anyway? The concept makes no sense at
all to me now. The idea of now, as opposed to the idea of then as
well as to ideas of past and future or seconds and days—all are
incomprehensibly meaningless. I cannot tell what time it is or
how long I've been lying here with my back bent in this awful
unnatural way. All I know is the pain. The pain is eternal. I have
always been in pain.

I hear the swift scurry of feet and the sound of a swinging
door—sounds again, only sounds. He's back and he says, breath-
lessly, "My God. There are cops all over your place."

So he's gone back there. The thought flies past: returning to
the scene of the crime.

Now it's known that I am gone. I wonder how it all played
out. I imagine Nino coming back from his walk, entering our
home, and realizing—with curiosity first then with growing
alarm—that I am gone. My heart goes out to him.

Do the kids know yet? Oh, God, please help my poor kids.

If there is any comfort here, it's that at least it's known: I am
inexplicably gone. Behind me I left my wallet, my rings, my car
keys. My glasses are still back there somewhere, on the floor,
where they landed when the man punched me.

They'll all know this is wrong. Nino will tell them—the
police, the detectives—that I'm blind as a bat without those
glasses. My coworkers will say I never fail to call in for work.
Never. Now they'll come looking for me.

But as quickly as this thought occurs, that's how quickly I

push it out. I cannot afford to hope. Don't want it. I am at acceptance now. To hope only to lose hope later would be unbearable. I need to stay at acceptance, at resignation. Hope feels treacherous to me now.

I DOZE, but it's more like going in and out of a stupor. In spite of the pain, I'm dulled. The worst thing, oddly enough, is the blanket that covers me, head to toe. I am still in my sweats, my sweater. The weight and heat of the blanket is horrible.

Then I hear a distinct pop, followed by the breaking of glass. A gunshot? At the second pop—yes, a gunshot—my body jerks up from the floor. Jesus God. Holy, holy shit.

Out there beyond that closed door he's screaming, screaming bloody murder.

Inside of me, I'm screaming, too, like the little rabbit. In seconds I'm braced again, rigid, keyed up, ready for it, waiting for him to come in and do it, kill me.

WHAT WILL IT be like? I think it must be like being flung from life into afterlife, wrenched from this place and thrown, at warp speed, into another, as the spark of life, the force of it, runs like water from a broken jar. Once again I reach out for my mom. Mom, be with me. Mom, Mom, Mommy, Mommy, I'm so scared.

But he doesn't come for me. I listen, and all I hear is the sound of a cigarette lighter flicking and flicking and the man breathing deep: inhale, exhale, over and over and over again.

I feel a warmth crawling down the length of my legs. I'm urinating all over his bathroom rug. I try to hold it in, but after a while I just can't. I want to cry. When he finds out, he's going to hurt me some more. But I can't help it. I'm like a child, offering up my little apology and hoping to be forgiven. I can't help it. Don't punish me.

Again, I try to calculate the hour. Certainly a night has passed.

I no longer think of what is going on outside—a search, a drag-net, even my family in their worry and fright. Can't do it. I haven't the emotional energy.

Nino, Melissa, Michael, I love you. And God help me, but I can't deal with thoughts of you right now.

I'VE LIVED THROUGH the night. I think of myself as I think of my patients, those who are at the brink but lingering on.

"Well," we'd say at daybreak, "she lived through the night."

The bathroom door opens, and I am jolted in an instant from used up, exhausted, half-asleep to wide awake and staring. He moves me—I am rigid, like a wooden plank, and I must be easy to move—from the bathroom to what seems like a small bed-room. New sounds make me listen up. A TV is on in the house—or is it a radio? It's soft at first, then he must have turned it up because it's suddenly loud enough for me to discern the words. I strain to hear the news. If police were at my house, won't it be on the news?

"Again, our top story: the death of a Newark man and the mysterious disappearance of his wife. Anthony Puglisi, fifty years old . . ."

The words, at first, won't fit together right in my mind. At first I don't hear, or refuse to hear, "the death of" preceding Nino's name. Then, the details. "Found shot to death in his home . . ."

"Anthony Puglisi, fifty . . . shot to death . . ."

"His wife, Debra, is missing. . . ."

So, I know. As the stranger raped me and ravaged me and ejac-ulated inside me down in our basement, as he dragged me back up the steps to the kitchen, as I worried that Nino would walk in on the crime then longed for him to come and rescue me, as a knife was pressed into the soft part of my throat, as I was bound and gagged and hauled like a sack of trash and thrown in the back of a car, my husband was already dead or dying.

I go cold, with a rush that goes from my toes to the crown of

my head. I think I might be sick and struggle to contain it. If I
vomit into the gag, I might choke to death.

"The victim's wife, Debra, is missing. . . ."

I don't cry. I'm frightened, like an animal in a trap. If I show
fear, the man won't like it. He'll make me pay. And fury? That's
an emotion I can no longer afford. I am in the presence of a murderer. I'm not allowed to feel anything about anything.

Oh, my God. He is really, really going to kill me. If I had any
doubts at all or any leftover hopes, they're extinguished now. He
has a gun. He's going to shoot me. But you know what? That's
better. It will be faster and less painful than a knife. Given the
choice—and hopefully I will be granted this small kindness—I
will ask him to do it that way. I hope he's a good shot. I will be
spared the river. I realize with a jolt that I am grateful for this.

Grateful.

The first cold rush of realization slowly recedes. I try not to,
but I think of my children. Michael: studious, serious, smart, and
disciplined. But so sensitive. Michael will torment himself with
the memory of our last hard words.

Don't do that, Michael. It was just an accident that we had a
quarrel on the last day. Don't carry that around, my honey, my
boy. Do not carry that.

And Melissa: beautiful. Like a flower. Nino used to call her
"my pretty little Melissa." But funny, too. She made her choice of
college—East Carolina U.—because she wanted to go to a party
school. And she made no apologies for it. My funny, goofy girl.

Don't let this steal all that from you, Mel. For Christ's sake, go
on and be happy. Don't let him kill you, too.

I wonder if they can recover from the loss of both Daddy and
me. I wonder, too, if my body will ever be found. The kids, especially, will need that. I console myself with the knowledge that we
have two cops in the family: my brother, Robert, a sergeant with
the Stafford Township, New Jersey, police, and Darlene's husband, Bill, who's a senior patrolman on the same force. They'll
find me someday. Robert, especially, will make it happen. This is

going to make him so angry. If he has to do it all himself, Robert will keep going till he finds me and brings me home.

Footsteps, slow and measured, approach the door. The door opens. I keep my head down, tensing for God knows what.

After a moment he says, "I'm sorry I had to kill your husband." His voice is flat and, despite the words, emotionless.

The door closes with a click.

I'm kept this way, hour after hour: bound, gagged, and blindfolded, lying on the floor. Being in one position for so long is tortuous: my muscles cramp up, my arms and legs get numb and tingly. My shoulders feel like they will pull out of their sockets. Every few hours, when it gets unbearable, I try to move. The best I can do is flip from side to side like a fish. It doesn't help much.

But physical pain is nothing next to the psychic torment. It's the waiting: the waiting for death, the waiting for the next rape. Thank God, I zone out a lot. Just go to a blank place where I exist but don't live or feel. There's not a moment I don't know what's going on—I haven't slept for twenty-four or thirty hours, however long it's been since he took me—but maybe this is where animals go when they know they're going to be killed. It's like exposing your own throat to the predator. After a while your body says, Enough. For God's sake just let this thing happen to me, because I can't take the waiting.

Every few hours throughout the day, he comes in. Doesn't talk to me, just opens the door, looks in, checks the ropes and the gag, and leaves. I freeze whenever he comes through; I don't want him to think I'm trying to escape, like in the car.

Why bother to try? There's no way I could get free from these new ropes—they're as big around as a man's thumb, the kind of coarse, strong rope you might use to haul a deer carcass. And they're tight as tourniquets. The blood to my left hand must be almost completely cut off, because the hand has swollen to twice its size. The pain feels like fire, the ropes like hot metal bands around my wrists.

He's here again. As he bends down to tug at the ropes, he starts muttering, as much to himself as to me. "I really freaked myself out last night. Saw that light in the window—I thought it was the police. They have this night vision light they shine in. . . ."

It occurs to me: the clicking from last night, the click-and-inhale sounds I heard from the next room. He was smoking crack. It would sound like that, wouldn't it?

The breaking glass. He was shooting out the windows.

The gag has loosened a little. He adjusts it, and I muster the courage to speak.

"Sir?" The sound of my voice is strange to me: meek, childlike. "It hurts. Do you think you have some Advil I could take?" At this point I don't care if he pumps me full of cocaine or heroin or whatever it is he takes. I want out of this body so bad.

He grunts, walks away, then, moments later, is back. "Here." He pulls me up to a sitting position, and I feel a tablet being pressed against my lips. Whatever it is, I'll swallow. Then, water.

Unbelievable. I said help. And he helped me.

"I have to get off these drugs. . . . Gotta clean up all that glass. . . ." His voice trails off.

I don't take much water; I'm so afraid I'll have to pee again. "Thank you, sir."

"Yeah."

How to make sense of this? He helped me.

"IT'S 11:59. Stay tuned for news at the top of the hour."

"And the big story is the murder of a Newark funeral director and the disappearance of his wife."

"It's 11:59. Stay tuned for news at noon."

"Our big story is the murder of a Newark funeral director and the disappearance of his wife."

"It's 2:58. Stay tuned for news at three o'clock."

IT'S MEANINGLESS, really, but each time I mentally correct them: Nino is a funeral planner, not a funeral director.

Then I correct myself. Nino was a funeral planner. To think of my husband in the past tense brings fresh horror, every time. Nino is. Nino was.

HE GOT AN ASSOCIATE DEGREE in marketing from Goldey-Beacom College in Delaware then earned his bachelor's at the University of Baltimore. Sales certainly wasn't a passion with him, like music, but Nino needed security. For him, it was an absolute necessity. No matter how talented he was—and he was very, very talented, maybe brilliantly so—Nino wasn't about to risk it all so he could call himself a full-time musician.

And a good thing, too. As the seventies and eighties rolled around, musicians really had a tough time of it. DJs were cheaper than bands and siphoned off most of the work. Though Nino continued to play as much as he wanted, he knew this was no reliable way to make a living. As a friend once remarked, "Musicians don't have jobs. They have gigs." And you never knew where the next gig was coming from.

It wasn't that Nino didn't like sales. He did, and he was really good at it, but of his many gifts, this was the lesser. When he switched to funeral planning (called "preneed" planning in all the brochures), he knew he was providing a good service that could save people lots of money, stress, and extra grief. That gave him a lot of satisfaction. But it was like a consolation prize. Given another chance (and assuming he could never justify his dream of making it in music), I think Nino would have gone to law school. It was his next best thing, the other dream. He didn't broadcast it all over the place; this one thing he pretty much kept close to the vest. Because by the time he was in his forties, my husband felt he couldn't start all over again. It was impractical, he said. It was impossible.

I disagreed, because I'd done it. I was thirty-five when I started nursing school. It wasn't a cakewalk by any stretch. Though I loved the work, lots of times I got by on just a few hours sleep, to the point that sometimes I didn't know what day of the week I was in. But even with two school-age kids and a job, I managed to graduate with honors and get my RN.

It was a huge affirmation for me, me who'd never had a big surplus of self-confidence. Later in life, I wondered why that was, why I should be that way. After all, I was nominated Most Studious at Burlington Township High School. In my senior year, I ranked third in a class of 150 students. But I never went to college, because people said I didn't need to go. I never got to be a phys ed teacher, though I wanted that more than just about anything. According to the wisdom of the time, girls just didn't have those kinds of ambitions.

Of course, that wisdom was changing radically by the time I was a teenager, but all the girls I knew were weaned on the old way. We weren't reading Betty Friedan and Germaine Greer or *Ms.* magazine. We didn't think women needed college degrees or careers, because they didn't need to support families. Women got jobs in the steno pool, worked a few years, then got married and had kids. That's what I was told, and that's what I believed, and that's what I did. It wasn't until years later than I realized how many options I had.

Not surprisingly, Nino's big thing with our kids was that they go for careers they were really passionate about. He said it all the time. "Michael, Melissa, you're going to work for a long, long time. Make sure you really love what you're doing."

In those exhortations, I heard his own unexpressed regret, his pain over all the lost opportunities. So I turned around and told him the same thing he told the kids. "Nino, do what you want. It's never too late. Go back to school." He didn't do it. It must have overwhelmed him, the prospect of starting from scratch and going from the comfort of being an expert in his field to the discomfort of being a novice. It wasn't easy, I knew, to be the middle-aged student in a classroom full of kids.

IT WAS ONE of those ideas that just kept tugging at my sleeve. I'd worked almost ten years in the medical field, and though my job was strictly secretarial—transcribing case histories from tape—I had a real aptitude for it. I loved the terminology (Latin, my Romance language), and when I realized I was beginning to "get" it: the dense case studies, the diagnoses, the treatment plans and therapies and everything the MDs were doing, I started to think seriously about nursing.

I enrolled at Delaware Tech, and when I started my first real class, I nearly panicked. Chemistry. Back in high school, I never took college prep courses. This was like asking me to read the Rosetta stone or figure out relativity.

When I got my grade—an A—I was positively giddy. Not only was it the start of a career, it was also the start of changes in me, changes that caused some resistance at home. From being certain of little else but my own shortcomings, my femaleness, and the ineptitude that went with it, I started to think of myself as an achiever. The always guilty mom and appeasing wife grew some assertiveness, and from the effect, you'd think a meteor had loosed itself from some other galaxy, hailed to earth, and crashed through our roof onto the dining room table.

Ultimately, I would start seeing a therapist, just to hear someone else say it was okay, even good, to look after myself, too.

MY CLOTHES ARE urine-soaked by now. I must reek. Yet sometime later in the day, when the light seems to have dimmed a little, he returns to rape me again. He rips my pants down and does it, and I am actually embarrassed by my smell. Then I ask myself, Why should I be embarrassed? The thought stirs a tiny sensation of anger, but it dissolves like a plume of smoke.

I'm limp. I simply accept. My mind feels separate from my body, and in my mind I repeat it, again and again: he is raping my body only. He is raping my body only. He cannot touch me. He cannot defile me.

Thank God, it's over fast. How many times now? And how can he stand the stench?

"I'm late for work," he says. His deep voice is terse as always.

"They're going to wonder if I don't show up. I never miss time like this."

Up until now, I haven't given a thought to the fact that he must have a job of some sort. Now I'm seized by curiosity. Where? What kind of work does this person do? It astonishes me to think of it: that he goes out and deals with other people, does all the things other people do, gasses up his car and buys groceries, punches in at work, picks up a newspaper, reads his junk mail, walks down the street, says hi to his neighbors. And all the time he is a murderer, and no one can tell. How can a murderer move so invisibly through the world? I can't see him, but if I ever do, will he look like a murderer?

He reinforces my ties, adjusts my blindfold, rewraps the duct tape over the washcloth in my mouth. Before he leaves, he cranks up the volume on the radio till it's near deafening, till I feel the noise is inside me. God. Maddening. Why does he have to do that? But of course I know why: should the gag come loose again, he worries that I'll scream.

What kind of place is this? Where am I that this raucous music draws no attention, no complaints? Last night, I screamed as he raped me. And nothing happened. Later he fired his gun and broke out the windows. Nothing. Are we far away from everything, in the woods, away from other homes?

But at least with the radio on, I get to hear the news, and I try to count every "top of the hour." As night falls, I listen for something new. Maybe something is going on out there or they have clues or a suspect.

I hear the same account, the identical words: "The death of a Newark funeral director. The disappearance of his wife."

4

My roses are dying. As I wait to call in for work, it comes to me: a sudden, certain knowledge that the four rosebushes I planted so painstakingly out front have begun to wither. The yellowing leaves drop, one by one; the colorful petals pale to white and cascade to the ground.

I have to stop it from happening this way. I have to do something. I race for the garden, but my legs are lead beneath me, and it takes forever to get there—like running through water or mud. Once there I scoop up the dead petals and press them together in my palms, as if I could make them all right again.

What happened here? What did I do wrong?

Kneeling on the ground, I sift the soil till it slips slowly through my fingers onto the garden plot. Gene dug this up with his rototiller, a plot about five feet wide and nine feet long.

I want to cry. I hate it when things die needlessly. Nino kids me about it, the fact that if I see a fly in the kitchen, I can't swat it, I have to kind of corral it toward the door and shoo it out.

"Well, Nino, why kill it? I don't have to squash it all over the wall. I can just let it go."

• • •

BUT WHEN I open my eyes, this isn't my garden at all. After a few seconds, I'm jarred back to time and place. The stranger's house. This small dark room. He hovers above me, a long shadow. Then he is pulling at the ropes. What is he going to do? Is it time to die yet? The prayers are going nonstop in my head, all the different prayers getting mixed up.

Okay, Deb. Okay, hon. Hold on. Here it comes.

And a silent plea to him, the man: make it quick.

When the ropes go slack, the air on my wrists and ankles feels like scalding water. He yanks me to my feet, but my legs don't work; I've been lying here for close to twelve hours.

Then I'm on a chair, and he's crouched there in front of me, tugging at the duct tape till it's off my mouth and down around my chin. Out comes the washcloth. For a moment it seems my mouth won't close anymore, like it's locked open. But no. With great effort, I can move it.

He turns on an overhead light then peels away the blindfold. I blink and close my eyes. A forty-watt, maybe sixty-watt bulb? It's like staring into the center of the sun.

I lift my head and turn in his direction. For the first time, we are face-to-face.

MOST OF US assume we'll get the standard threescore and ten years; I'm no different. I never thought I'd die young. And really, how ridiculous is that? I'm a hospice nurse. When I first started nursing, I worked in the neonatal ICU; my patients have included babies and young people in their prime, like Keith.

Yet I guess like everyone else, I lived in the illusion of my own security, as if a force field, an impenetrable bubble surrounded me and my family. Besides making a will when I was forty—it was Nino's and my first plane ride together, and I insisted—I gave little thought to the possibility, now a reality, that the bubble would burst.

Nino, though. Nino had a fear, a premonition. When I remember it, a chill walks straight down my spine.

During Easter Week, Mel came home from North Carolina. Nino was in his glory. Only Melissa—still his little girl, at nineteen—could barge through his characteristic reserve. She was the only one who could hug him, for no reason at all, without him stiffening or acting uncomfortable. She'd sit on the arm of his chair, her head on his shoulder. She'd cling to his arm, just like she did when she was a twelve-year-old. And though he sometimes pretended to find it annoying, he wasn't fooling anyone. Beneath his stern look, he glowed. He basked in it.

One afternoon, a few days after she drove back to college, I found Nino alone at the kitchen table, head in his hands. When he looked at me, his eyes were wet with tears; his look was inconsolable. I felt a thrill of alarm: my husband just did not cry. In fact, I couldn't remember seeing him in tears, with one exception. The day his father died.

"Oh, my God," I said. "Nino, what's wrong?"

"I just have this feeling," he said, staring up at me. "I don't think I'll ever see Melissa again."

Two weeks later, he was murdered.

AND NOW IT'S my turn.

But before I die, I will solve at least one mystery. I will see the face of my murderer. Without my glasses, I can't distinguish many features. All I see is a dark man in this too-bright room. He seems big, thick through the middle, with wide sloping shoulders, big ears, and closely cropped hair. I can't tell much about his clothes, only that they, too, are dark. But I can look for only a few seconds before turning away. He is going to kill me now, and I don't want to watch.

He says, "You can eat something if you want."

My fingers, linked together in my lap, tighten around each other. This isn't right. It's the same person, the same low voice, the same abbreviated way of saying things, but there is no mania here. There is no fury in this voice. No murder.

I don't know if I replied. He walks away then returns in about ten minutes with a plate of eggs and a cup of coffee.

I am in shock, my breath suspended. What to think about this? What to do? I have been on this precipice, looking down, for days; all my thoughts have been about preparing for the instant when I will be pushed over the brink and put to death. Now he offers me food. I wonder if it's a joke, some sadistic game: giving life only to take life away. But he puts the food and coffee on the desk beside me then seats himself on a chair across from me and looks on expectantly.

I haven't eaten since Monday morning, but the smell isn't enticing; I have absolutely no appetite. But I take a few bites of scrambled egg anyway and a sip of coffee. I'm afraid not to, afraid to refuse his generosity, for fear that he will become violent again. But when I drink the coffee, I realize this means I'll have to go to the bathroom again. Eventually he's going to get mad about that.

"I've been thinking," he says. "Thinking maybe I could let you go."

The next breath—when it comes—feels like the first breath of my life. The kind a baby takes. It has never breathed before and now can't get enough of breathing.

"Maybe I could let you out on the highway somewhere."

I was already dead. I've been dead for days. How can I come back so quickly? But I do. I try to tamp it down, the hope. He can't mean it. I can't have it, I mustn't wish for it. It's too late now.

But there it is again. Hope.

ONE OF HIS CATS walks into the room. He has four, just like me. If nothing else, he must take care of these cats; first, there's no cat smell in here, and this one—big and smoky gray—winds around the edges of the room and around his ankle without hesitation. No fear.

This must mean—I hope it means—there is some decency in this person. Maybe there's a decency strong enough to argue with the murderer.

It may also mean he didn't hurt my cats, Paddy and Homey, Tinker and Bandit. I want to ask if he left them alone, but I'm scared.

Oh, God, just let my cats be safe. In this moment, dear God, that's all I will ask of you. Let there be something left alive in my house.

AS MY EYES adjust to the light, I make more sense of the blurry images around me. We're in a small room off a hall. It looks like he's fixed it up as an office. Very orderly. There's the desk and a bookshelf and not much else. No clutter. But I can't be looking too much. Not at my surroundings and especially not at him. I know it's not safe to do.

For an hour or so, we sit here together, in hard-backed office chairs, almost knee to knee. I gulp down a bit more of the food, because he seems to want that. Then, again, "Yeah," he says. "I was thinking about it. Letting you go."

"Yes, please," My breath spills out with the words. "Thank you, sir."

He grunts, shrugs, goes off to another part of the house. He has things to do. He has to prepare. But really, how much preparation will it take? All he has to do is drive me somewhere and release me. It'll be my job to figure out the rest.

I wonder if I can walk any distance. My feet, like my hands, are swollen and achy. Instead of carrying me, they are like anchors that hold me to one place. But that's okay. That's more than okay. I'll figure it all out. I just want to exit this cage, see the daylight, get home to my kids, and be there when they take their father to his grave.

Kids, I'm coming home.

When he returns—he has been gone maybe forty minutes—the man is different. All I can see is the outline of him—my eyes are that bad—but there's something about the way he walks that tells me something has changed. He stands before my chair, looking down at me, and shakes his head. "Uh-uh," he says. "If I let you go, my life's over." He lifts his chin in what looks like defiance. "And I'm not going to jail."

"You won't have to." Don't let me cry here, God. "I won't tell anyone."

"Trouble is, you can identify me."

What? Then why did you take off the blindfold? "I wear glasses, sir. Without them, I can hardly see you. I swear it."

He lapses into a long, brooding silence.

Then: "You know this house."

I don't! "Sir, we could go in the car again." And back into the trunk. Just the thought makes me churn inside. "If you put the blindfold back on, then I wouldn't be able to see the outside of your house or the location."

"Don't know. I have to think about it." Later on, he comes up with a new reason why I can't go. The flocked wallpaper in the hallway. A previous owner had installed it. He loathes it, far more than you'd think a man would. The police, he insists, will be able to track him down if I describe it.

Oh, sure. I can just see myself at the police department, excitedly telling the cops, "Yes, he was a tall black man with a gun, and ropes, and duct tape . . . and this hideous flocked wallpaper."

Once again, I assure him that I haven't seen the wallpaper, cannot see the wallpaper, do not intend to tell police about the goddammed wallpaper.

I have no frame of reference for this. I am in polite conversation with a killer as he ponders the pros and cons of allowing me to live. We are negotiating for my freedom, my very existence. He throws out an objection; I try to allay his fears without sounding insistent or demanding. For what seems like hours, we debate. Do I deserve to live? Do the benefits for me outweigh the potential drawbacks for him? He goes back and forth, vacillating between letting me go and keeping me "a little longer" so he can figure things out.

That first giddiness—he's going to free me!—is gone, and I go very still inside. I had rejoiced at the thought of being driven out of here, left on some barren stretch of road. Day or night, I wouldn't have cared. I would have walked forever to be free, singing as the stones cut my feet.

I have deceived myself. And really, isn't he right? It's too risky to let me go. I've become a dangerous woman, if only to him. Damn me for daring to think I would live on, see my kids again, be with them as they bury their father. Damn me.

"Sir, I understand. I know you need time. I realize you're trying to do the right thing." He looks at me carefully, as though the words confound him. Should I go on? I don't want to say the wrong thing, but this is my life, and I am compelled to plead my case. "I know you're trying to be a good person," I add.

Another Zen-like silence follows. He stares at the wall, the window, and me, and I try not to squirm in the chair. When he doesn't reply, I decide to change the subject. Let's get back to safe territory. I blurt out, small-talking like someone on a bad blind date, "Well, what is it that you do for a living?"

His head comes up sharply. He snorts derisively, then a smile opens up his face. "Me?" he says. "I'm a criminal."

I need to find some neutral place to be during all of this. Cannot tolerate the journey from hope to despair and resignation then the inevitable journey back. It is draining me—of reason, of resilience. Need to stay strong. Can't do that if I'm throwing all my energy into feeling.

Feeling anything is taking too much out of me.

This is no conscious decision. But I submerge.

Abstractly—it's all an abstraction now—I can't help but marvel at this peculiar thing called self-preservation. This capacity human beings have to protect ourselves. Physically. Mentally.

We're not necessarily strong in crisis; at least, our strength is not something we can claim credit for. It's built in, part of the machinery.

I've heard those amazing stories of people who drown, spend as much as an hour underwater, then are raised and resuscitated. They survive because in crisis all but the most necessary body systems shut down. Respiration stops. The heartbeat slows. The body's surface temperature plummets, but the organism fights to sustain heat at the core, in the brain.

I recognize that I am submerging, and my emotions about being here in this place and in this situation with this killer are going under with me. I know it's something instinctive. I thank God for it—in the most abstract way, of course.

I am just going away for a little while. Wake me when it's over.

LATER IN THE MORNING, he suggests that I clean up. Do I have a choice? I'd welcome the chance to get out of these wretched sweats and wash, but the impulse to thank him tastes like mud in my mouth.

I thank him.

"You can take a shower."

"I'm feeling weak, sir." Oh, the "sir" comes so effortlessly. "I don't think I can stand up too long."

How to reconcile his "kindnesses" with what has gone before? He takes me into the bathroom—he takes me with him everywhere, as I'm no longer bound—and runs a bath. Then he tells me to take off my clothes. This is hard. The heat rises in my cheeks. Anger and shame assault me. I have never stripped in front of a man, not even my husband.

I do as I am told, then sit on the toilet, naked, hugging myself, until my bath is ready.

Before I step in, I show him the deep wounds on my wrists. The skin isn't skin at all—there is no skin left. There are deep grooves where the ropes dug in; the flayed flesh looks like bloody meat.

"Sir, do you think you might have some peroxide? Some Neosporin . . ."

He searches the medicine chest and the cabinet under the sink. "Here."

"Thank you, sir." You, sir, who have inflicted these wounds.

Steam wafts above the hot bath. He leaves the room briefly, for which I'm profoundly grateful. I could not bear for him to watch me wash between my legs, to see how much I want to be clean there.

The water feels soothing, bracing, wonderful. But no matter how I scrub—and I'm in there twenty minutes or more—I feel I can't get clean. The grime washes away, along with the sweat, urine, and ejaculate. But I'm still dirty, irredeemably dirty.

He looks in. "Are you finished?"

I'll never be finished. "Yes."

"Aren't you going to wash your hair?"

"I tried, but my arms and hands hurt. I can't raise them over my head."

"All right. I'll do it."

He pours the shampoo into his hand and washes my hair, rinsing it clean with water from a plastic cup. I want to shrink from the feeling of his hands on my head. Instead, I grit my teeth and endure.

Washing my hair. It's something I do alone, in my bathroom while bathing. For some people, it's something tender, the kind of thing that lovers do for each other. Until now, I never recognized it as the intimate act it really is.

Now I do. It feels like the first rape, and the second rape, and the third.

USING A Q-TIP, he applies peroxide and Neosporin to my wrists. He wraps them with gauze and secures the gauze with tape. He gives me a clean white T-shirt and a pair of his sweatpants, both way too big, and I jump into them fast—it appalls me to be naked before this man. As I dress, I catch a glimpse of myself in the bathroom mirror. Poor as my vision is, I can still make them out: the big, blue-black spots on my upper arms. His handprints. And the brutal-looking black eye.

Then he notices there is residual duct tape in my hair, bits of tape and glue he couldn't shampoo out. I don't mind, but it seems to bother him.

"I guess you could cut it out," I offer. I am so helpful. And so he does: chops out pieces of my hair with a pair of scissors. I watch as thick tufts of it fall to the tile floor. Nice. Now I have the layered look.

For some reason, he has become very talkative. Although there is no more talk of letting me go, he reveals much. I listen intently, careful to keep my expression meek and docile, with eyes downcast.

"I've got to stop doing all these drugs." The crack I know about. Click and inhale.

"I'll get them out of the house now, so if I'm arrested, they won't add any time for possession." As if they'll need to add more time to his sentence.

"If they catch me, I could get ten years." At this, I'm astounded. How can he believe he'll get only ten years for rape, murder, and kidnapping?

"I really hate prison." Oh, great. So he's been there before. What for? I could ask, and he might even tell me. But I decide not to. Don't undermine yourself, Debbie. If you know, it'll scare you. It'll bring all those submerged feelings—the fear, the anxiety—back to the top, and you'll be vulnerable again. That won't help.

I say nothing. Then he announces that he must go in to work—a full shift tonight—so it's back to my bondage.

He leads me to what must be the master bedroom and a king-size bed with dark green sheets. Looks like I won't have to lie on the floor this time. Before he ties my feet together, he puts a pair of socks on me, to cover my mangled ankles. The wrist ties go over the thick gauze bandages.

I sit on the edge of the bed as he prepares to blindfold me again. Again I catch myself in a mirror. And there it is, my crowning glory: my hair, cut all jagged and funny on one side.

5

As a kid I was always fascinated by wooden nesting boxes, the kind you open to find another box, then another and another; you keep opening them and think you'll never get to the last one. I once saw one in the shape of a woman, with a painted smile and two pink painted cheeks and some kind of painted peasant costume. When I opened her up there was a smaller woman inside, then an even smaller woman, then a teeny, tiny little woman.

I think of myself as that woman, the smallest one, hidden inside under layers of other women with painted, placid smiles. I am inside a box inside a box inside a box. The person I was last Monday morning, before the madness, has gone into hiding. She has been replaced by this accommodating Stepford creature who displays no anger at the death of her husband and no anxiety at the prospect of her own, agrees to be patient while the killer "thinks it over," and helpfully suggests how he can best escape detection ("You could let me go out in the country somewhere, someplace remote. I don't mind walking. . . . I can't see, so I can't tell police what you look like. . . .").

Nurse's training is part of all this. I have learned, over the years, to detach on command. I could not have continued in hospice if trauma and crisis turned me into a puddle on the floor.

I think back to 1985, when I announced to the family with great fanfare that I was going to study nursing. The skepticism was almost unanimous.

"Do you think that's the field for you, Debbie? You're pretty squeamish."

"Deb, get real. You don't have the stomach for that kind of job. It's a pretty high-pressure thing, nursing. Maybe you should stick to office work."

"How's someone like you going to deal with real pain, real suffering? You'll fall apart."

"C'mon, Deb. You can't even swat a fly. . . ."

It was upsetting—this chorus of naysayers—but they said nothing I hadn't already said to myself. I wasn't the tough type; what had I ever done in life to prove otherwise? I was just a nice little wife and mother who typed transcripts for a dollar a page. I couldn't change a flat tire or file my own tax return. When an emergency happened, I called for my husband. I wasn't built for Big Life, the kind that takes spine and steadfastness.

That I persisted at all was a wonder.

Strangely enough, motivation came from a very unlikely source: our family dentist. The year I started nursing school, I had a tooth just crumble in my mouth; this was odd, because I'm pretty religious about going in every six months like you're supposed to. When I called the dentist—a very nice, gentlemanly man who had been used and recommended by my husband's family for decades—he hemmed and hawed for days before agreeing to send me to a specialist. Even then, he'd refer me only to one of his associates.

Instead, feeling vaguely guilty about my choice, I went to another dentist entirely. After he got me in the chair and took some X rays, he shook his head. "Mrs. Puglisi," he said, "you've got abscesses in all four quadrants of your mouth."

"Doesn't sound good. What's it mean?"

"It means your dentist, instead of drilling out areas of decay, has been sealing over them. Just filling in on top of decay, without removing it."

"Why would he do that?"

"I have no idea. But the upshot of this is, if you don't do something, you could lose all your teeth."

At thirty-five? I was horrified, and so was Nino. But when I decided to file a malpractice suit—it was either make this guy pay for the damage or get a mouthful of dentures—his family erupted. Their disapproval was directed, not at this crackpot but at me, for daring to create a "situation."

I was hurt and baffled and so troubled I actually went to a priest and a counselor for advice before deciding to pursue the case.

Then I sued, and two years later I won the first dental malpractice suit in the state of Delaware.

Thirty-five years old, and this was the first time in my life I had ever talked back.

FROM INSIDE the smallest box, I watch the other me—Stepford Debbie—go through the motions. Obedience. Acquiescence. Head down, eyes averted.

"Don't you women douche?" he asks.

"What?" I stammer. "No. Well, if you think I should . . ."

"What brand?"

I'm amazed I can think of one: "Massengill. Massengill. That's fine."

"Okay." Later he returns with the douche—a vinegar formula, no additives, no "summer breeze" smell—then watches as I use it. His eyes on me at this moment as I perform this act make me feel utterly whorish. Like the most flagrant whore, the most faithless, adulterous whore. I wonder with disgust if it turns him on. It can't possibly. But this is the same man who had sex with me within minutes of murdering my husband.

As I finish douching, I think to myself—and say silently to him—You're not fooling me. I know exactly what's going on. I am washing away all the evidence. All the DNA has just gone down the drain.

Even so, I'm elated to have him out of me, all the traces of our sex.

IT'S LATE AFTERNOON, and I am back in his bedroom, where I guess I will spend the night. He leaves me tied up, but—this surprises me—neither blindfolded nor gagged. The shades are drawn, and the room is dark. From another part of the house, his music revs up again: Power 99, Philadelphia's rap station.

I'm sure he's still around. I may have earned some points for good behavior, but I don't think he'd leave the house without gagging me. An hour later he opens the door and looks in. Just checking. And me, good girl that I am, I'm just where he left me. Ropes intact. Haven't tried anything, haven't tried to wriggle free. Keeping my promises.

Later still, he sticks his head in again, this time to say he's going to this job of his, whatever it is.

"I'll be awhile. I've got a full shift tonight."

Before he goes, he switches the radio from rap music to WJBR, an easy-listening station. The DJ, a silky-voiced woman called Delilah, plays nothing but love songs, interspersed with calls from listeners who make tremulous dedications, talk about loves lost and reclaimed, and wax romantic about some special "someone."

It's hard to hear. The thoughts come flooding in, unbidden, unwelcome—of Nino and all the years we shared. From the time we were silly kids, crazy in love with each other and heedless of the odds against us, to the predictable early years of struggle, when we forgot our passion in the quest for stability. Then the kids came along, and for a while, that was enough; we were a family at last. When Nino held the babies high above his head and took them for their "flying lessons," racing around our living room as they squealed with pleasure, I thought I could never be more content.

Then life intervened. What's that saying, and who said it? "Life is what happens when you're busy making other plans." In midlife, Nino and I were still working hard; we spent precious little time together. Like so many people, we got caught up in the day-to-day. We went to the job. We came home. We waved as we passed each other on the way to the next thing. How differently would we have lived our lives if we'd known?

We talked a little about retiring and threw out Florida as a possibility. But as Nino grew older, he wondered if he could tolerate warm weather year-round. He did say he'd love to get a part-time job at a marina. Everything was boats, boats, boats.

"Well, we could always go back to Galena," I ventured. "Let's go back to Maryland and live like hicks in the sticks. That way we can still be close to the kids." I knew Nino would never let those kids get too far away from him. His life revolved around M & M.

Tucked in there among the years of routine was the briefest idyll, for which I'm so grateful; though here and now, in the killer's house, I could curse the memory, which—along with this treacly music—makes me want to weep. The year the kids turned thirteen, we flew alone, just Nino and me, to the Bahamas. Our first trip in aeons. There in the islands, we really reconnected. Drank fruity pastel-colored drinks and got matching sunburns, swam in the hotel pool, and slept together on the ivory beaches. Danced like sweethearts, cheek to cheek, at the funny little club nearby.

I hoped when we got back that we would keep hold of that new bond. But we soon slid back into our workaday routines, our opposing schedules, our nearly separate lives. Hi and bye. When I tried to initiate more romance, Nino made it clear he thought that was kid stuff or special occasion stuff. I didn't buy it, and I told him why: it was because of my dad's parents, my Nana and Pop Pop. Even in their sixties, they still sat together on the sofa, hand in hand, smooching like a pair of kids. Sometimes when they walked together, I'd catch Grandpa reaching out to pat Nana on the behind. Once I even caught him goosing her! At the time, I was scandalized. I didn't think old people were supposed to act like that. But by the time I'd been married twenty-five years, they were my role models. I wanted nothing more than for my husband and me to become like these crazy old people. I hoped when we both stopped being so busy it would happen that way for us, too.

Now any chance for that has been taken from us.

Damn it. Damn it! I can't be crying here. When the man gets home, he'll be able to tell. He'll get mad at me.

It's the unfairness of it all. That's what gets me. Didn't we always do what we were supposed to? Nino and me, we did our jobs, raised our kids, got them started on the right path. And this was supposed to be our time. Time to rekindle, time to be a couple again. Didn't we deserve it?

All gone now. All the years ahead—wiped out.

I snuffle into the sheets, wipe my nose on them, shake my head to clear it. Okay. Had to do that. Did that. Stop now, before he comes home.

Once again, I am rigidly in control.

IT'S A PECULIAR THING, not to plan. This is a revelation to me. I have always lived by lists, with one foot in the future. Now, for the first time, I know what it's like to have no list and no reason for one. There's not a thing to do tomorrow, because tomorrow isn't going to happen. Well, it will but only for others. I won't be here. Someone has decided I do not get a tomorrow.

The Sunday before, Nino and I had been full of lists and plans for the future. Nino, in the midst of his springtime ritual, was readying the boat for the water. He spent his day off at Skipjack Cove in Maryland, flat on his back under the hull with a scraper and a paintbrush. We had rented a slip for the season, and Nino was counting the days till we could ease the Pug Boat out of dry dock into the waters of the Sassafras. Sunday at dusk he came home tired and wind-burned and covered from head to toe with motor oil and paint. But he was all smiles and eager as a boy. I loved to see it. "I can't wait to take her out," he said, and I knew that from now on he'd be checking the skies every day, waiting for the first break in the weather. Even weekdays, when he had to go to the office, the first thing out of his mouth was always, "Aw, man, what a great day to be on the water!" or "I'm telling you, this rain better let up before Friday."

The slip at Skipjack cost twenty-five hundred dollars. It was the first time we'd rented one for the whole summer, and Nino wrestled with what seemed, to him, like a huge extravagance. More than once he said, "I should have my head examined, putting out all that money." But I was just thankful he let himself have a little fun. This wasn't my idea of paradise—living out of a cooler, washing up in a communal shower, sleeping below deck on a bunk lined with four inches of foam—but for Nino, it was serenity and sanity and consummate joy. When he was on the boat, he was a happy, happy man.

And despite the rougher parts of roughing it, there was a wonderful simplicity about our weekend life. At night the gentle rocking of the boat at anchor was like a return to the cradle. I loved opening the hatch and staring up at the stars. There were always a million more stars in Maryland. Sunday mornings I'd scramble eggs in the single frying pan, and Nino would even drink instant coffee and powdered "whitener" without grumbling.

For him, this was heaven, and the Sunday before he died, he couldn't wait to get back there.

GOOD THING I cried. It helped. Now I must be resolved. God, I need your strength. I've come this far, but my work has just begun. There has to be a good side to this man. I swear I'll find it and do whatever it takes to make him know me. If I make him know me, know my humanity—even *like* me—I might make it impossible for him to kill me.

Don't let this person finish me off now, God. I told myself I was ready to die. What I didn't know was, I'm not.

He comes in after midnight, muttering loudly. Very tired, he says. Has to get some rest. After untying my ropes, he takes off his shoes and shirt—leaves the pants on—and lies down next to me. His big right arm comes up around me then falls across my chest, where it will stay throughout the night.

I dare not move, lest I disturb his rest. I lie motionless on my back, staring at hairline cracks in the ceiling plaster. They seem to move into shapes and forms. If I connect the dots, I imagine I see the shape of a creeping wolf and a falling tree. It's just like when Michael and Melissa were kids and we used to look for pictures in the clouds. There in one corner is what looks like an outstretched hand.

He sleeps fitfully, but his arm is always there, clasped around me as if I'm a favorite stuffed toy.

If I lose consciousness at all, it's only moments at a time, and sleep doesn't restore me. Sleep isn't sleep; it's passing out, it's sheer physical depletion. I have been emptied. I wake at the slightest motion or sound, and struggle to remain still.

The long night gives me more time to think, more time than I want. Here I am, locked in the embrace of the man who murdered my husband. At one time I might have considered this the final indignity. But I've thought that many times these past three days: "This is the worst, the pain." "This is the worst, the rape." "This is the worst, the fear." He has always managed to prove me wrong.

Rape hasn't been the most dreadful part of this. If I am the recipient of any grace at all, it's the fact that, for all his voracious sexual appetite, the man is easily satisfied. He does nothing but enter, heave, then roll away. If he ever attempted to arouse me—or, oh, God, kiss me—I know I couldn't keep from recoiling.

The hours crawl by, and spears of light and shadow move across the room, making the pictures in the ceiling shift and change. The wolf becomes a person, gender indeterminate, who crawls on all fours. The hand, reaching out, becomes a face in profile, smiling broadly. The fallen tree stays a fallen tree.

In the morning, he is perturbed. Can't sleep like he used to, he complains. Afraid I'm going to try to get away.

"No, no," I protest; doesn't he believe me yet? I have worked so hard for his trust. "I wouldn't do that, sir. I promised you I wouldn't."

Before he dresses, he requests a "sexual favor." Of course. The daily rape.

He crawls on top of me, and I open my arms.

I tell myself that if I survive, this can stay my secret, forever— this pretense of wanting it, liking it. How could I ever tell? No one would understand. But if I must feel guilty, at least I'll have the rest of my life to do it.

He rolls off and lies back on the bed. "Do you want to suck my dick?"

I freeze, fixing my eyes to the opposite wall, pretending not to hear him. I had worried about this, about what I would do if he ever wanted it. A no would anger him. A yes would certainly invite more of the same. I say nothing and pray he won't make me. He doesn't.

Isn't this the way men are with prostitutes? There are unspoken rules: Do not kiss, do not touch. The only parts that collide during that kind of transaction are the sexual organs. He seems to know this etiquette. Has he been with prostitutes then? I could now be an incubator for the AIDS virus. He has raped me, and raped me, and raped me, five times, six times—I've lost count.

But though the idea crosses my mind, it doesn't take hold. Doesn't become a fear. In the hierarchy of my fears, the threat of AIDS doesn't even register.

6

IN THIS HOUSE, the telephone does not ring. Days pass, and nothing—no one comes by or knocks on the door. This is an isolated man. On Thursday, though, before I am let up and out of the bedroom, I hear fragments of a conversation coming from the next room. He is talking low, almost whispering.

"I've done something. If I get caught, I'm going to need your support."

So he has a confidant. But it's not someone to whom he can tell the details of what he's done. The "something."

HE IS GOING FOR take-out, he says. Do I want anything in particular?

"Would you mind getting a newspaper, sir?" To my surprise, he agrees.

Information has come sparingly these last few days; within my box, I have lost touch.

What is going on out there? I have imagined a marauding army of police, roving the countryside with guns and dogs in search of me. I have imagined a noose pulling ever tighter around the man, as investigators get closer and closer to the place we are. But the cavalry hasn't arrived. My mind begins to tiptoe around the possibility that this will be my reality from now on. This strange half-life, in this small, neat house. I'm reminded of an old movie, *The Collector,* in which a deranged man takes a woman from her world and locks her up in his, as one might cage a bird or a butterfly.

I cannot be more than a few miles from my home; that I know. The drive on Monday took fewer than fifteen minutes. I keep thinking, Either we're in Bear, a little town about five miles out of Newark, or we're close to it. It's maddening to realize that no matter what's going on out there, it's most likely happening close by. Maybe right outside that front door.

By now I think I could reach that door blindfolded.

This has become my work. Each day, when he unties me and lets me out into his living space, I try to construct a mental blueprint of his bungalow: where windows and doors are located, where there is furniture, where he keeps his portable phone.

"I GUESS THIS is something you have to develop a taste for," he says, when I leave the collard greens on my plate. He's brought home a special "treat": barbecued ribs, baked beans with rice, a side of greens. Soul food.

"I really appreciate your kindness, though," I say, and force myself to swallow some rice. "It's good."

He is in an oddly jovial mood. Eats up and finishes off what I leave over. Jokes around with me. "You know, I think you're getting too expensive to keep."

And he laughs, as if this is humor we can both appreciate.

Perhaps this is the source of his good mood. He has brought home a copy of the *Wilmington News Journal,* our local paper. On the front page, the words—in huge block letters—nearly shout.

WHERE IS DEBRA PUGLISI?

And underneath: WIFE OF MURDER VICTIM STILL MISSING.

And under that: POLICE ADMIT THEY HAVE FEW CLUES. A detective is quoted as saying that the investigation is "like looking for a needle in a haystack."

This could *not* be today's newspaper. They must know something by now. But there is the date, just big enough for me to see: Thursday, April 23.

Suddenly I am light-headed, like someone has punched me in the face. How could it be? The man took me almost four days ago. Picked me up and threw me in the back of his car in the middle of the afternoon. At the time, people—literally, dozens of people—were milling around the neighborhood. I'd seen them all: Gene Nygaard on his lawn, on the cell phone. Joe Strykalski walking his dog. Kids stepping off the school bus and walking down the street. Construction workers, building the new part of Academy Hill, directly across the street from our house.

How did it all go unnoticed? A strange car parked on the lawn. A strange man tossing a life-size bundle in the back.

But people don't look for danger in Academy Hill. They look for it in the run-down neighborhoods of Wilmington. But not Academy Hill. Academy Hill is Mayberry.

There is my picture—I'm glancing over my shoulder and smiling. There's Nino's photo, a professional black-and-white portrait. He wears a suit and tie. He looks handsome and serene and helpful—your friendly preneed planner.

The man reads aloud from the news article, and shock is heaped on shock. With little evidence and no leads, the police actually theorized that I was in league with the killer—or was the killer myself. The speculation: I had grown dissatisfied in my marriage and taken a lover. Together we conspired to do away with my husband. Again, it's like the movies, like *Double Indemnity* or *The Postman Always Rings Twice*.

What has happened to my real life?

Terrifying, sickening. How could anyone consider me a suspect? Quick, angry tears spring to my eyes.

No, Debbie. Get a grip now. I clench my fists so hard they

hurt. I focus on the pale half-moons at the base of my fingernails. The tears recede.

Is he a stone, this man? How can he fail to see the wreckage he has made of our lives? But he seems to take pride in the fact that he has confounded the investigators.

"Puglisi case has 'more questions than answers.' " "County police are no closer to determining where Debra Puglisi is, or who killed her husband." "As a suspect in her husband's murder, 'She hasn't been ruled out, but she hasn't been ruled in.' "

The newspaper account also includes details of my husband's funeral, scheduled for Monday. On Sunday, there will be a memorial service, with an empty chair next to the casket. An empty chair for me.

Alarm runs through me like a current. Have they stopped looking for me? But I'm alive!

The man chuckles. He sounds pleased and amused, as if someone has just paid him a great compliment. "Looks like I've just committed the perfect crime."

I ASK FOR permission to use the toilet. In the bathroom, behind the half-closed door, I gaze at my mirror image. The black eye looks more horrific, if that's possible; the color has congealed to that sickly purple-yellow. My left hand looks like a rubber glove that has been blown up or filled with water; it looks like it's about to burst.

With my right hand I reach up to smooth the short, sticking-out ends of my hair.

My hair will always be brown; it will never get to be gray. In everyone's memory, I will always be this age. One day, years from now, my children will be older than their daddy and I ever got to be.

That night it's a domestic tableau turned inside out. We are just another couple at home, chatting over dinner, watching the evening news. He is seated on the black leather sofa; I'm on the love seat across from him. One of my bracelets is on the coffee table, which strikes me as vaguely sacrilegious. How'd it get there? I want it. But I dare not reach out to get it. It wouldn't fit my wrist now, anyway.

Though Nino's murder and my disappearance are still the lead stories on TV, they pass without comment from me or the man seated across the room from me. He watches with mild interest, as if this is of no real importance; as always, I take my cue from him. There's a shot of my house, with yellow tape running all around the perimeter. I see the flag hanging outside the door, with an embroidered house and the word, WELCOME. There's a photo of Nino and one of me, too, me standing with my patient, Keith. We're hugging each other and smiling into the camera.

Oh, Keith. You always managed to smile, even when you were dying.

Then, the worst. It's my father and my brother Robert, talking to some reporter from *Action News*. I have to restrain myself from reaching out to them.

They're outdoors somewhere, perhaps near the new construction at Academy Hill. Robert, wearing a windbreaker and baseball cap, looks exhausted. I cannot clearly see his features, but the posture is all wrong. He sags as if under some ponderous weight. Dad stands next to him, looking on. His gray hair is askew. He seems shrunken into himself. I know he has been crying.

"She would never do anything like that," says Robert, and his voice in my ears is a heartbreak. He sounds so worn, so sad. There is no indignation in his voice; it's as if he feels the suspicions about me are too preposterous to be taken seriously, much less vehemently denied.

"My sister wasn't the type to hurt anyone," he says quietly. "She was a nurse. She dedicated her life to helping people. And the family—they were like the Cleaver family."

Robert is referring to me in the past tense.

They do not mention Michael and Melissa, and I'm relieved. I have not mentioned them to the man, even when I thought doing so might evoke some sense of compassion in him. I won't

use my children to appeal to a killer. I don't want him to know
they exist. He is not good enough to occupy the same world with
them. He is not good enough to hear their names.

Later, we watch an episode of *ER* (lady's choice). Then he pops
a movie in the VCR.

"This is a great movie," he says. "It's my favorite."

I have never seen *Fargo,* but it doesn't hold my interest, and I
start to nod off. He decides it's time for bed.

Later, he snores next to me, arm wrapped firmly around my
shoulder. I stare at the ceiling, praying to my family.

Don't stop searching, I think, trying to psychically will the
information to them. I'm still alive.

Find me.

And the hours pass. In the pale blue early morning hours, I
feel a tickle start way down in my throat. I have to cough. Reflex-
ively, not thinking, I start up in bed, knocking his arm away.

He is up in an instant, rising up in the bed, towering above
me. Screaming. "Are you trying to get away? Think you can?" He
raises his arm as if to strike me, and I fall back on the mattress.

"No! Sir, no! I had to cough—I'm sorry!"

"Bitch! Stupid bitch!" His rage—enormous, fearsome—fills
the room. "I knew I couldn't trust you."

No matter how I implore—and I implore all through the
night, hands clasped before me, saying I didn't mean to disturb
or alarm him—he will not be reconciled with me.

"Please forgive me. I'm so sorry. I didn't mean to do it."

"Shut up, bitch. You were trying to get out of here. So don't lie
to me."

"No, it's not true. I had to cough—"

Here I am, prostrating myself before him, begging for his
indulgence. I've done nothing but everything he's ever demanded
of me. Now he's raging, stalking around the room, shouting,
thrusting his finger in my face. My offense is unforgivable. I had
to cough.

Way down deep, something that's been dormant for days
begins to stir, to reassert itself. I want to push it back down. It's

roughing up my smooth, noncombative surface. Once again I find it hard to maintain this plastic composure of mine, the niceness to him that lets no insult in, no matter how grievous.

This shouldn't happen—I had buried this—but I am getting really mad. I breathe deep, choking on words that are so ready to be said.

Cool it, girl, cool it, I tell myself, squaring my shoulders. Not now.

It's nearly daybreak when he relents. The torrent of accusations, so loud and furious they almost feel like blows, come to an end. But I know we've rolled back the clock. All week I've worked so hard to win his trust. I've been obedient and deferential; I've yielded to him sexually. Now all my gains are lost, swept away in a second.

For the rest of the day, he is extravigilant, just as he was at the start. He constantly checks up on me. All of a sudden he makes it a practice to leave the house then return before I've been told to expect him. He's attempting to catch me trying to undo the ropes, trying to get away, trying to stay alive.

I'm being tested. Any sign that I'm thinking of escape and he'll kill me.

Then, a terrible thought. And I know even before it's fully formed in my mind that my hunch is absolutely, indisputably right: he knows damned well I wasn't trying to escape. Does he think I'm that stupid, that I would leap up from the bed he was in and try to make my getaway, through locked doors?

No. He's like the lover who fabricates a fight so he can justify ending a relationship. He's trying to get mad at me. He's trying to think of a good enough reason to kill me. If I am treacherous, a liar, a bitch, he can kill me and remain blameless to himself.

The pieces fit together and the picture becomes clear. All his plans have been laid out for me, if I dare to look at them. I'm "getting too expensive." I'm a threat to his safety. I'm his undoing.

And another thing. It's Friday now. When I was a teenager, first out among the working, Friday was the day people cashed their checks, the day some people started the party. TGIF. Friday was time to hit the bars and get loaded. This man, I know, is transformed by crack cocaine, which turns him from a neat neurotic into something monstrous and murderous. Crack gives him permission to commit murder.

For all his supposed remorse about drug-taking, is he going to stop now, when he is under what is probably the most intense pressure of his life? Of course not. He's going to turn to drugs again, and it makes sense that it will happen on a Friday.

So I lose. Is it going to be death, then? I've been so close to death these past days, and several times I've thought I could do it with courage. But now I just want to get free.

Sunday is Nino's memorial service, with the chair alongside the casket. It's a lovely gesture that simply horrifies me. I wish I didn't know about it. According to the news, the family is planning to put some of my personal effects on that chair—I guess my wedding ring and maybe one of the crystal angel pins I wear to my patients' homes. I know, also from the news, that Nino's folks and mine have pooled their resources to buy a double plot at Saint Patrick's Cemetery. A place for him. A place for me.

I'm already dead. I hear it on the noon news and the nightly news. I hear my killer read it out loud from the newspapers. Only in Nino's obituary is there a hint of hope held out for me. Whoever composed the obituary—and, thank you, God, included me among the survivors—thought to add, "Please remember Debbie in your thoughts, and pray for her safe return."

Oh yes. Please pray.

I'VE COME TO know this name, and the voice that goes with it. A detective named Domenick Gregory of the New Castle County police department is the head of the investigation into my disappearance. On TV this day he reiterates to the press that the task force assigned to the Puglisi case still has "no solid leads." The investigation, he says, is "ongoing."

He says an eyewitness report of a black male wearing a baseball cap near a green car on the Puglisi lawn is being checked out. But unidentified fingerprints in the Puglisi home—our dream house, now a crime scene—have not turned up in any regional or national criminal database.

The tire tracks leading to the front door have not yet proved useful, he says; tires are not easily matched to a make, model, or year of car.

Yes, Detective Gregory tells reporters, his team is still devoting itself full-time to the search.

Yes, he concedes, the outlook for the missing woman is not promising.

My children hear every word of this, and it must be so excruciating for them. I hear every word of this, and it's like somebody who knew me very well devised just the right way to drive me slowly insane.

ALL WEEK I'VE suppressed my anger, denied it, because it could not serve me. I thought acquiescence was the way to control my controller. And it worked, too, for a few days. But it's not working anymore. He is going to kill me anyway.

I can't beat it down anymore. Now I'm consumed by it—the greatest, biggest, all-encompassing anger—and I begin to think, No. You will not win. I'm screaming at him in my mind, and the anger grows and grows, till I feel as tense and powerful as a clenched fist. No. My children are waiting for me.

In my mind, I see them both: Michael's handsome face, the intense brown eyes behind wire-rimmed glasses, the querulous half-smile. Michael is stubborn and self-effacing and driven, and his perfectionism drives him and me both a little crazy. Then there's Melissa: long silky hair, wide dark eyes, slim as a willow switch. She's hardheaded, smart. Sometimes my adversary, sometimes my dearest friend.

The man looks in at me. Just checking.

You asshole.

I will remember this moment always, when I first said it about him.

Asshole.

The instant the word takes shape in my mind, I know I've reached a turning point. If nothing else, this will set me free, this rage, and I let it take hold of me. I welcome it. God damn this fucking asshole, who kills and destroys with impunity, even pride ("the perfect crime").

That he thinks to joke about his criminal prowess with me— knowing my desperation, knowing I'm afraid to die, and knowing that my family is suffering—makes me want to beat him bloody with my bare fists. Asshole. Son of a bitch asshole. You don't get to decide when I live and die.

The thought of my kids burying their beloved dad and doing it without me ignites me. Despite my bondage, and the near impossibility of my situation, I'm inflamed by fury at him, by love for them.

I'm needed at home. I have never been needed more. I have to get there in time for Nino's memorial.

Over the course of five days, I've made peace with the possibility of death. Now I'm ready to risk it. The moment I make the decision, the fear drains away, a blessing from God. It's life or death, today, now.

No one is coming to save me. I will have to rescue myself.

"I'VE MISSED A LOT of work this week," he says (implication: my fault). "I better go in for my shift tonight."

He hustles me into the bedroom—"our" room now—and spreads the shower curtain across the bed.

"Before you go," I begin, tentatively.

"What?"

"I'm worried about my hands." I hold them out for him to see. They are massive. Grotesque. The ropes have carved deep scars in my flesh, and my left hand is nearly twice its normal size. As a nurse, I suspect severe nerve damage, maybe tissue death.

"I'm in so much pain," I say.

Later on I think of this moment and wonder what good thing

I had done in my life to deserve the beautiful mistake he made then. It was a mistake for him. For me, it was all the blessings of God. Somewhere up above fate was conspiring, at last, in my favor.

His idea: to replace the ropes with handcuffs. I sit on the edge of the bed, listening as he phones half a dozen pawnshops in the area. I can tell by his side of the conversations that he is being turned down, but he catches on quick; he realizes he has to pretend to be a cop or security officer in order to get them. Finally he finds someone willing to sell him what he needs: two sets of cuffs, one for my wrists and one for my ankles. He's happy: just five bucks apiece. A real bargain.

When he returns, he's tickled by an exchange he had with the pawnshop owner, who asked him if he wanted the cuffs for some kind of sexual bondage.

"I told him, 'Yeah, something like that,' " he says, chortling. Then he clasps the handcuffs around my wrists.

I know at once that I have far more flexibility with these than I had with the rope ties, which had been nearly impossible to budge. I look at him then look away fast. Though my heart beats a little faster, I'm careful to keep my expression blank, bland, subservient. And when he checks the cuffs on my hands ("Y'know, I'm not sure these are tight enough") I press my wrists together to keep him from seeing that there is a little give in the chain.

He pulls my arms and legs behind me then links the handcuffs with a length of rope.

It's five or six o'clock when he leaves. I lie awake in the dark, wanting to move, wanting to try, but so afraid. It's become his habit to come and check up on me. What if I test this, see if I can really move better with the handcuffs, and he walks in?

An hour passes, and I lie on the bed, in paralysis. I rebuke myself: move, damn it. Do it. But I cannot.

And thank God for it. Before the second hour passes, he is back. Just as I suspected, he comes back and looks into the bedroom. Only when he sees I haven't moved does he leave again.

I'm acutely aware that this is it: my last opportunity.

I have prepared myself. I will not let my children bury their father without me. Either I get out of here or I die.

My decision, this time.

The countdown has begun.

I CLOSE MY EYES and try to visualize the placement of the ropes, where they meet the cuffs, where the rope is knotted in the hog tie. Then I feel behind me, along the rope line, till I find the thick knot. It's tied so tight. Can I undo it?

The rope is twiny and rough under my fingers; the knot thick as a pig's knuckle. I work feverishly to loosen it, but it just won't give. Oh, my God. Just loosen up!

Twenty minutes pass, maybe more. I work. I *work.* I am damp with sweat; the sweat has soaked through my T-shirt onto the shower curtain.

The rope. It won't come loose. Shit. When he comes back and finds this thing half-undone, he's going to kill me. No matter what, I've played my hand. I can't pretend I wasn't trying to get away. God damn it! God *damn* it!

Every few minutes I must stop, steady myself, breathe. And back to work.

Something is happening. The ropes are not as tight. But the knot is still intact.

I tug. Please. God, give me the strength.

Finally, in one graceful fluid motion, the knot gives, pulls apart, falls away. My arms and legs are still handcuffed. But I can move.

Slowly, painstakingly, my heart hammering in my chest, I slide from the side of the bed, find the floor with my feet, and rise. I'm so weak, my head feels wobbly on my neck.

One foot, Debbie. Just go.

I shuffle in the dark toward the nearest open door and lunge forward. It is suddenly, perceptibly darker, and shirts and jackets on hangers flap into my face. I've walked into a closet. Now my composure dissolves. The terror I haven't allowed myself to feel for five days wells up. I'm panicking.

Debbie, get hold of yourself. You've come this far. Don't give up now.

For a moment I have the distinct feeling that someone is here with me, encouraging me. In a familiar, tender voice, my husband whispers—I literally hear him whisper, "Hang in there, honey."

Nino, I'm trying.

I back out of the closet and search for the door to the hallway, which leads to the dining area. Then picturing the table where the killer usually leaves the portable phone, I inch ahead. Behind me, I feel for the edge of the table, then the receiver.

It's still there. I lift it, turn and see it light up in my hand.

God's grace.

I drop to my knees. Cannot see the damned thing, it's behind me. Just have to figure this. Beads of sweat trickle down my rib cage as I search the keypad.

Think hard, girl. How are the numbers configured? Where is the number nine? God, I use the phone a hundred times a day, and I can't remember. Then: yes! Third down from the top on the right-hand side. One is on the upper left-hand corner.

For the rest of my days, I will never be able to recall just how, with hands cuffed behind my back, I managed to hold the receiver and punch in the numbers.

It's now 8:50 P.M., Friday, April 24, 101 hours since I was kidnapped.

"Nine-one-one," says the crisp voice of a dispatcher. "What's your emergency?"

7

I KNEEL AND LEAN in close to the phone, which is now on the floor.

"Please."

"What's going on there, ma'am?"

"Please help me. This is Debbie Puglisi. Please."

I have imagined this moment, or some version of it, for days. I've dreamed of this, tried not to dream of this. Deliverance. I am closer to home than ever.

But he might come back, the killer. So please, hurry.

"This is Debbie Puglisi."

But for the man on the other end of the line, who has the impersonal voice of someone at directory information, my name doesn't seem to register. It's like, Debbie who? I thought people were looking for me.

"He kidnapped me," I hiss into the phone, trying to speak low but needing to make him know what is happening. If the man comes back and finds me here, in the living room, on the phone, he will murder me, I know it. It's a peculiar thought, but I think it: if he sees I have broken my promise to him, he will kill me even harder. He will make it more horrible than it has to be. I can't let that happen now, not after I've come so far.

"He killed my husband. Please! My name is Debbie Puglisi."

"Just a minute, please. Hold on." And then there is a click and the sound of a dial tone, followed by a brief silence. Jesus Christ! Have we disconnected? Luckily, I do not have time to react to this (I was actually transferred to another line) before a second voice comes on—another man—and he, too, speaks in the clipped, professional monotone that so unnerves me. In time I learn that this is the emergency dispatcher, an officer named Steven Conrad. He asks me who I am and what is my problem, and I have to say it all over again: "I'm Debbie Puglisi. He kidnapped me, killed my husband. Help me." I know they all think I'm dead—does he think this is a prank?

"Where are you now?"

"I'm in his home." Please, believe me. Please, get here before the man comes back. "I think it's somewhere in the Bear area. Please come get me. My hands are tied behind my back."

"Where is the man now?"

"He's at work, I think. But he might come back."

"So you're alone now?"

"Yes, but he might get here before you do. Please!"

"How long have you been there?"

"Since Monday night."

"Do you know who this guy is?"

"No, I don't know him. . . . Please help me." What's wrong? Why don't they know who I am? Why don't they come and get me?

"You say you're handcuffed now?"

"I was handcuffed on my hands and on my feet. Oh, Lord have mercy. Oh, my God. I want my children. I want my children."

"So you said he's at work now?"

I won't know till much later that by some technological miracle, the killer's address has flashed across the dispatcher's screen and police are already on the way. To me, it still feels like the dispatcher is trying to determine if this is a genuine emergency.

"He said he had to go to work," I whisper. I cannot speak loudly—what if the killer comes in another way, like through the garage, and hears me?—but the result is that I feel I'm strangling on my fear. "He tied a hog tie from my handcuffs to my feet. And I worked and I worked and I got the knot undone."

"Okay. So you don't have any idea who the guy is?"

No! I clench and unclench my cuffed hands and bend into the receiver. "I think his first name is Don. I don't know his last name. Are they almost here?"

"They're on the way. They should be there in a couple of minutes."

A couple of minutes. When every second is a lifetime. I scan the black squares of windows in the living room, back and forth, fearfully, obsessively. Don't let me see headlights. So scared to see that. Not until I'm sure it's the police.

His questions are never-ending. "Did this guy tell you anything about why or what's going on?" Of course, he is just trying to focus me, keep me occupied, keep me from becoming hysterical. He also wants to make sure I don't feel alone while I wait.

"Ma'am?"

"He said he saw me in my yard and he wanted me. He waited in my house, and then my husband came in and he shot him." Tears are spilling down my face, into my mouth, falling off my chin. Saying it makes it so real. "He killed my husband. He shot him."

With every passing moment, I tell myself that God would not beckon me back to life if he did not intend for me to live it. I need to believe that. Heaven would not be so cruel to me or my kids.

"I want my children." I want so much to hug them. I promise if I get the chance I will hug them so tight, kiss them so hard, breathe them in, cry with them about Dad, and love them so thoroughly that if we're ever wrenched apart again, they'll have all the love they need for the rest of their lives.

"Ma'am," he says, "do you see the car outside? They should be pulling up outside, any minute now."

I do see something: lights, the tops of them, crawling along the lower edge of the living room windows, getting closer. White lights, not red or blue lights. It makes me think: the killer. Coming to check on me. The lights stop moving right in front of the window.

Oh, my God. No, no, no, no.

"Please!"

He says, "Okay, stay calm now." There is a pause when he seems to be listening to someone else. Then he's back with me. "Okay, we should have an officer pulling up outside now, so if you hear something, that should be one of the officers."

There are footsteps first, heavy steps like the killer has, and I press myself against the door of the foyer closet, where I have been crouching. The footsteps are followed by more footsteps and some kind of skirmish, then there is a sharp rap at the front door. Whoever it is, I am separated from them by one door.

Inside, I cower. Later I learn that when I didn't respond, they looked around briefly, then prepared to leave without further investigation. Thank God for the dispatcher. I can hear him hollering into the phone on some other line. "She's inside! She can hear you!"

It's time. I am on my feet, scrambling for the place where the lights are. These are safe lights. "Help me!"

"Just stay calm," says the 911 man. What is he, crazy? "He knows you're there. . . . Can you hear him outside?"

I edge toward the door, steps from freedom now, and finally erupt in the shrillest scream. Later, when I hear the tape—and that god-awful shriek that sounds nothing like me—I know one thing for sure and for good: I can scream. I can scream good. "Help me!" I say. "Help me! Help me!"

All kinds of shouting outside that door, then, "Ma'am, stand back. Get away from the door."

I stagger back, out of the foyer and back into the dining room. There is a sharp report, louder even than a gunshot, but it's a cop, kicking at the front door. Once, twice, and I can hear him go "oomph" every time he kicks. Then I hear a big boom that is the sound of splitting wood, and the lock gives way. The door bursts open, and the light from all their cars floods the house like klieg lights.

Uniforms. I'm surrounded by policemen, all in their uniforms. "Help me!" I scream. They need to know that we, all of us, are in danger now. The man could come home at any time. He's a killer. We've got to get out of here. They are all bending over me. Arms are reaching down to me. "It's okay," says a voice. "You're okay."

"Ma'am, we're here now. You're safe now."

"Help me!"

"It's all right. He's not coming back. You're going to be okay."

"Help me, please." I collapse into myself, my head drops into my chest. I comprehend, slowly. But even after I have stopped screaming, I still hear it. Who is that? It sounds like another person screaming somewhere close by.

"Someone shut that thing off!" says one of the officers, and I realize, dumbly, that it's the house alarm. The alarm system is screaming away with a hot intense sound that sputters now, then blips, and finally stops.

"Take me out of here, please."

"Hang on, ma'am. Relax. Let's see if we can get these cuffs off, okay?"

Lights go on in the house. Police are all around. One is down on one knee beside me, his hand on my shoulder. I see uniforms, badges, brown-clad legs walking by but no faces; even when I look at them I can't see what their faces look like. But they all speak with the same voice: soft, soothing, strong. "Calm down, ma'am. We're going to get these handcuffs off you. Okay?"

"I'm Captain Hedrick." The officer holds a big tool that looks for all the world like a pair of hedge clippers. Is he going to use these on me? It looks like a weapon, and instinctively I shrink from it. "It's okay," he says, squatting down on the floor. "I'm going to use these bolt cutters to cut the chains, then we'll get you out of here. I'll be careful. It won't hurt." The chains snap easily, but the cuffs won't release; I thought the police had some kind of universal key that opened any kind of cuffs.

"Oh, God, get them off me!" This is too important to me, to lose these handcuffs.

"I'm sorry, we can't get them off quite yet," says Captain Hedrick. He turns to the other officers. "Look, we'll figure out the handcuffs later. Let's just get her to the hospital, okay?"

THEY CLUSTER ALONG the sidewalk, with mouths and eyes literally agape: a woman in a quilted robe, a man in pajamas and a windbreaker, people swaddled against the cool night air in sweaters or afghans. The police carry me on a stretcher toward a waiting ambulance, and I crane my head to both sides, disbelieving.

We are in the prettiest little neighborhood, on a tiny tree-lined street with neat little houses side by side. Why, the nearest house cannot be more than fifteen feet away.

How could all this go on without someone hearing or noticing? But their shocked expressions—even with my poor vision, I see those mouths and eyes—tell me they knew nothing.

Just as my neighbors in Academy Hill saw and knew nothing. This killer—this asshole—was an extraordinarily lucky man. Then I changed his luck.

AT CHRISTIANA HOSPITAL, I am treated for dehydration, a black eye, a broken toe, and severe lacerations of the wrists and legs.

My family has been notified; they had traveled, all of them, from North Carolina and Virginia, Florida, and New Jersey, for Nino's funeral. For the first time this week, I allow myself to feel weary, and the feeling is bliss, so wonderful I don't want to end it by going to sleep. By now the kids know I'm okay. This feeling of safety and protection—I could get drunk just on this. Knowing there are miles and miles and dozens of police officers between me and the asshole who did this to me and my husband.

■ ■ ■

"WE HAVE TO ask you to take off your clothing then drop
them in here." A man who has introduced himself as New Castle
County Detective Mike Walsh holds out a kind of plastic gar-
ment bag. He is careful not to touch the bag's interior, and when
I get the things off, I'll notice he does not touch them either.

We are in a square, fluorescently bright room off the ER.
Walsh and another detective, Tony DiNardo, look on expectantly
as I start removing the asshole's T-shirt and sweatpants. God. So
cold. And here am I, completely naked in front of two strange
men. My skin is paper-white under the lights.

"Thank you, Mrs. Puglisi. Now, we're going to take some pictures. Could you stand on this sheet?"

I look at Walsh, who is opening a camera bag. Pictures? He
looks back, steadily. "I'm sorry, Mrs. Puglisi."

I hobble over to the flat white sheet, which has been spread
across the linoleum floor. My broken toe is just starting to throb.
Till now I didn't even notice the pain. I am beginning once again
to inhabit my body and feel what it feels.

The detectives are gentle with me and very reluctant to ask for
each successive awful thing. "Turn right. Turn left. Now this way.
Thank you, Mrs. Puglisi." They take a series of forty-some photos to document everything that has been done to my body. I
shudder from embarrassment, from the chill. Hospitals. They're
like supermarkets. Always freezing.

Walsh is understanding. "We want to get this guy, and we
need to gather all the information we can," he explains. Okay. So
we pretend—by unspoken, mutual agreement—that this is not
as degrading to me as it feels. I understand, of course, what this
is—it's critical business, the first machinations of the law. Later
on, when I think of these first few hours, I can almost hear the
massive bureaucracy creaking into gear. This is evidence-
gathering. I am the evidence, and the evidence is all over me,
inside and out.

They record and document every inch of my body, every limb from every angle, dozens and dozens of pictures; and I swallow each protest, fixing my eyes on a spot on the wall and focusing there. Thanking God I can't see. I pretend they can't either. This is not my body, anyway. In this context, I am evidence, as much as my house and the killer's house are. This, in a peculiar way, is a comfort. Somewhere out there, I hope the asshole is being photographed in the same way.

I have suddenly become so good at this, disconnecting from what is going on around me.

HE HAS BEEN taken into custody, Walsh tells me, and, ever so briefly, relief and satisfaction invade the numbness inside. How'd they do that? But, of course, once they got his phone listing and got into his home, it was short work to find out who he is and where he is employed.

Yep, says DiNardo, the guy was seized on an assembly line at the Chrysler plant, where he is employed to make car doors. Detective Gregory, with a police dog and a half dozen other officers, all of the men dressed in factory clothes, walked right up to him on the line. Gregory took him down in a big bear hug. Right now I have nothing more than his name, Donald A. Flagg, and age, forty.

When I hear the "A" is for Anthony, it makes me sad and angry.

My husband's name is Anthony, asshole. How dare you share anything with my husband.

"Can you spell your name?"

"P-U-G-L-I-S-I."

"Your first name?"

"Debra, D-E-B-R-A."

"Debbie, we're starting this interview. It's approximately 12:56 A.M. on Friday, April twenty-fifth."

DiNardo corrects him. It's after midnight, he says. It's Saturday. Instinctively, I scan the walls for a clock. Has midnight really come and gone? Then it's the next day. The day after. I was in the killer's house yesterday, not today. If I had the strength, I'd jump up and down. This isn't happiness; happiness seems a small, mean, ephemeral thing now. I wonder if I will ever feel it again or if I want to. Happiness is for other people. From now on, for me, for a very long time, it will be extremes of joy and pain, separated by long desertlike stretches of that nonfeeling. Like anesthesia.

We are in yet another room, where we have been joined by two nurse examiners, Kathy Rainey and Bill Marshall. They are called SANE nurses (sexual assault nurse examiners) and are specifically trained in the debriefing and examination of rape victims. When Bill walks in, I nearly leap up and kiss him—the man looks uncannily like my brother Gary: tall, lanky, with sandy hair and wire-rimmed glasses. It's hard to look away.

The interview continues.

"Did his penis enter your vagina?" This is Walsh.

"Yes."

"Were you lying on your back?"

"Sometimes on my back, sometimes on my thigh."

Over the next few hours, we cover, it seems, every minute of the five days, the 101 hours, from the moment I walked from the garden to the kitchen at Academy Hill to the moment I dialed 911 from the killer's house. Walsh and DiNardo want to know everything, from the color of the toothbrush I used and the kind of food we ate to the killer's sleeping patterns and the tenor of our conversations. Then there are the sexual acts, in all their variety. This must be the first time I've counted up. Eight. Eight rapes. Eight "sexual favors."

"When he sexually assaulted you back at the house, that was vaginal intercourse?"

"Vaginal and anal."

"And anal," Walsh repeats, monotone, scribbling; and I can't help but think of that assault and the quiet screaming that sounded like a petrified rabbit. "Again, back to the house," Walsh continues. "Did he penetrate you digitally?"

"Yes."

"Do you think he used K-Y that first time?" This is Bill Marshall.

"No, no. It was—everything was so fast. So in my house he did not."

Kathy Rainey gnaws on the end of a pencil. "The other time when he did use K-Y, did he just rub it on himself or did he rub it all over you or how did he do it?"

The memory sickens me. His glee. His delight. "He rubbed it all over. In fact, the first time when he got a good look at me when I was on my back, in his house, he goes, 'Oh, whee, I've got a hairy one here.' " I force myself to look at them straight-on. Shame. I feel it. I won't yield to it.

Kathy tells me the police will go through his trash, the heat ducts in the house, the drains, everything in their search for evidence. "They'll go through his vacuum cleaner," she says.

"I SAID, 'I do see the goodness in you.' And I said, 'I really don't think you're a really bad person.' "

"You did what you had to do," says Kathy.

"I did."

"Right. You did the right thing."

I did. If you asked, I might tell you everything else I did. Letting that man touch and probe me without a word of dissent. Without a murmur, unless it was one of pretend pleasure.

But you don't ask, Kathy, so I don't volunteer the information. Will I ever tell that part? How I gripped him with my body to make sure he ejaculated because, God knows, if he didn't—if he was frustrated sexually—it might be the death of me. To my mind, he had to have good sex. I wanted him to. Because I didn't want to die.

No, I can't tell. No one will ever understand.

I remember from my Catholic studies a saint named Maria Goretti. She was canonized, as I recall, not for great good deeds but because she resisted a rape attempt. The would-be rapist killed her, and ever after she was held up as an ideal of womanly virtue.

There goes my chance at sainthood.

Should I deplore my actions in that man's house? I pretended to like the man who killed my Nino, pretended to welcome his touch when in fact it made me want to wretch.

If you asked me, Kathy, I might tell you all this. But you don't. You make it so easy for me. All you ask is, "Did his penis enter your vagina?"

"Yes," I tell you. "It did."

NEXT STOP: a cubicle alone with Bill and Kathy, who conduct the internal exam. They take pubic hair combings, vaginal swabs, anal swabs. When the speculum comes out, I feel the clench in my stomach. They soothe me throughout, warning me in advance about what is next.

MY ROOM IS under guard, as is the entire hospital, lest some enterprising reporter storm the place. There's a cop at the door, and he looks in on occasion, nods and smiles and touches the brim of his hat, so courtly. "Just wanted you to know I'm still here. If you want anything, just holler." I've always liked policemen, and of course Robert and Darlene's Bill are both cops. Now I love them.

Later I learn that reporters and TV crews have swamped the hospital; they get this information, breaking news, from police scanners, and I wonder, Does someone listen to those things twenty-four hours a day? The news vans and cameras reach the hospital before the ambulance does. I think I hear the hammer of chopper blades somewhere up above. News media are so numerous that the police and the hospital staff decide my family members will actually have to use a password to see me.

Police ask me to choose it. I think of Nino and the last time I saw him as he walked from the garden to the house.

I sit up. "Tell them roses. The password is roses."

And they surge in, Dad and Barb, my cousins, nurses from Delaware Hospice. I can tell by their expressions that I look pretty bad: battered and beat-up, with my hair chopped off on one side where the killer cut out the duct tape. I don't care.

I'm touched to see that my coworkers are wearing yellow ribbons and crystal angel pins, like the pin I often wore when I visited patients. They later explain that they started wearing them just yesterday, in a concerted effort to send me love and power; and I wonder ever after how much their prayers helped me to finally escape.

Dad's arms around me are like a dream. As I look at his face, seamed with age and anxiety, I want to tell him, "I never, never thought I would see you again. You look beautiful to me." But I am overcome. I just revel in him. When he breaks away, he is so emotional that he must find an armchair.

Here is my sister Darlene, looking jubilant. "We're so proud of you," she whispers, clasping my face with her hands and kissing me a dozen times. "We are so proud."

Here come my kids. Michael first, then Mel, looking dazed, arms lifted, smiling and crying. One after the other, they slump against me, their arms around my neck, murmuring words I can never remember.

I let them hug for a minute, loving it, then I push them away. I want to see their faces. Both are thinner and paler than before, Michael with his short hair standing straight up, Melissa with bluish hollows under her eyes.

"I'm sorry," I tell them. Instantly they shush me. But I want to say it. I'm sorry for their sorrow and sorry I was not here throughout it all. Melissa says it's okay; all the family was here, and my younger sister, Jane, was a great stand-in mom. Racing from her home in Barnegat, New Jersey, she virtually moved into the Comfort Inn, leaving her own kids to the care of her husband, Jed. When the tension grew insufferable, she tried distracting the twins, inviting their friends to the motel, taking whole gangs of kids shopping and out to eat. Otherwise, their time here could have turned into a deathwatch.

And for their sake, Jane, who is typically quite emotional, dis-

guised her fright under a steely calm. She told them, morning
and night, that I was alive. The very fact I had not been found,
she insisted, meant I was alive. Sometimes she almost believed it.
And she refused (as others quietly advised her) to start preparing
them for the worst.

"Mom is alive," she said. "She's coming back to you. And right
now she needs us to hold on to our faith."

"She never gave up," Melissa says. Thank God for Jane.

After all the hugs, we suddenly burst into laughter. Like it's
Christmas or something. They are solicitous. Is there anything I
need or want?

"Oh, Jesus, yes," I say. "I know it's a hospital, but can I get a
beer?"

Yes, I can.

Just before dawn, a Dr. Saunders comes in to check on me.
I've been watching TV—the news—and he snaps it off. "No," he
says. "You need to sleep. Your body needs to sleep. If you don't
sleep, you don't get out of here."

"But I want to find out what happened to me." I almost laugh.
How ridiculous it sounds.

Dr. Saunders is affable but strict. "There's always time to
watch TV later."

I consider arguing with him. Right now I'm in no mood to
obey him or anyone else. But he's right to say there's time. There
really is.

How wonderful. There is time.

He orders a Valium, and I accept it. Soon I'm engulfed by
a sweet, languid warmth. I drift away and dream about nothing
at all.

8

AGAINST DOCTOR'S ORDERS, I have left the hospital to attend Nino's viewing, slipping out a back entrance to avoid the news media. A police escort drives me to the Comfort Inn, where the family has been staying for the past week. It is within a mile of the crime scene at Academy Hill.

At the motel my sisters hover at my side like bridesmaids, helping me dress, tending my hair, helping me slip into the one black shoe and one foam slipper I will wear today. Even when I walk into the bathroom, they trail in my wake, as if they can't stand to lose sight of me. When I come out again, they're waiting, practically breathless with waiting. It's like time stops in the few minutes it takes me to wash my hands or use the toilet. And every time they look at me, it is with something like astonishment.

It reminds me of the morning I married Nino, when my attendants fluttered around me the same way, like moths, in dresses that rustled like wings. They fluffed out my voluminous veil. They made sure I was well stocked with borrowed and blue. Darlene, just fourteen then, was thrilled to be among them, one of the big girls in the long flowing gowns.

That day—so long ago, not so long ago—I was the big event,

the first of the three Engel girls to marry. I was a baby of a bride, just twenty-one, but we all played grown-up that day. We wanted so much to be grown up.

As I prepare for my husband's memorial, I realize that again I am first—this time, the first widow. Grown up at last.

"Here, Deb, let me get that zipper."

"Thank you."

"Let me comb your hair—does that hurt?"

"No."

I don't need a mirror. I see myself best by looking at Jane, Darlene, and my stepmom Barb. Sometimes they look full-on, locking eyes, like they can't believe I'm here; other times I catch them peeking, surreptitiously, like they can't believe how awful I look.

When I do stand at the mirror, I'm stunned, repelled, bitterly amused. Here is the femme fatale of all those newspaper accounts. I look like a bedraggled crone, with chalky skin, a shapeless black dress Jane bought in haste at a nearby mall, the blue-and-black contusions from when he beat me, and my funny-looking hair.

A stylist was kind enough to come to the hospital to do a last-minute salvage job. I guess she was trying for some kind of gamine look, but the best she could do was chop off the longer hair to match the short hair, where the asshole cut out the duct tape. End result: my hair is impossibly short, shingled up the sides. My hands are swathed in thick white gauze, so it almost looks like I'm wearing mittens; my left arm is in a sling. The mall dress has short sleeves—how could Jane have known?—so it doesn't cover the marks on my upper arms. Like the bruises on my head, they, too, are almost black by now and shaped like thick fingers. Well, at least they match my black eye. I am coordinated.

"Debbie, it's twenty to three." This is Darlene. She and Jane and Barb have gathered at the motel room door. It's open now, and they stand there expectantly. Unwilling to rush me, I know, and prepared to wait me out.

"Isn't there something more to do before we leave?" I ask. Still unsteady on my feet, I blunder around the beige-and-blue motel room with the patterned carpet and fake oil paintings. I'm certain that something is still undone, and I try desperately to figure out what it is. "Do we have everything?"

I look at my sisters. Their faces are so kind, so full of pain for me. They know I don't want to be ready. The process of *getting* ready was easy, still a step removed from what we have to do now. But *being* ready? Unthinkable.

I wish so much I could cry. Why can't I cry? Maybe crying would dislodge the great, awful ache inside. But I have no tears.

"Debbie? We have to get going."

I guess we do. I know the sorrow that waits for me, and I can't do a single thing to keep it at bay.

I don't want to be ready, Lord, not for this. Please, let this cup pass.

Dad leans into the doorway, then Gary behind him, then the twins. Damn it. Isn't there anything else to do first? No. It's time to go to the viewing. Ready or not. As they shepherd me through the door, the lightbulb goes off over my head. This could be a new motto for me, a whole philosophy summed up in a few words. Ready or not.

MICHAEL, MELISSA, AND I stand at the threshold of the chapel, along with Melissa's boyfriend, Jeremy. We hold hands, draw a collective breath, then look down the long carpeted aisle to the open casket, where Nino is just visible, his head elevated slightly. Melissa sways on her feet, and Jeremy tightens his grip around her waist.

I didn't expect to see my husband right away; I thought he would be completely inside the box, and I would still have time before I had to see. But there he is, his gray hair gleaming under the lights.

The casket is flanked on one side by flowers, hundreds of them, dozens of arrangements of lilies and carnations and daisies, so many that the perfume is almost sickening. Nino's bass guitar rests on a metal stand nearby—his sister Dolores's idea—and then there are the pictures of him, a veritable gallery of photos showing Nino as he was in life. There he is with the kids, on the bandstand, at the helm of his boat, and throwing back his head and laughing that great, big laugh that when it got going could almost collapse him.

The three of us stand at the entrance as if rooted there. We finally make our way to a pew halfway down—a way station— where we kneel for a moment, pretending to pray. Then some-one—Mel?—stands up and starts walking toward the coffin, and we all fall in. We stand and walk and keep walking and don't stop again until we're there, with Nino. Ready or not.

Oh, thank God. He looks well. I've been so scared, thinking that the bullet had mutilated his face. But he looks well. I peer down, scrutinize him, but I cannot tell where it struck. God bless Sharon, Nino's friend and associate at Beeson's, who prepared him. She fixed him for us.

At least I'm here, Nino. As if from an aerial view I see this self-same image, the three of us standing here, and absent myself from the picture. This almost took place. I almost didn't make it. Another few days and he would have been put in the ground without me there, and even if I managed to live on, I would have been denied this.

"Daddy looks wonderful," I whisper to Melissa then add, "You should be proud, sweetheart."

She nods, almost imperceptibly. Of everyone in the family, it was this little girl, my teenage daughter, who took control of the arrangements after her father's death, with Jane's help. Melissa chose this casket, chose the tie and sport coat Nino is wearing, planned the service, and decided—in the most fitting remem-brance of all—to park his beloved Boston Whaler on the lawn of the funeral home, dressed with a spray of flowers. Now, as she looks down at the father she loved, this strong girl seems thin and so vulnerable, as if at any moment she could go up in smoke.

See how much she loves you, Nino.

"Mom? I want to put this in with Dad." Michael holds out his hand, and there on the flat of his palm is one of the many medals he's won in track. The same medals he used to toss in the sock drawer and refuse to display. He bends close to the casket, slips it in, steps back. He is icy white. He looks baffled. And I can tell—by the way he bites his lip and by the exertion in his brow—that he is trying with all his might not to cry.

See how much he loves you, Nino.

I've decided, after much deliberation, to keep Nino's wedding ring. After the first few years of marriage, he'd stopped wearing it anyway, simply because he hated wearing jewelry. He doesn't need the ring. I do.

Now the last thing, which is a much better thing to give him. The night before, at the motel, Mel pulled out an old knit throw I bought a few years back at a curio shop in Chesapeake City. Woven into it are images of all the rivers that end in the Chesapeake—the Bohemia, the Sassafras, the Elk—and all the harbors and islands and lighthouses that mark them. The Chesapeake had been Nino's heaven on earth.

"Don't you think Daddy should have it?" Melissa asked.

Now she tucks it in around him, tenderly, as if to keep him warm, and her tears fall onto his face until it looks like they are both crying.

JAY BEESON OPENS the doors at four o'clock. I am eerily aware that this viewing was supposed to have been for me, too. I was to have been eulogized right along with Nino. Being here is like attending my own wake.

I have never seen so many people: our families, and our neighbors from Academy Hill and friends from different lives and times in Maryland and New Jersey. They wait, some of them, from midafternoon to dusk in a reception line that twists around the block, and I see them all. Dad and Robert break in every half hour or so to demand that I get off my feet, take it easy, sit one out, use the wheelchair that's always at the ready.

"Guys, I can't do that. They've waited all this time. I feel okay.

Really." I do, too—buzzing along on numbness and adrenaline. Let me just keep going. I know there is a crash ahead. Let me do what I can till it happens.

Lots of Michael's track buddies are here. It's odd and sweet to see them, some looking like brutes with their shaved heads and big-shouldered bodies, holding each other up and crying like little kids. At one time or another, Robb Munro, Mike DiGennaro, and Steve Scarborough had been Michael's roommates, and they had become second sons to Nino. This morning they are so respectful and so fumblingly eloquent.

"Mr. Puglisi was such a cool guy."

"Mr. Puglisi was always cheering us on."

"It'll be so weird when he's not on the sidelines. With that stopwatch!"

That makes me laugh, and I notice that people turn to see why. That was Nino. He'd crouch at the chalk line with that watch and just scream for his boys—not just Michael, but all of them—trying to motivate them to slice a fraction of a second off their times.

I look a little down the line, and at first my gaze moves right past a big guy in a rumpled suit coat with hair almost as gray as Nino's. He's very familiar, but who? I'm foggy. Then I look again, and I know: Bill. Jesus. It's really Bill Sharp. He looks straight at me, into my eyes. He dips his head in acknowledgment and lifts his hand. I'm astonished and pleased enough to feel it through the numbness.

We haven't spoken in more than twenty years, but I've heard about him from time to time: Nino's friend, my former boyfriend, my first love before I met Nino. Bill had run a service station for years and years, then a couple of nightclubs in Wilmington. He had been married and divorced. The clubs had done well, then not so well but from what I heard he was still in the business and no wonder. That shoe that fit perfectly. All his life Bill had been the consummate host: expansive, generous, eager to see people having a great time.

Now here he is, in middle age, still handsome, wearing a grim smile. His expression seems to say, "Well, the shit doesn't get any deeper than this, Debbie." Agreed.

He is in front of me now and holds out his hand. "Debbie, my God," he begins. "Damn it. Poor Nino."

"I can't believe it's you, Bill." It is months before I discover that Bill—who mostly shuns TV and newspapers—learned of the kidnapping and murder just hours before the viewing and raced to get here in time.

"Nino would have loved that you came."

He puts his arms around me and hugs, carefully—like everyone, he seems to think I'm frail, a Dresden doll that will shatter at the slightest pressure.

"Debbie, call me if there's anything you need," he says, and his eyes bore into mine, letting me know he means it. "Promise to call me, okay?" He won't let go of my hand till I nod. Then he turns and vanishes into the crowd.

PEOPLE DON'T KNOW what to say. "I'm so sorry," they say, then they say, "I'm so glad." Two different winds are blowing at once, crosscurrents of emotion that do not coexist easily. There is such grief in this room and such jubilation. The service is a peculiar blend of mourning and joyful reunion.

"I'm so sorry about Nino. But how wonderful. You're alive."

"What a terrible tragedy. I'm happy to see you."

I feel it. I'm buffeted by it. I am here. My heart continues to beat. I do not have to die yet. I can reach right out and touch Michael's arm or smooth Melissa's collar. I am elated about this, to be with them, to know they don't have to do this alone. But here is the man with whom I spent most of my life, and he is dead. How can I feel good? How dare I?

Here comes Kathy, my dear friend Kathy Manlove, who was also one of those bridesmaids the day I got married. I step into the circle of her arms, and she hugs me gently, minding my bad arm.

"I'm so happy to see you, oh, God," she breathes. "So happy."

Later that night, as we prepare to leave, I am astounded by the commotion outside: reporters, photographers, news vans, people hefting microphones and big white lights on their backs; and I remember what I had forgotten for a day. My husband's death is news. It's an event, a media spectacle. As we emerge cameras whir and flash, and news people with handheld mikes try to lure some of the mourners into the spotlight. Dad and my brothers form a kind of human cordon leading to the car, protecting me from the press like bodyguards.

Then there are the party crashers. These are the people who might go out of their way to watch a building burn to the ground or see bodies carried away from a car wreck. From behind my dark glasses I see their eyes looking back, probably hoping for a moment of melodrama to make this thing really good. I'm not particularly upset by this. I can only wonder at their fascination.

I have become some kind of bizarre celebrity. Nino's service has all the excitement of a Hollywood premiere. Dad opens the car door, and I slip inside, like a celebrity stepping from a red carpet into her limo.

MONDAY, THE DAY of Nino's funeral, is sunny but so cold. Puzzling to me. It's April. It shouldn't be this cold out. I wear the black dress again, this time with a sweater.

Feels like wintertime.

At church, the casket sits in front of the altar. Closed now. It jars me. Final, more final, most final. Bit by bit, we lose more and more of him.

Husband, I will never see you again.

I am so cold.

"WE REMEMBER YOUR weed whacker, your twelve-miles-per-hour lawn mower, your sheer determination to finish what you set out to do with the fewest obstacles in the shortest possible time." Jay Beeson, speaking his eulogy from the podium at Immaculate Conception Church, makes us laugh with his description of Nino, who had been his best friend since they met in the elementary school chorale. And he's right on the nose with his characterization: Nino was impatient, driven, an over-achiever, a perfectionist. A man who raced through life.

Now that impatience seems prophetic. Somewhere down inside of him, something whispered, Go fast.

Nino knew.

The episode in the kitchen a few weeks ago ("I don't think I'll ever see Melissa again") was not an isolated one. He had been saying things like that for years, and for years I had laughed it off or hugged it off or shrugged it off. "Don't be silly," I'd say. "You're big and healthy, and you'll live to be a crotchety old man. We'll be old and crotchety together."

Lately—strangest of all—he'd become convinced that the length of his earlobes portended an early death. His earlobes! I don't know where he got that one—some old Italian supersti-tion?—but he was always asking me to check out his earlobes. "Do you think they're longer than usual? Do you think one's longer than the other?"

"Nino, for crying out loud! Your earlobes are perfectly fine. Good God."

It was exasperating. It was funny. It was just the way he was. But for all his fretting about death—death coming suddenly, pre-emptively, in balls of fire, sudden mudslides, or falling anvils—Nino did nothing to prepare himself or the family for the consequences. He was a funeral planner who didn't plan his own funeral. And despite his conviction that he would die young, Nino refused to buy a lot of life insurance. Oh, he made the ges-ture, got the minimum plan; but if he was genuinely concerned about his health or his fate (he was an awful smoker), he didn't guard against it with insurance. I guess it was his way of hexing the hex.

He knew. He must have known. Maybe he thought if he got ready for it, it would seal the prophecy.

It happened anyway. Ready or not.

■ ■ ■

MELISSA IS PRETERNATURALLY composed. Quiet, poised, her spine straight as an arrow. She cries just once, when her friend, Tory Windley, sings a soaring a cappella version of Schubert's "Ave Maria," one of Nino's favorites. Tory later says she never thought she'd get through it without breaking down. But she knew Nino was a perfectionist as a musician, too—she knew he'd accept nothing less than her best. So she stands up there, stares wide-eyed at the ceiling to keep the tears from spilling, and pours all her heart into it, singing in a faultless pure soprano.

The church is filled with flowers, some left over from Easter services. The pallbearers are my brother, Gary, my brother-in-law Bill Sillitoe, Dan Gorman from Elkton, Stuart Ross from Nino's old job at Harrisburg Paper, our nephew Joe, and Kathy Manlove's son, Ernie. They assemble with near military bearing around the casket, grip the brass handles, flex their shoulders, then move slowly in cadence to the rear of the church.

The kids and I follow. Melissa is still calm. Michael cries openly, so hard that his whole body shudders. Together we walk Nino out of church and to the waiting hearse.

At Saint Patrick's Cemetery, I place roses—one white, one peach-colored—on the coffin then turn away, unable to look at that hole in the ground. Behind me, Melissa leans down to hug the box containing her father's body. I don't see it, but I do see the people who see it, and their faces crumple. They look as if they have been simultaneously struck.

The final prayers seem without end. But I'm glad. Don't let time pass too quickly today. Because tonight when the sun goes down, my husband will lie, dark and alone, in his grave.

9

THERE IS A WHIRLWIND around me, but I find myself strangely unmoved. I began to notice it at the cemetery, when people reached out and held me and sobbed and I realized I did not fully share their dismay, their grief, and disbelief. Instead, I felt like an observer of this drama. I looked on dry-eyed at the tumult. Not quite part of it, certainly not the central figure.

In theory, I know what's happening. As a nurse, I'm up on Kübler-Ross and the classic literature on death; I know the textbook steps that accompany tragedy or loss or trauma: shock, denial, anger, depression, blah, blah, blah. I have the drill down and watch myself to see where I am on the scale. Prevailing wisdom says I will ultimately reach a stage called acceptance. Oh, sure. Accept this? How can I, when I can never not know what happened to my husband? Hard as I try, I will never lose the image of him turning a corner and meeting his killer, feeling the cold barrel of a gun pressed dead center to his forehead. And hard as I try—and I *am* trying—I will never completely believe the murmured reassurances of doctors and police officers and friends who say, "It was so fast. He felt nothing. He was there, and then he wasn't."

And even if I believe, does it count as consolation that Nino was dead before he hit the floor? How do I accept that at all, much less accept it as a good thing?

Acceptance. The idea makes me want to laugh and cry all at once, but of course I do neither. I feel things only in the abstract. I can only think of what I would normally feel. In fact I feel nothing.

Bargaining. That's another "stage." I did that in the asshole's house, when I made deals with God, pledging to be a good person, a better person, a kind and churchgoing person if he would allow me to continue breathing. God answered my prayer—I hear that ad nauseam, how God answered my prayer and the kids' prayers and everyone else's—but I find it hard to conjure up much gratitude. I am chilled inside, at the very core. He said he would kill me, the asshole, and he did. I look alive, but inside I have just ceased to be. I am killed, too.

Maybe this is shock. If so, I won't argue with it. It's a safe place to be. I see the wreck of my life from a distance, as if through the wrong end of a telescope, and there's little I can do but appreciate the buffer. Later it will be time to feel. Then, I'm sure, I'll wish for nothing else but to stop feeling.

In this altered state I find I am capable of much busy work. Maybe that's what shock is for. Between Monday, the day of the funeral, and Friday, when Dad and Barb spirit me off to Florida for a "good long rest," I accomplish a lot. Visit the Social Security office to file for my whopping $255 death benefit. See our attorney, Bruce Hudson, to probate the will. With each paper I sign, I feel I am signing Nino's death certificate, again and again. Closing his coffin, again and again. Making him more dead every time. But I do it. Death is a business. Death and widowhood are scrupulously documented. I am conscientious. Let's get it all done.

Up until now, part of me still believed in miracles, and that part insisted, all the way to the churchyard at Saint Patrick's, that my love for Nino was enough to make this all unhappen. I didn't quite know how the miracle would play out, but I left that to

God, the merciful God I have always loved. It didn't happen.
There is no waking from this nightmare. Every so often I shake
myself and say, out loud, "He is gone. So stop it. You can't call
him back, ever again, not even once." I wonder when the last
time was that I told him, "I love you." Had I said it recently? We
were old marrieds; that wasn't a daily thing anymore and hadn't
been for a long time.

But you knew, didn't you, Nino? You knew I loved you, didn't
you?

At the register of wills, a clerk regards me disdainfully and
snaps, "What are you doing here? It's too soon. Come back in a
month."

A month. In a month Nino will be even more gone.

Everyone is packing to return home. I am astounded when
Michael and Melissa elect to return to college right away, but
they are firm: this is what Daddy would want. Gary's headed
back to Virginia, Dad, Barb, and me to Florida, everyone else to
New Jersey. But one thing first. I want to go home, too. When I
announce my intentions, there is a chorus of objections.

"You know, you don't need to do this," says Darlene, rubbing
my hurt hand between her own as she rewraps the dressing. We
are still at the Comfort Inn, and luggage and carryalls are piled
up at the doors. "Why are you doing this?"

"I need to."

"Don't you think it should wait a while? You're still at the
beginning of this. It's still sinking in."

"Dar, I just need to."

Dad is against it, too, loudly. "Not a good idea," he says, in the
gruff, laying-down-the-law voice he used to use when we were
kids. "What are you trying to do to yourself, Debbie? Don't go
there."

But it's all I want. I can't *stay* there—home is still a crime
scene—but I want to see it. The pretty Cape Cod. Our dream
house. That hasn't changed, at least for me. It's still our dream
house.

And I can tell the twins think it's a perverse idea. Go home?

That place doesn't deserve to be called home anymore. When I tell them, Melissa looks away with a shiver and Michael shakes his head, looking just like Nino when he would disapprove.

With the family so up in arms, I get defensive. Don't blame my house. My house is innocent. I'm going there.

From the outside, you'd never know. The yellow crime-scene tape has been taken down, but all around the neighborhood are yellow ribbons, on mailboxes and fence posts; and in our yard, a collection of now listless potted plants with faded notes attached: "Praying for your safe return." "Thinking of you at this difficult time."

Inside, though. I walk through, with Dad and Barb close behind (once they knew I was serious about coming home, they quickly fell in). All we can say is "Oh, my God," "Oh, my God." Panels of flooring and carpet and wallboard have been ripped up, removed for evidence. A fine black film—"Fingerprint dust," says Dad—covers the windowsills and windows, doors and door locks, appliances, kitchen tiles, and countertops. Every surface is sooty with it, down to the couple of cups and glasses left in the sink, and the fish tank in the dining room.

Fish tank! I press my nose to the glass, and Fishie is right there on the other side, his pinkish fins undulating in the cloudy water. Still alive. So there are still things to thank God for.

"Fish, sweetie! Fishie boy. I'm so glad, so glad." I am surprised to hear the catch in my voice. "We've got to get him out of here." Dad looks at me, worriedly. "Dad, please, let's not leave him here. He'll be so lonely."

"Okay," he says softly. "We won't leave him behind."

The dining room. Here is where it happened—I know it because I was told, but I also know it because a huge piece of wall has been lifted right out, exposing the wooden studs. The floor, too, is bare down to the wood subfloor; carpet and padding gone. Nino was shot right here ("He didn't feel a thing") then dragged through the hall to the bedroom, where he was later photographed with a coroner's tag around his ankle.

Worst of all, the bedroom. The bed—mine and Nino's—has

been stripped to the mattress. They probably wrapped Nino in the sheets—pale-green sheets I'd just bought to go with my green-and-pink flowered quilt. The quilt—my would-be shroud—is in an evidence vault somewhere.

The police have invaded my house, even more than the asshole did. I know this is what needs to happen. But these are our things. I am suddenly possessive, angrily so. I want them all back. I have no idea that they are irretrievable, don't know until I see them in court, sectioned-off and presented as exhibits, like something out of Perry Mason.

My sheets. I want them so bad.

Nino is really dead. I am still able to be amazed by this, to be surprised at the thought that it's really true.

Now that I have seen the house, I know it even more than I did the day before.

As we continue our walk-through, Dad tells me that Darlene spent hours, when she knew I was coming, on her hands and knees, scrubbing Nino's blood from the floor. I am filled with horror and gratitude. God bless that tough little sister of mine.

Nothing has been left undisturbed. The Beanie Babies, once heaped up on chairs and along the sofa back, have been crammed into plastic bags; they gape out at us like preserved specimens. Books and framed photos are all shoved around or stacked up in corners. Sofa cushions have been upended, and no one thought to right them again. There on the floor, on top of a bunch of magazines, is a picture taken last Christmas, our first and only in this house and our last as a family. Nino and the kids and I are so happy, so oblivious. The kids and I have on our say-cheese smiles; Nino, with his arm around my back, looks happy and relaxed. I pick it up. Did no one think to treat this more carefully? It might have gotten broken.

From the outside, this looks like the home I lived in. But it's not home anymore, I know that, and I know that I'm no longer the woman who lived here. All the good, sweet memories of my life with Nino are mixed with the others—the horrible ones.

Though part of me still wants to keep the house, Nino's life insurance was just enough to cover the burial and pay off some small accounts. We had always talked about taking better care of one another that way, but it never got past the talking stage. Now my situation is precarious. I know that somewhere down the line, the house will have to go.

But I'm not finished saying good-bye to this place. Day after day I return here, and friends—Gene and Karen next door, my sisters and my dad, all my nurse friends—are upset with me. "Don't go there." "I won't." But I'm lying to them. Time and again I sneak back to sit in my rooms, trying to believe the unbelievable.

"IT'S THE BEST thing to do. Let's just get this thing behind you."

Dad and Barb and I are flying US Air to Florida, where they live in a retirement community in a little town called Stuart. It's the first of May, which stuns me. Already, the references have changed. I thought it would always stay April.

Over peanut-butter crackers and Styrofoam cups of coffee, Dad pats my arm reassuringly. "Let's just get out of this town and relax, far away from it all."

Right. With Nino's body still cold and fresh in the grave, with our home being chopped apart by criminal investigators. But there is no arguing with family. I go not just for me but for them. They, too, have suffered at the hands of that asshole. They need to feel they are helping. By helping me, they feel a sense of their own control in an out-of-control situation. My father, especially, needs to take care of me, to take me to a safe place where he can pamper and love and dote on me and make it all better—as better as it can possibly be at this point.

As we descend to the airport, I recall that Nino and I once fantasized about retiring to Florida. We told ourselves we'd get a little place on the water and live like beachcombers. Nino would get a job at a marina, where he could live like the sailor he was at heart. Now Florida is my first stop as a widow. I am still trying that word on—widow—hating it, rejecting it, and wishing there was some other way I could identify myself. But come to think of it, there are many: I am a crime victim. A rape victim. A single mother, a single woman. And in the news media at home, I've been transformed into some kind of heroine: a woman of rare courage and fortitude, with a "will to live." Most of all, I'm touted as a "survivor."

Well, I can't dispute that. The asshole didn't kill me fast enough. I did indeed survive. But don't tell me about courage and strength, because any minute now I am going to come apart.

They are rewriting my history, turning my life into a triumph over adversity, and all I want is to be my old, everyday self, before courage became a necessity. I don't want to be seen as courageous or congratulated for it. I just want to go back to being ordinary.

We arrive in Stuart just in time to change and drive to Shrimper's, a favorite place along an inland waterway. It's happy hour, and we decide to get *very* happy. Lounging on the outside deck with our toes bared in sandals, we order drinks and appetizers and enjoy how the breeze blows through the palms. We talk about everything but what matters and order more drinks. Alcohol therapy, and I'm all for it. Right now wine, and lots of it, is highly medicinal.

The waitress plops down another glass of chardonnay and clucks with concern when she notes my bound-up hand. "Gee," she says, "What happened there? That must have hurt."

AROUND MY FOURTH day in Stuart, the prosecutor, Jim Ropp, calls to see how I'm doing.

"Fine, thanks." I still say that when people ask how I am. Fine.

Before we flew down, I had to clear my trip with the deputy attorney's office. I found I was not a free agent, was not even permitted to travel out of town without giving my phone number to all the appropriate people. Lucky for me, though, since they found me tied up in the asshole's house and since the asshole confessed to kidnapping and homicide, I was no longer a murder suspect myself. I figured that was a step in the right direction.

I try not to be flip with Mr. Ropp, who is solicitous and I'm sure means well. But I am beaten-down and on edge, and I am tired of the niceties. What stage am I in now? I'll call it "pissed off and disgusted." It's only aggravated when Ropp starts talking about the complexities of this case. (Complex? I thought it was pretty straightforward myself.) He says he wants me to prepare myself for the murder trial and wants me to be aware that this isn't going to be an open-and-shut case.

"Why not? What more do you need? For God's sake, this guy confessed to murder, kidnap, and rape! What else does it take to convict him?"

Ropp's voice is measured, careful. He tells me he understands my view, but the murder suspect is entitled to a fair trial, and his counsel will do everything they can to defend him.

My head swims. It never entered my mind that this case did not begin and end with Flagg's jailhouse confession. Ropp is telling me that this is just the beginning of a long, long process. Someone, some lawyer, is going to defend this evil person— defend evil itself—and blame evil actions on extenuating circumstances. What will it be? An unfortunate upbringing? Child abuse? That old standby, mental illness? I think of the asshole, laughing and telling me with pride, "I'm a criminal." Does anyone doubt it now?

I double over, the phone in my hand, and start bawling, shrieking. Dad comes from nowhere and seizes the receiver and starts yelling at the top of his lungs. "Who's this? What the hell did you say to my daughter? Damn it, don't you people know she's gone through enough?"

I already know the answer to that one. No. I haven't gone through enough.

When Dad hangs up the phone, he suggests a quick remedy. "How about a nice glass of wine?" he says.

10

WHEN I RETURN from Florida, the consensus among my sisters, brothers, and others is: don't live at Academy Hill. It's too soon. You're too raw. Stay with us, or rent. You can't stay in that house (in lurid newspaper parlance, that "house of horrors," that "house of death"). They cannot understand how I crave the shelter of my own home, the embrace of things that are familiar to me—my sofa, my kitchen chairs, my pillows.

But my house is still being fixed, so I bunk with the Nygaards until the end of May, walking over every few days to see how the repairs are coming along. It won't happen overnight. These repairs are funded by the Crime Victims Compensation Fund and implemented by the insurance company, so there is a fair amount of bureaucracy involved. But by the end of the summer, I'm assured, my house will look as it always did, as if nothing terrible had ever happened there. It will be normal again.

I find that I'm expected to return to normal just as quickly or at least pretend to. The family has decided, by silent, mutual accord, that Nino's murder and my disappearance are subjects to be scrupulously avoided. It recalls that timeworn definition of dysfunction as the elephant in the living room that everyone sees but no one will acknowledge. It's bizarre, almost funny, as we go from day to day, reading from our heavily edited scripts, so mindful that we mustn't say certain words, mustn't speak certain unspeakable things.

For my part, I want to talk about all the bad things that happened; I crave it as one would crave food or water or air. I want to take my loved ones there with me, into Flagg's house, to live and relive with me each violation. I want them to see, to know; I want to open this wound and let it bleed until it bloodies us all.

But it doesn't happen, because no one will permit it. I soon learn that when I broach the subject, the people closest to me—my sisters and brothers, Dad and Barb and Sue—scatter, sometimes literally fleeing to another room. Avoiding talking. Avoiding me. Or else they change the subject gracelessly, so when I begin, "That first night in his house . . ." someone is likely to reply, "So who wants pork chops for dinner tonight?"

Perhaps they believe they are sparing me. I know they are sparing themselves, and I find this deeply upsetting. Don't they know how much I need to tell this? It's like when we were little and I'd run home from the playground to tell on the bully. Of course, this is worlds bigger than that, but so is the need to tell. I want to tell on the killer, and no one will let me. I have stories, horrors I need to share in the hope that they will lose some of their power to horrify, but they are left inside.

I feel left alone, leperlike.

The rest of the community, however, is hungry for the tabloid details. I remember with a twinge of shame how I used to love a good true crime story. Used to love watching "the big story on *Action News*"—the sensational crime du jour. Had I not been the victim, I would have thought this story was a really good one: helpless woman, predatory man, plenty of sex. The plot has been around as long as the dime novel, and with the extra fillip of drugs and murder, it's especially titillating. It seems I hear the 911 tape—and that woman's voice, shrieking—every time I turn on the television. I cannot leave my home or shop in a mall without someone looking my way with morbid interest.

But those closest to me are least able to share my burden. They shrink from the violent details. They quietly discourage me from talking about it. And because I was raped, it's even worse. No matter how often that word blares from the headlines—"violent rape," "brutal rape"—no one wants to talk about it.

It's often said that rape is an act not of sex but violence. I hear that misguided sentiment many times from well-meaning friends, and though I usually nod and even thank them for their insight, it begins to rankle. Rape is the perfect expression of both sex and violence, one masterstroke of cruelty and degradation. When friends try to separate out the sex, I want to say, "Trust me on this one. It was sex, too." And it was. The most intimate act, perverted beyond recognition.

In the past, I had never talked much about sex, except jokingly, with girlfriends. Even then, I wasn't one to dish. The topic was too personal. How to do so now? If I am to talk about the crime with my family or anyone else, I have to talk about sex. No wonder they head for the hills.

It's too much to expect my dear, devoted father and my protective brothers to know in graphic detail how their daughter and sister was harmed and debased. Robert and Gary, at all times my champions, are uncomfortable with disclosure. My sister Jane, so loving but so sensitive, can't handle it at all, and I won't impose it on her. As for the kids, I wouldn't think of confiding in them. They have enough hurt to last them a lifetime and more. If I tell them about the assaults, I will create images they may never be able to forget. No, there is no way to talk about these things.

Only Darlene allows me to talk, and when I do—sobbing one afternoon into my butter sauce at Red Lobster—I can tell, from the grim set of her mouth and the hurt in her eyes that every word is a blow. But she takes every blow willingly, and I am grateful to her.

One day I come to know that despite their silence, my family never failed to love me. They couldn't bear to hear what happened, because they loved me so very much. But for now, language has become a minefield. Words—of comfort, advice, solidarity, outrage—often go unspoken. Other words that used to be ordinary are suddenly tainted. Once a girlfriend making small talk about her bratty teen says, like a thousand times before, "I could just kill that kid."

Then her eyes fly open. She claps a hand over her mouth. She falls all over herself in apology. "Oh, my God, Debbie, I'm sorry. I didn't hear that till it was out. . . . I can't believe it. . . . I'm so insensitive."

THROUGH NEWSPAPER ACCOUNTS and conversations with friends and family, I've begun the process of putting together what everyone else went through while I was gone.

I am especially disturbed when I learn exactly what happened to my kids the day their dad died and I vanished. On that Monday, shortly after Nino's body was found, Michael was among the first to be informed. Taken from his dorm at the University of Delaware, he was driven to the New Castle County police station and questioned for hours. It's hard for me to imagine how horrifying that must have been for him. He was asked repeatedly if his mom and dad had had an unhappy marriage (in keeping with the theory that I had committed the crime).

Melissa, at East Carolina U., was watching a video at her own dorm (the movie: *Alive!*). When she answered a knock at the door and found police officers and a counselor there, she thought she was about to be busted for having beer in the fridge. The police told her that her father had been killed and her mom was missing. Melissa fainted.

Then there are our friends. Shirley Brogley, her daughter Jennifer, and Nanci Osner found Nino's body. Shirley and Nanci were so alarmed when I didn't call into work that Monday that they actually stopped at the house, where they knocked on the front door. Seeing Nino's Jeep out front, they assumed someone was home, so when no one answered, they walked around the house to the deck and peered through a window. There they saw a man's body on the floor, with a coat thrown over his head.

They ran next door for help. Gene Nygaard rushed back with them and went inside to investigate. He is the one who found his friend. How dreadful it must have been for him. As I listen to all these accounts, it hurts me to know how much it hurt them. I am also astounded when Nanci tells me about her own trip to the police station, where she and Shirley were interviewed. As they paced nervously in the hall, Nanci heard a female police officer remark, "Well, you know how it is in these kinds of things. It always turns out that it's the spouse who did it." What a callous, ridiculous comment. Did anyone say something like that to my son or my daughter? The idea infuriates me.

I also learn about the killer. This Donald Flagg, who is forty and unmarried, was employed with Chrysler in Detroit; in 1980, when he was laid off there, he came East.

He is generally described as a quiet, responsible man, a hard-working sort who had a girlfriend but lived alone and took good care of his property and his cats. He liked gardening. He had just built a new tool shed and willingly lent out gardening tools to his neighbors. His lawn is described as always carefully mowed and edged, with bags of mulch neatly stacked near a covered barbecue. The week he held me captive, he did some yard work that Wednesday afternoon when I didn't know where he was. As the newspaper reports, he "smiled and waved to neighbors as he mowed the lawn to its usual perfection." Neighbors waved back.

"I thought he was a nice guy," one of his Wellington Woods neighbors tells the newspaper.

" 'He wasn't acting weird or anything,' " says the woman next door, who saw him during the week. " 'I feel kind of bad because I was playing with the kids outside, and all that time she was in there.' "

On the job at Chrysler, he got high marks. He was known as a conscientious employee, with no absenteeism in more than two decades. No wonder he was so unnerved about missing work. He could lose his good-attendance star.

But this is also in the news: in 1989, while drinking and

smoking crack cocaine, he imprisoned a female friend, Rosetta Shepherd, in a motel room for more than twelve hours. He did not physically harm her but refused to release her, despite her pleas. It was not until 3 A.M., when he shattered a window in the motel room, that she managed to break free and call police. According to the *News Journal,* the episode "now looms as an eerie foreshadowing of the murder, rape and kidnapping that Flagg allegedly committed."

He was arrested, but the charges were dropped by the State of Delaware. The incident was considered a misdemeanor.

There is more. Soon he is implicated in a crime on April 17, three days before he came to Academy Hill. A man broke into a Newark apartment where a twenty-one-year-old single mother was sleeping on the living room sofa. He woke her, then forced her to supply her own lubricant, and, as her young son slept on in another room, he raped and attempted to sodomize her.

According to the *News Journal,* police also suspect Flagg in the unsolved murders of two prostitutes found along an industrial highway in lower Delaware. Those crimes were committed in the early 1990s.

How cruel, if he did all these things. How pitiless to prey on helpless women. The report about the prostitutes, more than anything else, makes me want to cry. I suppose such women must have been hardened by life, made desperate by circumstances, but I can't help thinking that each and every one of them was once someone's baby, somebody's little girl. They didn't deserve to die that way.

THE TWINS TRY, valiantly, to pick up where they left off, as if nothing had come along to disrupt the smooth flow of their lives. They are back at college, working hard, trying, as I am, to blot out their pain with nonstop activity.

We speak regularly by phone, once or twice a week, and we are always careful to fill the conversation with talk of grades and sports and job prospects. There is seldom a word about sad things, like Daddy or losing our home. If we run out of chatter, I can almost hear the mental wheels grinding as we, each of us, cast about for fresh topics of conversation. Our ground rules: Keep it safe. Keep it cheery. Keep smiling. Don't let each other hear the sound of hearts cracking open.

Just three weeks after we bury Nino, Michael is scheduled to compete in a 10,000-meter race at Northeastern University in Dedham, Massachusetts. Though he's not in top form and hinted that he didn't feel like racing, he decides to go ahead, and I take part of the blame for this. I've been encouraging him to carry on, in the mistaken belief that it will be good for him—a victory of his always-strong will over personal disaster. His teammates are urging him on, too, for a very practical reason: they need him. Though team members run as individuals, their scores are tallied together.

I travel up by car. On Saturday, race day, I huddle on the sidelines with Coach Jim Fischer and his wife Kathy Carroll, a psychologist. I clutch a cup of coffee, very aware that I am standing in for Nino, who never missed a race. When I see my son, I give him a big smile and thumbs-up, wondering if this is what Nino would do and hoping it will encourage him.

The flag comes down, and the pool of runners takes off. Michael starts out fine, but soon I sense that he's in trouble. His stride is not as powerful as usual. He seems to lack coordination. His chest heaves as he tries to keep up with the pack, which is edging swiftly past him. When another runner advances from behind, he stumbles—unbelievable for my son—and his head falls back. I can see the look on his face—stunned, angry. I can see him clench his fists, again and again, as the field sails by.

Michael comes in fifth. But after passing the finish line, he does not stop. He simply runs on. I crane my head, trying to follow with my eyes as he sprints into a stand of trees at the end of the field then disappears into the woods.

I am wrenched by guilt and grief. Oh, God. Of course this is traumatic for him, but I made him try anyway. Racing was something he and Nino had shared since Michael was in high school.

Why did I urge him to do it? I throw my coffee cup to the ground, take to the field, and follow him, crying and calling his name.

Don MacKelcan, the father of Michael's friend Katie, grips my arm and holds me back. "Debbie, let him go."

"He's suffering," I cry, trying to wrest myself from his arms. "Oh, my God. Let me go to him."

"He needs to be alone," says Don. "Give him that. Let it be for a little bit."

Later on, Michael admits he was run down but insists he ran off because he was disgusted and embarrassed by his showing. Not because of the brutal killing, just weeks before, of his father.

AFTER SOMEONE YOU love dies, holidays can be unbearable; and birthdays, too—all those Hallmark moments. But the firsts—the first Christmas, the first next birthday—are especially hard.

We have plenty of milestones to get through and little time to prepare. June 7 will be Michael and Melissa's twentieth birthday, and it will be hard for all of us to celebrate without Nino. Worse, July 3 will be Nino's birthday, what should have been his fifty-first. But the first and perhaps the most difficult date is May 19, less than a month after Nino's death. It's our twenty-fifth wedding anniversary.

Way back before the crime, in February, I'd gotten that night off from work, thinking Nino and I would be going out to dinner and wondering what dress would look good with the diamond earrings he gave me.

When the day arrives—it's a Tuesday—the normalcy of it all staggers me. The sun in the sky is an affront; for God's sake, I think, at least let it rain, like in some Brontë novel. But I can't will the sun away; it glints lemon-yellow in a big blue sky, as if to spite me.

Spring. In our family, it means nothing so much as the official start of boating season, which peaks in summer and always lingers way into fall. Nino adored it. I think he liked the preparations as much as the act of boating itself. I used to quip that for him, getting ready—spending ten-and twelve-hour days at the marina, scouring the underside of the hull, then striding the dock and surveying the horizon with a knowing scowl, all in the company of other seafaring, manly men—all these were more fun than boating itself.

I force myself to turn from the window of my room at the Nygaards'. I walk to the bathroom to comb my hair, which now looks almost normal—my regular wash-and-wear pageboy.

Miserable as this day is, obscene as it feels, I am resolute. I will celebrate.

I meet my own gaze in the mirror, noting the fresh lines around my eyes and a slight but pronounced droop at the lids.

"Celebrate, damn it."

The refrain in my head has become: give nothing away to the killer. Not a minute, not a day. Certainly not our anniversary.

Melissa and I have arranged to meet Nino's sister, Dolores, at Schaefer's Canal House, the place we also celebrated my in-laws' fiftieth anniversary, and my mom's retirement. Nino and I went there often, for steaks (him) and seafood (me); it's one of "our" places.

That reminds me. I will have to start deleting words like "our" from my vocabulary—"our" and "we" and "us."

Also "husband."

Also "wife."

Funny. This anniversary was the day we argued about, Nino and me. I was sentimental, I wanted the rented hall, the caterer, the big to-do. Nino was practical, he wanted to conserve. It was an argument we'd had all the years of our marriage, in one way or another.

How senseless it all seems today.

WE HAD ALWAYS loved Schaefer's, located just where the Chesapeake and Delaware Canal meet the Chesapeake Bay in Maryland.

At that juncture, the channel is deep enough to accommodate all the big boats, and when one went by, every light in the restaurant would be dimmed so people could see the boat lights blinking on the darkness of the water. I remember seeing some of the tall ships go by. And once Melissa (who worked one summer as a dockhand for all the pleasure boaters) saw a spectacular yacht said to be owned by Jane Fonda and Ted Turner.

Schaefer's is also close to all our summer havens—the Sassafras and Elk Rivers; the beautiful Bohemia; our favorite towns, Galena and Chesapeake City.

This day we have a nice-enough lunch; we are each of us determinedly upbeat. We clink glasses in a toast to Nino and have a tiny cake. When we part—this merriment wears thin after about ninety minutes—Dolores and I hug tight. We make lavish promises to stay close and stay family, despite the tragedy. After all, Dolores and her brother Rick are Michael and Mel's godparents.

I don't know it, but it will be years before the kids and I hear from Dolores or Rick or Nino's mother or any other member of his family.

"I can't assure you that you'll regain full use of your hands, Mrs. Puglisi." Dr. David Sowa is a hand surgeon referred by Dr. Saunders at Christiana. Our first consultation takes place on May 20, a day after the anniversary, a month to the day since—well, since.

The doctor examines my hands, especially the left, which is swollen and almost arthritically stiff with a bluish discoloration of the fingers. His touch sets off a tingling that runs along the underside of my wrist like a traveling electric shock.

He is cordial, candid, and guardedly optimistic about the return of function to my hands. But, he adds, it will take a while, weeks or even months, before he can give me a true prognosis. "From the constriction of those ropes, you have partial- and full-thickness burns to the wrist. Now full-thickness burns can require skin grafting, and I don't know yet if that will be necessary in your case. But your scarring is very likely permanent."

So these are mine now, these thick crimson scars. They look like bracelets or the brands they use to mark cattle. And unlike the varicosities on my legs, also caused by the ropes, I have to look at them every day. When the swelling goes down, perhaps I can wear real bracelets to hide them. It never occurs to me—couldn't possibly, at this point—that one day I will value these marks, the same way a soldier values his stripes.

Dr. Sowa's diagnosis is reflex sympathetic dystrophy, or severe damage to the median nerve of the left hand. In lay terms, that means the nerves in that hand have been crushed. His advice: I need to take a course of pain management at the Wilmington Hospital Pain Treatment Center, where I will receive a series of injections for the pain along with extended physical therapy. He also agrees to prescribe a drug called Nortryptyline, which I ask for because I know it's used by lots of hospice patients for nerve pain. It's also an antidepressant.

It takes a long time to start working—seven to ten days—but it takes the edge off both the pain and the misery. A good thing, but then again, I have been using physical and psychic pain to pay my debt to Nino, the debt I owe for surviving him. How to pay now? I have not nearly filled my quota.

At the pain clinic, I learn that I must receive injections of local anesthetic in, of all places, my neck, to erase the pain in my left wrist. I'm not afraid of needles, and I have a fairly high tolerance for pain in general, so the idea doesn't bother me until the anesthesiologist touches the needle to that spot. It's the very same spot where Donald Flagg held a knife to my throat.

Suddenly, surprising myself and thoroughly alarming the doctor, I begin to whimper then explode in noisy tears.

I had forgotten it. That feeling, that pinprick in that soft place, when I lay on the floor of the foyer and thought, with great certainty, that the man who had raped me was about to slit my throat.

I HATE MY physical therapy. It's so simple as to be absurd. I have to plunge my hand into a bucket of sand then try to name or describe whatever is buried in there. But though I can tell when I encounter something—if nothing else, I can feel the mass—I can never figure out what the thing is. It makes me so mad I could scream.

"Then just pull out the object," says the therapist. "Don't go crazy. Believe me, the fact that you can feel it at all is a good thing."

So I pull it out, and it's always something so recognizable, like a coin or a marble or a Ping-Pong ball. And I look at it and want to throw it out the nearest window.

IN APRIL, Nino and I had received an invitation to the upcoming wedding of a friend, Stu Ross. In May I call to ask, "Can Melissa come in Nino's place?"

Stu is Nino's old friend from the paper business. The occasion of his wedding is bittersweet, for many reasons. Stu's first wife of many years, Lizanne, died in 1997, in her fifties after a brief illness. It was devastating for Stu.

Before and after, Nino was a wonderful, stalwart friend. The night Lizanne took a turn for the worse, Nino rushed to join Stu at the hospital, and after she died, he made a point of keeping him busy.

We had just moved back to Newark. Sometimes on a Saturday, Stu would stop by for lunch. He was so lonely. When six months passed, I remember Nino saying, "C'mon, Stu, it's time to find yourself a date. It's time to move on." But neither of us was prepared when Stu found Nancy and after a brief courtship proposed to her.

We were both taken aback. It was so quick. But how could we begrudge Stu this new happiness? He had mourned earnestly and hard, and it was lovely to see the smile return to his face.

"Well, I'm happy for him," Nino said. "Still, it seems pretty fast . . ."

"Nino, sometimes people who've been happily married are even quicker to form a new bond." I was only parroting something I'd read in women's magazines, but I liked the theory: it sounded so nice and hopeful. And who was I to say it was untrue? Marriage suited Stu. And Nancy seemed like a marvelous girl.

At the wedding, Melissa and I share a box of Kleenex, but it scarcely stems the tide. For me, it's especially beautiful to see two people, not dewy-eyed children but adults, both of whom have weathered their fair share of heartache, dare to trust again in happy endings. Here is proof, sweet and sentimental, that people can start over again.

BUT FOR ME, new beginnings must wait for the dispensation of justice. Nothing can happen until that happens first, and I am filled with both relief and trepidation when the process finally gets under way.

I meet Jim Ropp, the deputy attorney general who will prosecute Donald Flagg. Jim assures me the case will almost certainly go to trial within a year and says for that I'm lucky. In a bureaucracy where nothing moves swiftly, that's lightning quick. But I can't help asking why, with the killer's confession, the law can't just declare him guilty and toss him in jail.

Theoretically, I understand. Justice is famously blind. There is still a presumption of innocence, despite an Everest of evidence. Legally, until shown otherwise, Donald Flagg is innocent, though the confession came right out of his mouth. He's innocent, though police found me beaten and handcuffed in his house. He's innocent, though he owns the gun that killed my husband.

This process, with all the checks and balances, was constructed by a conscientious legal system. Without it, justice would be arbitrary and random—not justice at all. I know this, but certain things drive me crazy: chief among them, the fact that right now each and every action committed by the suspect is alleged, alleged, alleged. Donald Flagg allegedly murdered Nino. He allegedly kidnapped me. And don't forget all those alleged rapes.

I learn to loathe the word "alleged" so much I can practically taste my own bile each time it appears in the newspaper, preceding the word "killer" or "kidnapper." Alleged.

A friendly reporter tells me, "When I started covering crime, I created a macro on my computer keyboard for the words 'alleged' and 'allegedly.' Saves lots of time. And Debbie, even if he did it in the town square in front of a dozen cops with video cameras, it would still be 'alleged.' "

I want to speak about all this. I am growing angry, and I have much to say. But the day before I am to meet reporters at the office of my friend and attorney, Bruce Hudson, the judge in the case, Norman A. Barron, hands down a gag order. Too much pretrial publicity, he says. It could create unfair prejudice against the defendant. The gag order makes me feel as if my views are unacceptable, that the legal system is more concerned with protecting Flagg than protecting me.

Bruce tries to placate me. Judge Barron, he insists, knows that any supposed bias in the community—bias in my behalf—could jeopardize the trial, compromise its integrity. It's the kind of thing the defense will seize on to derail the whole process. If the asshole is convicted, Bruce cautions me, his defense team could claim that pretrial publicity prevented him from getting a fair trial. So Judge Barron by imposing a gag order is protecting me as much as Flagg. But as a victim, I have an acute need to speak my grievance. To be told to shut up and say not a single word against my attacker is frustrating and infuriating.

The next step when it happens seems almost foregone, and there is a depressingly inevitable feel about it. I had even joked about it, bitterly, to Robert, saying, "Watch him go for insanity." When he does, I am not surprised, just overwhelmingly discouraged.

At first I absorb the news quietly. Later on in the day, I grab the car keys and jump into the car. This has become my chief mode of response when things get too maddening—just take off, hardly noting the route I take. I just drive and drive and cry and cry, pounding on the steering wheel. That someone could publicly proclaim without a hint of embarrassment that the murderer of my husband need not take responsibility for his actions—it's like being slapped. No, it's worse. It's like being raped again.

The asshole has no history of mental illness, but now, according to his public defender, Brendan O'Neill, the truth will be known. His long-suppressed paranoid schizophrenia will presumably explain and in part mitigate Donald Flagg's coldblooded, coldhearted, point-blank murder of a good, innocent man who was getting ready for his afternoon nap.

It comes on me like a fever, this primal hatred unlike anything I've ever felt, and it makes me realize I never knew what hatred was. I didn't know there was a feeling like this, a feeling this strong, dark, and overwhelming. It is a foul thing, sickening me from the inside out.

For days while I was gone, everyone's question was "Where is Debbie?" Now I'm asking myself the same question. I had always thought of myself as a decent, caring person. To me, kindness was always as important as honesty, maybe more so. I can hardly believe I am capable of ardently, earnestly, passionately wishing another human dead.

But cruelty up till now was always theoretical, a concept. Just like hate. Now they are real, the monsters under the bed coming into the light of day. I feel possessed by them. I feel monstrous myself. Because now *my* hatred and *my* desire to punish feel as strong as the killer's must have been at the moment when he pulled the trigger. But he didn't hate us, did he? How could he? He didn't even know us. And sometimes, this realization—that evil can be so casual—makes his crime all the harder to bear.

One day I see our faces—mine and the asshole's—in photographs in the *News Journal.* They are the size of two postage stamps, positioned side by side. It looks as if we are together. The newspaper slides out of my hands to the floor. I call my brother

Robert, in New Jersey. My voice is wobbly. "Robert call them at the paper," I beg. "Tell them not to put his picture next to mine." And they never do again.

THOUGH I AM still staying with the Nygaards, I often wander over to my house after the workmen are gone for no other reason at all but to sit awhile by myself and give Gene and Karen some privacy. One evening as I lock the door, I turn to see a young dark-haired man standing on my doorstep, head tilted querulously to one side. "Mrs. Puglisi? Debbie? Hi, I'm a reporter for the *Wilmington News Journal.*" He hesitates a moment before extending his hand.

I'm not mad that he's here, but I'm surprised he would show up like this, unannounced, at the home of someone who was recently assaulted and raped during a break-in. Doesn't he realize I might be a little jumpy if a strange man comes to my house? Then there's the gag order. I couldn't talk to him if I wanted to.

But then again, where's the book of etiquette on this stuff? Maybe people don't understand that crime victims don't want people coming up and saying boo, and I realize I have to make allowances.

The reporter wears a sad smile, like a mortician. He says, "I really don't want to take up your time. I just wanted to tell you, you know, I've had people in my family who've been through crimes, and I really feel bad for you and your kids." The sun is setting in the sky behind him, so I have to squint to see his face. What to say? "Well, okay. Thanks."

His smile widens. "And, you know, no pressure or anything, but if you ever want to tell your story, here's my card."

"Oh. Thank you." I file the card away. I never call him. Later, when I start catching up on all the accounts written while I was missing, I come across a four-page Sunday feature written by this same man—written before he ever met or spoke to any member of the immediate family. In it, he conducts an in-depth dissection of my life and marriage, starting with my so-called broken home—my parents' divorce, my dad's remarriage and second divorce. It's maddening—not because it depicts us in a poor light (though in places it does) but because it gets many facts correct without getting anything right.

With a few names and dates and plenty of imagination, the reporter weaves a tale bearing very little resemblance to reality. There are our pictures: Nino, me, and, worst of all, our kids. Where did the newspaper get their graduation photos? It makes me helplessly angry to see Michael and Melissa exploited. Yes, there we are. But when I read the article, I scarcely recognize us.

Sure, I didn't grow up in the perfect family. And divorce does not occur without some rancor and hurt. But every single one of the adults in this group—Dad; Mom, when she was living; my stepmother Sue Regars—maintained very decent, warm relationships. To this day, Dad, Sue, and his current wife Barb are all friends. But according to the reporter, the Engels are the poster family for dysfunction.

That's nothing compared with how he portrays me and Nino. In his version, Nino married me on the rebound, after a devastating breakup with an "exotic, olive-skinned beauty"—his former girlfriend, presumably his true love. He had written a ballad for this girl. In essence, the article suggests I was Nino's second choice in life, the first runner-up. The writer also quotes someone who describes my husband—Nino, the committed homebody, the consummate family man—as an "Italian stallion."

I can't believe my eyes. Oh, yes, it's good reading, I guess, like a Danielle Steele potboiler is good reading. It's juicy. But it's bullshit. And thousands, maybe hundreds of thousands of people are out there reading it and taking it as gospel. Worse, it's right there for my kids to read. I call Michael at school and tell him to ignore it.

"Why?" he asks, a trace of suspicion in his voice. "What's it about?"

"It's fiction," I snap. "It's about a bunch of strangers. Don't read it. And for God's sake, let's not say anything to Melissa."

Down in North Carolina, she might miss it altogether if we don't tell; the last thing she needs is to read about her father's supposedly lively love life.

Kathy Manlove urges me to shrug off the story, and the dozens of others like it, like the one in a Delaware County paper with the headline SEX SLAVE HORROR.

"You've gone through so much worse than this," she says. "Why let it get under your skin?"

"But it's all untruths," I say. Same as that stuff about me being this wondrously brave woman, this miracle woman. It's not who I am. These stories are not who we are.

Maybe I should rise above it. If I measure everything against the crime, nothing will ever bother me again. But what happened to my family didn't endow me with immunity against the little things. I still feel them.

I want to tell Kathy, Don't expect me to be this paragon. Don't make me out to be this wonderful person. And please don't ask me to be brave, because I'm not.

I NEVER HAVE been. All my life I've thought of myself as this little, quiet thing. "I am Dorothy, the Small and Meek." As a girl, I was the shy, studious child, the best-greased cog in the family wheel. I was the one who never caused too much ruckus. Mom and Dad never had to dog me to clean my room or do my homework; I just did it.

In school I was the stereotypical bookworm. But I never won any admirers for my scholastic ability; if anything, straight-A kids were invariably tagged as weirdos, teacher's pets, or brown-nosers. And with my slight figure, pixie haircut, and cat's eye-glasses, I had not one but two jeering nicknames: "Four Eyes" and "Stick."

Becoming a cheerleader was my big hope for a Cinderella transformation, but even that didn't help my image. I was chosen only because I could do a clean split, was little enough to throw around, and light enough to stand atop the human pyramid.

I had always allowed others to tell me who I was and what I could and could not do. The dreaded pixie hairdo stuck with me till I was out of high school, simply because Dad didn't want me to grow my hair. Though I despised the look, I never stood up to him. I never demanded my hair rights. And no college for me, because I was a girl; my destiny was the steno pool, and I accepted it, reluctantly but meekly. Later, even my husband, with his knee-jerk way of downplaying my abilities ("Debbie, if anything ever happens to me, you'll never make it") convinced me that, deep inside, I was still that tremulous child, all alone in a big strange world, unable to take care of herself or anyone else.

So when people applaud me in these months following the attack, using these big shiny marquee words to describe me, I want to look around to see who on earth they're talking about.

This heroine, this cartoon superhero, Debra Puglisi—the fierce survivor who confounded a drug-crazed murderer and escaped—is unknown to me. Debbie, the person I meet in the mirror each day, is worried and scared. When I see the handprints on my arms, fainter now but still visible, I feel the killer has never let go of me.

11

By June 1 the repairs on my house are still unfinished. I am feeling restless and guilty for imposing on the Nygaards for so long. So I ask the kids if they'll go with me to stay for the summer with Dad and Barb at their second house in Manahawkin, a little bayside town along the Jersey Shore.

They're all for it, and within days we make our getaway. This, I think, will be medicine for everyone. A time to be close, a time to talk and think and breathe and heal, away from the memories—and the media hubbub—back in Delaware. Soon we will all go our separate ways again. Right now we need, and want, a little time to be still and together.

For me, it's wonderful. Blessedly uneventful. So safe. Dad is my caretaker, tender and indulgent. He becomes Daddy again, and I am a pampered little girl, home sick from school; all I have to do is whimper and he appears, my own personal genie, ready to do my bidding. I haven't been fussed over like this in years, and, oh, how I revel in it. Every day is chicken soup and chocolate pudding and my favorite shows on the TV.

In retrospect, I see the total regression. I'm forty-six years old and all I want is my daddy. I guess I need someone to make me believe that everything is going to be all right again. Who better?

I also have my kitties, Bandit and Paddy, who live like little kings on a screened-in porch overlooking the water, and stare hungrily at a flock of mallards that comes by each day to be fed. (Homey, my outside cat, has since moved to my sister Jane's.)

Our routine consists of placid, lie-about times, alternating with periods of frenetic activity and forced merriment. We eat out a lot and gorge on vast quantities of comfort food. Dad barbecues every night but Thursday ("Moose Night"), when he and Barb and I drive to the local Moose Lodge for steak sandwiches or big burgers and trade chips for free drinks.

Barb and I shop daily, trekking from Wal-Mart to Kmart and back, where we load up on Beanie Babies, picture frames, bedsheets, shampoo, and tons of other stuff we don't really need. I buy loads of knickknacks, thinking I'll really pretty up the house when I get back. And for some reason I keep the washer and dryer going constantly. As long as I stay busy, my mind can't wander to it—the event. Or, as we obliquely take to calling it, The Thing that Happened. So every day, sometimes twice a day, I track down dirty laundry from everyone's room and do load after load of wash, sort, separate, and fold, then start all over again. I crave routine and order and work like an automaton, mechanically, taking great pleasure in building tall, neat piles of sweet-smelling clothes and sheets and socks.

But after a couple of weeks, this familial cocooning at Dad's, with five of us shoehorned into a three-bedroom rancher, starts to become oppressive. The twins feel neglected and, surprisingly to me, lonely. At first I don't see their restiveness. I'm still dulled by shock, and preoccupied with me. I don't notice the way Michael sprints to the door first thing every morning, sometimes in the afternoon, too, to run for miles along the edge of the lagoon. It doesn't seem out of the ordinary to me, because running is part of his routine; also, he's training for cross-country in the fall. But this summer he runs with special intensity. Like he's trying to run away.

Nor do I see the way Melissa gradually separates herself from our group, growing more and more withdrawn, sullen, even angry.

I keep thinking family is the best refuge for them—what else but? Naively, I assume (and I will do so again and again) that we are the best people to take care of us. I think any distance between me and my children or between any of the members of our family will dissolve now, to be replaced by strong, fast, appreciative bonds. After all, we almost lost each other. I envision a new level of relationship in which we treasure one another all the more, nothing is taken for granted, and every second is heaped up with meaning, with the things that matter.

It doesn't happen. We are not magically transformed into the perfect family. All the little strifes and strains that existed between us before the crime remain; sometimes, they intensify. Why, for example, am I amazed that the Puglisi family has cut us off? The one I was closest to was Nino's father, Anthony Sr., whom I adored. Now, with Nino and his dad both gone, the rest of the Puglisis have chosen to break that bond. It might have been fine with me—I knew they were hurting—but they cut off the kids as well, and that makes me not just sad but angry.

And Michael. Like Nino, he had always kept his feelings in check. Since the crime he is not suddenly a wellspring of emotion; if anything, he has become more silent, more reserved, more strenuously self-contained. He is the man of the family now, and he strives to protect the rest of us from the fallout of his grief. Instead, he throws all of his passion and pain into exercise. It takes me a long time to realize then accept that he does not turn to me for emotional support. He's a teenage boy. He needs his friends, his running buddies, and college friends far more than he needs his mother, just as Melissa needs her boyfriend, Jeremy, back in North Carolina. All I've accomplished by dragging them here is to remove them from their real, everyday support systems.

I can give them mother love. It's not nearly enough. And even if it were, I am incapable of giving it in full measure.

This first summer, the focus is on me—the broken one, the beat-up one. And no one, including me, remembers to take care of the kids. I *have* my daddy. Michael and Melissa have *lost* theirs, suddenly and horribly. I don't see the enormity of their sorrow and need because I'm too caught up in my own. Then one day the veneer of a close, insular family, finding shelter in each other at a time of crisis, comes apart. It's sudden, it's big, and it's loud.

We've brought Nino's Boston Whaler—a small, very portable boat that doesn't need more than a hitch to haul it around—to Dad's for the summer. Like Nino (unlike Michael or me), Melissa is a boater, and I think it'll be nice for her to be able to go out if she wants. When Dad and I decide we should keep it tied up off the dock, Melissa disagrees.

"A boat that size shouldn't be kept in the water," she says. "You just put it in when you want to use it then take it back out again."

Maybe she's right, but it seems a small matter to me. Why not keep it ready to go? After all, we're doing this for her.

"No, Mom," she says. "Dad would agree with me. It doesn't belong there. And I know more about boating than you guys."

I note the hostile tone in her voice and bristle. Just like that we're facing off, as we have always done. The events of the past few months, which I was certain would bring us closer—along with all my pledges to treasure and cherish each moment with my children, forever and ever, amen—are forgotten.

"Well, Melissa," I say, surprised to hear the fury in my voice. "Just this once, let's make Pop-Pop happy and put the thing in the water. Okay?"

"It doesn't belong there," she shoots back, equally furious. "Does anyone in this family listen to me or care what I think about anything?"

"Melissa, all we are trying to do here is keep you happy! Why do you have to be so difficult, especially now?"

And we're off, in one of our legendary mother-daughter squabbles. Soon we have an audience, as Dad, Barb, and Michael converge from other parts of the house to find out what's wrong.

By this time, Melissa and I are shrieking at each other, saying mean, hateful, hurtful things. Finally, shaking with anger, I turn, grab my car keys, and race from the house. Behind me, I can hear Dad shouting, "What the hell did you do to your mother?"

I practically tear the hinges off the door of my car. I climb in, gun the engine, and speed off, crying so hard I can scarcely see the road.

Mel and I had been at loggerheads from the time she turned eleven; between eleven and nineteen, it had been one pitched battle after another. Only recently, when she met and fell in love with Jeremy, had we called a détente. With the natural rebellion over, she found to her surprise that she wanted to talk about womanly things with her mother. We've just begun to develop a real friendship.

Now we're back at square one, sniping at one another about silly things.

Before the end of the day, Mel and I have said our apologies, but the relaxed summer vacation is over, and that fight is like a storm warning. I wonder, if when this thing is over, we will still be a family or if the idea of family will be as precious and meaningless as Nino's belongings, which I will soon sort out and give away.

HERE'S A PAIR of holey blue jeans, pouchy at the knees, saggy in the seat, and soft as cotton. Here are dingy T-shirts, thin and flannelly and so worn they're practically transparent. Here is a tuxedo, Nino's Friday night uniform, on a hanger with two or three pressed white shirts with pleated fronts. And here, sheathed in plastic, is a twenty-year-old leisure suit in basic brown polyester. I can't help shaking my head. Nino never willingly threw things away, even if all they did was rent space in his bedroom closet.

It is August, and I am once again a resident of Arizona State Drive. By now every trace of the violence that took place here just a few months ago has been expunged, like magic. The floorboards and wallboards have been replaced, recarpeted, painted over, sanitized, till the place looks once again like a model home.

The fingerprint dust is gone, the gore and blood have all been airbrushed away, so all my rooms are perfect and pretty once again. The sofa cushions are plumped, and the Beanie Babies are back on display. And, just as I'd planned, the rose bushes are visible from the window near our breakfast table. But they're not nearly as nice as I had hoped they'd be. Even in full sun—because the sun, inexplicably, does continue to shine—their heads droop, as if the transition from Gene's yard to ours was just too jarring for them.

I have changed one thing. It's that WELCOME sign, the colorful banner that once hung on a flagpole outside our side door, with a happy little gingerbread house embroidered on it. That's now gone, with a vengeance. The day I came back from New Jersey, I ripped the goddamned thing down with my bare hands, nearly breaking the metal dowel in half.

For now, by all appearances, I have resumed a nearly ordinary life. With summer on the wane, the kids are headed to school, and next month, I'll be going back to work, too—a financial necessity and, I think, a necessity in every other way. I need the semblance of normalcy, and I also need to make a statement (to myself, if no one else) that I will not be destroyed by this crime. In the meantime I practice doing ordinary things. Getting up. Having food. Driving in my car. Smiling at my neighbors, some of whom gape at me as if at a ghost.

I take in the mail and try to ignore the clutch in my stomach when I see something addressed to Anthony Puglisi. But I'd better get used to this; it will continue for years, and every spring, the IRS will send curt letters demanding that Anthony Puglisi file his tax return or face a substantial penalty. I wish ardently that they would call. Like the telemarketers, whom I used to suffer with a certain amount of grace. But now I have lost all patience. When the calls don't let up—when they keep calling to sell Nino on a new phone plan or newspaper subscription—I begin to use blunt force.

"Good evening, is this Mrs. Puglisi? May I speak to Mr. Puglisi? I'm calling from Sears to tell him about—"

"Mr. Puglisi is not here."

"Okay, I'll just call back—"

"Don't call back. Mr. Puglisi was murdered in April." Click.

I've known the desolation of losing someone I love with heart and soul—Mom—but I guess I forgot the crushing, animal pain of it all. What hits me each day, like good-morning slaps in the face, is the silence. Silence in the house where there had been daily conversation about news, the kids, the jobs, friends, and what's for supper. Now there is silence in every hour.

No man here.

I can so easily conjure images of Nino, seated at the island in the kitchen, getting in my way while I made dinner, sneaking to get something from the fridge after vowing to stick to his diet. And Nino now, in the dark, arms linked at his midsection, with Melissa's afghan pulled up to his chest.

For a time, one thing worked to keep this stuff on the shelf: being in New Jersey, away from where it happened. At Dad's there was hardly anything that said Nino out loud—the boat, but that was all. I was not assaulted daily by reminders. But now I am back, and every day I must face the things that make me think of my husband. In the morning, his razor and shaving cream, which I cannot bear to toss in the trash, and the mirror in our bedroom, where he would sometimes stand behind me, combing his hair while I put on lipstick. It is so jarring to see just me there that I start using a compact if I want to wear makeup. But why wear makeup? Who cares if I'm pretty now?

At night I go to sleep, still occupying just one side of the bed, here in the room where my husband lay for so long after being shot and where investigators probably stepped over him as they measured blood spatter and bullet trajectory. Did he die here? Though the coroner insists otherwise—Nino died instantly, he says, in the doorway of the dining room—I suspect this may be a kindly, well-intentioned lie, designed to spare me further pain. In too many of the accidents or crimes I hear about, the victim "died instantly." How can they be sure?

It's funny, but I sleep okay. No dreams, good or bad. I wake refreshed in the morning, ready to do the same things I did the day before. Like a hamster on a wheel.

I am trying to get back to my "ordinary life." On the surface I manage a pretty good approximation. But there is no ordinary left.

ON THE CLOSET FLOOR, among a motley collection of sneakers and loafers, I find a pair of old canvas boating shoes. Once white. Now scuffed and grayish and frayed around the sides. Nino wore them for years, till the tread wore out of the soles and the heels were nearly walked away. Again, practical Nino. But when it came to his clothes, it wasn't just a matter of practicality. New clothes were stiff, he complained. They felt starchy. They had edges. It took lots of washing and wearing before things got good and broken-in, and broken-in was just how he liked them. When I slide out of my pullover and into one of his sweatshirts, I catch a whiff of sweat and soap and tobacco, along with something herb-y and Italian-smelling, like oregano. Nino never wore cologne except for gigs, and I always joked that Good Seasons was his version of Old Spice.

I recall the first time I saw him in a tux, shortly before we married, when I tagged along like an adoring groupie to one of his gigs. He was so young, and he looked so elegant. I was proud to be with him and watched other women watch him, as he strode to the bandstand and picked up his guitar. Oh, how I loved that man.

Past tense. I hear it in my thoughts and instantly admonish myself.

Love that man. I love him. I do and I will. Always, Nino. Always.

Among the jackets and shirts and suits flapping on their hangers, I'm reminded of stumbling into that other closet, in Wellington Woods, on that Friday night in April. Something of that

feeling, that terrible fright, returns to me now, as I begin the ritu-
alistic parceling off of Nino's things. Yet I am driven to do it, and
immediately. When we were kids we called it "hurting a hurt"—
that perverse impulse to wiggle a loose tooth or pick at a scabby
knee or look straight at something dead along the roadway. Of
course I knew the sight and scent of Nino's clothes was going to
hurt. But I wanted to see and smell and touch and hug them. I had
to. Soon it would be too late. His imprint will start to fade. I have
to fill myself up with it. It will have to last a lifetime.

So many people—Karen Nygaard, Kathy Manlove, and my
stepmother Sue, Dad's ex-wife—offered to help me with this
task. But I waved them away. I wanted to be alone with my husband. And when I come across these old shoes, I'm thankful to
be by myself. I kneel on the closet floor and hold one shoe to my
chest and just rock, back and forth, back and forth.

Nino, always.

We were just kids when we first said it. And though by midlife
we were no longer the most passionate couple in the world, it
mostly stayed true for us. Nino and I continued to love, "till
death," just like we promised. He was not demonstrative, but
sometimes he still held my hand. He still called me "Sweetie."
We never parted without a kiss, even if it was just a peck. We
were one thing, Debbie-and-Nino. It was like one word. To the
kids, Mom-and-Dad, inseparable.

But not inseparable after all. In a few minutes, at the whim of
a stranger, it was all irretrievably gone.

I think of amputees who still feel the sensation of that missing
arm or leg—the "phantom limb." In the same way, I still feel
Nino's presence—not just in my mind but actually, physically. In
bed at night I embrace the space beside me and fantasize that I
feel the weight of his arms around my waist. Then, too soon, the
space feels empty again. Each night I lose him again and again.
Realization sweeps over me like the crash of waves, like the waves
that once knocked me off my feet at Long Beach Island.

Each second of the day I know for a fact that my husband is

dead. But every so often it can still come around and smack me
like something new and shocking, feeling fresh and horrible all
over again. Nino is dead. It's like I am hearing it for the first time,
with that same bewilderment and disbelief.

Does it scare him to be dead? From time to time, I think of
him in a locked box under the ground, and I want to go there
and rescue him from that. He can't be happy in that place, my
Nino who was so much a part of the living. I think of him and
wonder if he's hurt and confused to be parted from us and cold
from being in his grave.

Thank God for Mel, who thought to wrap him in his favorite
blanket.

And wherever he is, does Nino blame me? The killer wanted
me, not him. He said as much in his confession. He was looking
for a woman to kidnap and rape; that woman was me. And as
much as I suffered at the hands of that brute, Nino was the real
victim. He got in the way. He died as a result. I wrestle with this
knowledge every day. I tell myself—as everyone else tells me—
that I'm not responsible for the actions of Donald Flagg. But it
doesn't work. This burden of guilt does not respond to reason. I
feel I owe a penance for surviving.

It's made worse, somehow, when I hear myself lauded in the
papers and on TV as a "hero." I don't deserve accolades, not for
heroism or courage or anything good. I am the reason my husband met his murderer. I cannot escape that truth.

I've heard the term survivor's guilt before, applied to people
who walk away from car wrecks and plane crashes and house
fires. It's a feeling of, Why me? I'm no better than the one who
died. Maybe I'm not nearly as worthy to live. But I did live, and
I must atone for that. But how?

One way: pain. My physical pain is not yet gone, and it is a
great distraction, an almost welcome relief. Whenever I want to
cry about the searing pain deep in my wrists, I remind myself it's
insignificant next to what Nino endured. I turn this into a sacri-
fice, my way to make amends. In every moment of pain, I tell

myself I'm taking back some of Nino's pain. Every spasm cancels out in some cosmic way a portion of his pain. Because even though he's dead, I feel that his pain is ongoing, like a record that stopped at one place and keeps repeating.

As long as my own pain continues, I continue to pay off my debt.

12

"I KNOW THIS isn't easy. But you have to bring yourself to look at his face."

I choke back my objections, brace myself, then turn and look straight into dull black eyes with yellow-tinged irises. The man looks massive: mountainous shoulders, a thick chest, jug ears, and a big, bullet-shaped head that's tilted back slightly so he seems to be staring down at me, ready at any moment to lift his hand.

Instinctively I look away, but my new therapist says no, don't. Be strong. Try. If I'm to confront this man in court, she says, I must first confront him—or, at least, his mug shot—here, in her office. This is vital work, she says. My work. Much as I want to shuck it off, I have to do it if I expect to get back some semblance of normalcy or tranquility.

And, oh, how I want those things.

"Look at him. Try, Debbie."

Her words are only meant to be encouraging, but all I can hear is the challenge inside them.

I dare myself. I dare myself.

It takes all my courage. Therapy is not a soft thing, a weak or self-indulgent thing, the way Nino used to think. I'm a veteran. I first saw a therapist when I sued our dentist and again after the kids left for college. Nino scoffed, but it wasn't all hugs and handholding and affirmations. It took honesty and character and grit. It helped me take a stand about things, at home and in the wide world, when it would have been a lot easier to live with my discontent. Therapy, first with a psychologist named Dr. Jeffrey Faude, helped me demand lots more of myself and others, until I was no longer willing to accept the role of handmaiden in my own home.

It was my primer. This will be graduate work. Now more than before, I know that the healing process is not something that happens to you, it's not something you get, from a doctor or counselor or anyone else. If I'm to recover, it won't be a passive process. I'll have to work at it and participate all the way.

All right, then. I've been through worse. Once upon a time I judged tough times by the malpractice suit, saying, "If I could do that, I can do this next thing." It was my high-water mark of being strong. Now I have a whole new measuring stick. One hundred and one hours in hell.

"Look at the picture."

I lift my eyes. I close them. I open them. And suddenly I'm grateful I was so unseeing during the five days at Donald Flagg's house. Now I can see. Holy Jesus! The man would have scared me to death.

Though I'm seated, I'm aware of a weakness behind my knees, a rubbery feeling in my limbs. It takes everything I've got to keep my eyes level with those of the killer. "Debbie, this is a fight for your life," the therapist says. "Don't look away. The rest of your life will depend on what you do starting right now."

Her name is Dr. Constance Dancu, and she is the founder of the Center for Cognitive and Behavior Therapy in North Wilmington. It was Kathy Carroll, a psychologist and the wife of Michael's coach, Jim Fischer, who recommended I see her, right after Michael's disastrous race in Massachusetts. I knew Kathy was right. It was time to find out what was going on inside me and inside my children.

For months the kids and I have stumbled along, trying to cope. When we talk at all about the crime, we use words like "acceptance" and "recovery" and "coming to grips" and "getting over it." And to others it probably looks like we're doing a good job. At home I'm upright every day, writing my usual to-do lists, making all the noises and movements that are indicative of life. At school, the kids are just as stoic. They don't falter in their studies. Their grades don't take even a dip.

For my part, I have begun to congratulate myself on my resilience. Didn't everyone think Debbie Puglisi was this meek little thing? Well, look at me now—all I've been through, and I bounce right back. Cool as steel. The hero in the newspapers, that's me.

I'm Spartan, and proud of it. The kids, Michael in particular, are Spartan, too. Let's keep this show on the road. Let's do it for Dad. That's the spirit.

I remember learning about real Spartan culture in grade school. The story that left the greatest impression on me was that of the Spartan foot soldier who stole a fox and hid it under his cloak. He was so determined to get away with it unnoticed that he carried the fox around like that and showed no sign of pain when the fox—as the teacher told us so graphically—began to "gnaw at his vitals."

We are like that foot soldier. Michael, Melissa. Me. Underneath, we're bleeding, dying, going crazy in a hurry. We've tried so hard to put ourselves together again, but it isn't working. Underneath is desperation and confusion and the knife edge of grief. Gnawing at us like the Spartan's fox.

After Massachusetts I knew we needed some kind of professional care, and we needed it fast. I encouraged the kids to find crisis counseling at school. Thank God there were resources for them there. Melissa bonded at once with her counselor and found almost immediate relief in the process. Michael was more hesitant, but he found reinforcement in an unexpected place: among his track buddies. I was touched to learn that they suggested group sessions with a counselor at the University of Delaware. The guys went as much for themselves as to support Michael. At least their gesture got him there, and though he discontinued therapy after a few tries, he was more receptive to the idea. I made him promise to consider going again if things got too stressful, and he said he would.

As for me, I heeded Kathy's suggestion and made an appointment with Dr. Dancu.

Before I met her, I had no idea what to expect. Dr. Dancu was a leader in her field. Her stature in the medical community impressed and even intimidated me, but in fact I found her very approachable. Petite, blond, sixtyish, with a soft, firm voice and unassuming manner. Her office was distinctly unofficelike, with a couple of comfortable chairs under low lights and no desk at all, at least not where we were. And—important to me—she spoke in plain language. I liked and trusted her from the start.

Of course she knew my history. Like everyone, she had followed the crime over the months, but at our first consultation she asked me to go over it all again. I was glad to—still so willing to talk if someone was willing to listen.

"It's nuts," I said. "I escaped from that place, but most of the time it's like I'm still there. In the house, with him. I still feel like I did then, all bottled up. And even when I try to feel other things—when I know I should feel things, when I know just what I would feel under any other circumstances—it's like my own reactions are just out of reach."

It's true. Despite the storm racketing around me—Nino's death, the media furor, the pending trial, and the thorough dismantling of one family and four lives—I remain at the storm's eye, in the dead-calm center. I am chronically dulled, lifeless. I still find it hard to weep; when I do, it is almost like I'm an actor on stage, weeping drops of glycerine. There is a dam inside me, shoring back oceans of—something.

Something poisonous.

Part of me wants it to stay that way. I'm afraid of what will come out if the dam bursts. "Someday," I tell Dr. Dancu, "the walls are going to give way, and then, look out."

Not just the pain is elusive. All the good and generous impulses, too, have been tamped down, put in some emotional cold house. The love and passion I have for my kids, the wild maternal protectiveness that drove me out of that killer's house and back to them, is now unavailable to me—and so to them.

Scholastically the kids are doing well, but every time I speak to either Michael or Mel, I sense the strain that still underlies their chatter about professors, classes, and campus life. I sense it, I know it's there, but I can't seem to muster a response. My children are in turmoil, and I, the quintessential mother hen, cannot lift a finger to help them. It's as if I'm sedated all the time.

The only thing I'm really aware of, I tell Dr. Dancu, is a vague unease. I jump at loud noises and voices. My peripheral vision is suddenly acute, and I find myself very aware of what is going on beside me or slightly behind me. I have a compulsive need to know what's happening in the 360-degree circle that surrounds me. I am always on my toes, and it's draining.

I anticipate her diagnosis before she pronounces it. Dr. Dancu, who is board-certified in the study, diagnosis, and treatment of post-traumatic stress disorder, is one of the most prominent practitioners in her field.

"This craziness. Is this what PTSD is?" I ask her.

I took a psych rotation in nursing school, so I already know a little about post-traumatic stress disorder, which can affect police officers, firefighters, soldiers back from the war, combat nurses, incest survivors—anyone who's lived through a terrifying event or seen death and destruction close-up. I know for example that it's not diagnosed straight off but must linger for at least a month after the traumatic event before it can be identified. That is the "post" in "post-traumatic." It kicks in after the shock wears off.

"You meet most of the criteria," Dr. Dancu says.

■ ■ ■

ONSET OF post-traumatic stress can be delayed for months, sometimes years. People with PTSD can walk around for a long time looking and feeling close to normal. That's thanks to the shock response. On the bright side, shock can be construed as a wonderfully effective protector in the first stages of trauma. Shock is a shield, protecting human beings in crisis from the onslaught of a natural response—abject terror—because terror, in most cases, will not aid in the victim's fight to survive. Terror is disabling. I lost any sensation of terror within the first few hours of my imprisonment. Mentally I went to that place of detachment, where I could think, evaluate, and try to construct an escape.

Without shock I would surely have become hysterical. That would have frightened the killer, who was already so jumpy he was shooting out the windows of his own home. I have no doubt it would have caused my own murder.

So in a way I have to thank my body. My body, my mind, my organism, like everyone's, is instinctively smart. In a near-death situation, it played dead, like a possum that crosses paths with a dog. When I was first kidnapped, Dr. Dancu says, my task was simple and clear-cut: live through it. Get out alive. Don't waste energy on feeling. It's as if I lived in suspended animation, emotionally.

Will my body, that instinctive organism, awaken just as naturally? I see no evidence for it. My deadly encounter is over, and yet I am still deadened. I don't know if I want to come to life again. I don't know if I know how. Life as I knew it once has been shattered, and sometimes I wonder if I'm strong enough to rebuild it. But I have to try, and I face this task with more dread and more determination than I have ever felt about anything.

And week by week, both Dr. Dancu and Dr. Faude, who already know me so well, help me learn more about what happens mentally and physiologically to many people during and after a life-threatening event. They tell me how people react, which, in fact, is how the body and mind are designed to react. Ultimately they will show me how people can learn to recover.

They are my professors, and I think of this time as being back in school. I was always a good student. After I am diagnosed, I run down the list of symptoms and check them off, one after the other. I quiz the kids on what they're experiencing. I haunt the library and prowl bookstores, looking for literature on the subject. I know this will be the most important lesson I will ever learn.

So begins my crash course in PTSD.

Post-traumatic stress disorder is the most recent medical term for the cluster of responses that can follow incidents of severe trauma. According to most definitions, including that used in the American Psychiatric Association's Diagnostic and Statistical Manual of Mental Disorders (DSM), PTSD is an anxiety disorder precipitated by "an event that falls outside usual human experience that would be markedly distressing to almost anyone."

The National Institute of Mental Health reports that, in the United States, about 3.6 percent of all adults from eighteen to fifty-four experience PTSD in a given year. It is more common (up to 30 percent) among war veterans and also afflicts survivors of terrorism, rescue workers involved in the aftermath of disasters, and people who have lived through accidents or violent crimes. Even those who merely witness traumatic events can be affected, along with families of victims.

The difference in PTSD versus some disorders, like rape trauma syndrome and generalized anxiety disorder, is that PTSD includes "reexperiencing" the event with flashbacks, nightmares, or explosive responses to "triggers," an unfortunate term for things that remind one of the trauma.

Like the time I cleaned out Nino's closet. I remember the sudden panic when his shirts and suits flapped in my face. It put me back in Flagg's closet the night of my escape. All of a sudden, in the middle of my oasis of nonfeeling, I was thrust back to moments of pure, primal terror. Though I never lost sight of where I was—in my own home—my mind screamed, Get out of here *now*. It happened another day, when I happened to glance out the window and saw a strange man walking across the lawn. It was like an internal bombshell went off. I flung myself against the door and worked the knob to make sure it was still locked. I ran through from the kitchen through the rest of the downstairs, checking all the other locks. Only then did I look out again and recognize the meter man.

Melissa has begun to have nightmares: fierce, leaping images of bad men, with her father at their mercy. Soon her fear of nightmares becomes fear of sleep itself, so she fights to stave off weariness. The hardest part, she says, is seeing her father made helpless. "I always think of Dad as strong," she tells me. "My hero. I can't stand to think of him that way. Not able to stop them from hurting him. I want to save him."

For her, the shock—that welcome shield—is wearing off far too quickly, and I want to kill the asshole. Here is my tender-hearted daughter, who wants only to be close to her dad in her dreams. But she dreams only of his violent death.

Then there is Michael. Though he debates it with me, insisting that he's doing just fine, I'm certain my son has clamped down on his emotions so strongly that they are coming out in other ways. He has begun to experience unusual lethargy and aching throughout the muscles of his body. As an athlete he has trained himself to work through discomfort, fatigue, and even pain. But now the exhaustion brings him down, and the sudden enforced inactivity depresses him.

Still he says, "Mom, I'm fine."

Dr. Dancu surprises me by saying, "Normal. It doesn't feel good, but it's normal. I know it's hard to believe, but all of what you describe—your fear, Melissa's nightmares, Michael's physical symptoms—these are normal patterns of response."

The literature concurs. The primary symptoms of PTSD are avoidance or emotional numbing (got it) and increased arousal (irritability, hypervigilance, the exaggerated startle response—got that, too), as well as panic attacks, depression, suicidal thoughts, substance abuse, feelings of alienation, mistrust and betrayal, and anger.

Check, check, check. In every other sentence, I see myself and my kids. I am definitely in the "emotional numbing" category, and I like this twilight sleep, where nothing hurts too much and every wrong can be assuaged with busyness, a shopping trip, or a couple of glasses of chardonnay.

But I know everything I suppressed in those five days is on the doorstep, demanding my attention. Whenever I start to think of myself as an exceptionally good survivor, something, some odd little thing, knocks me right off kilter again. Example: the day I pick up a bag of peanuts and am suddenly, utterly, seized by fear, greater than anything I felt even when I was in Donald Flagg's house. What's going on? Then I see it, I get it. On the side of the bag is the expiration date: April 20, 1998.

Time and again I ask Dr. Dancu, "Am I normal? Is it normal to feel so crazy?"

She assures me that what I'm going through is commonplace, expected, and absolutely necessary.

The kids and I are not the only ones going through this. The trauma has radiated from the center, where we stand, to our extended family and on to the greater community, like the aftershocks that follow an earthquake. All of us are on the fault line, dreading to hear the earth split beneath us.

I read about an increase in the sale of security systems since the crime and a higher incidence of women purchasing firearms. People are buying more dogs. It reminds me again just how many victims there are, beyond Nino and me. This crime, like all violence, has shaken the neighborhood, the workplace—it's like a virus, spreading from one person to the next till dozens or even hundreds of people are affected. They, too, have been traumatized and made afraid. The people of Academy Hill are now uneasy in their secure suburbs. Some of the people in Wellington Woods, in Bear, are putting up FOR SALE signs. It makes me angry and sad.

I wonder if the asshole is proud of the havoc he has wreaked.

PTSD is more likely to affect those who feel, rightly or wrongly, that they bear some responsibility for the disaster.

Here's where survivor's guilt comes in. I still feel guilty for Nino's death, personally culpable to the point where I have to restrain myself from apologizing to the kids and to Nino's family and to his close friends for making this thing happen to them. Dr. Dancu spends a great deal of our time together repeating that I am not responsible. We actually argue about it, with me trying to explain to her why I am. Yes, the killer was after me. But not only that. If I had only locked the door to our house, this never would have happened.

"I left it open," I say, and it comes out sounding like a moan. "I left the door open, so anyone could walk in."

"Debbie," says Dr. Dancu, "how many people lock all their doors to go out to the front yard for an hour? People leave doors unlocked all the time. It doesn't result in someone being murdered."

"But *I* left the door open, and someone *was* murdered. *I* left the door open."

"Yes, you did. You left the door open, and Donald Flagg walked in and killed your husband. Then Donald Flagg kidnapped, tortured, and assaulted you. Tell me, are you willing to take the guilt from his shoulders onto your own?"

"No!"

"Then don't do Donald Flagg's work. Don't torture and assault yourself."

Her bluntness shocks me. For the moment what she says makes sense, and I want to cry from sheer relief. I didn't do it. Later, when the moment passes, I find it easy to argue myself back into guilt. Survivor's guilt does not respond to reason as much as to *repetition* of reason. Dr. Dancu has to work with me again and again on this one issue, and it is months—months of self-flagellation, the most punishing remorse—before I can acknowledge without reservation that I did not cause the death of my husband. Before I can say with conviction, "Someone else killed Nino."

Like Melissa, I am also tormented by the way Nino died. The image of him being shot, of him falling back, the sound of his body hitting the floor, the sound of the asshole dragging him down the hall and tossing a coat over his face, the idea of his blood soaking the carpet and dripping down into the basement, reruns in my mind without mercy—as if I must somehow accompany him there, as if I must join him and feel everything he felt. Once again Dr. Dancu addresses it in a most unmysterious way: just by talking sense and saying what I know is true again and again, till I believe it.

"Debbie, remember when you first walked into the house, how Flagg hit you?"

"Yes."

"What do you remember about that moment?"

"All I remember is feeling something then being knocked to the floor."

"Did you feel any pain?"

"No, not at first."

"Did you know what was happening?"

"No, it didn't kick in right away."

"Now think of Nino."

"Please. I can't stand to."

"I know," she soothes. "It hurts, because you love him. But do this. Think. It will help. The gun was fired at very close range, you know that. Nino had no time to respond or to do battle with this man. It all happened very quickly. It was instantaneous."

"But what if it didn't happen that way?"

She doesn't try to persuade me. She simply starts again, asking the same questions as before. "Think it through. What did you feel when you were hit?"

"Nothing. Just—nothing, for the first few minutes."

"Did you feel fear?"

"Not right away."

"Now," she repeats, "think of Nino."

"Oh, God." I shake my head back and forth. "It hurt him. It hurts him."

"What happened to him was so sudden, Debbie. Yes, he might

have seen his killer for a second, but it didn't even register. There was no struggle or fight. The police have told you that."

"I keep thinking they're trying to spare me, saying he didn't suffer so *I* won't, but what if he really did know and was frightened?"

"Debbie," she says, patiently, "what did you feel when you were struck?"

And so it goes, week after week, the same questions and answers until I really accept that in all likelihood Nino did not suffer.

This near knowledge does not bring the comfort it should; instead it makes me feel, more than ever, that I must suffer in his stead.

I LEARN A LOT from my doctors about the condition known as post-traumatic stress disorder. During the Civil War a similar set of symptoms was called DaCosta's Syndrome. Over the years the condition has also been known as hysteria, nervous shock, and the tongue-twisting traumatophobia. After World War I, they called it shell shock: following World War II, combat fatigue, or war neurosis.

I'm surprised how often these names—hysteria, neurosis— imply a judgment of the survivor. As if some of us are tough enough and others aren't. It's untrue that a truly well-adjusted person (I considered myself that) will emerge from a brush with violent death as stable and well-adjusted as before.

Dr. Faude says the reason I can now feel so suddenly fearful has nothing to do with weakness. I am not overreacting, nor am I imagining a threat that isn't there. For me, it is. It's a sort of knee-jerk neurobiolgical response that starts in the part of the brain called the amygdala that interprets incoming sensory information. The amygdala's job, he says, is to "sort out clues or reminiscences of the bad experience, highlighting them as a way of avoiding them." In other words, I'm on constant high-alert, even though I'm no longer in danger.

Post-traumatic stress disorder is not simply a set of psychological reactions. It is chemical. It is biological. It involves mental and physiological systems, the mind and the body.

A traumatic event releases a flood of chemicals into the system, starting with an influx of adrenaline that gives people the energy to take flight (if possible) or stay and fight (if necessary). The fight-or-flight response is as natural to humans as to animals in the wild, a gift of God and nature that enables us to survive the first moments of an attack. (A third type of response is "freeze," which I did when the killer first knocked me to the kitchen floor.) The object of every response—fight, flight, or freeze—is survival, at any and all costs.

Once survival is accomplished, the traumatized person is likely to continue to produce high levels of epinephrine (adrenaline) and norepinephrine, natural opiates that remain in the system for some time post-trauma. This may account for the disconnect between survivor and reality in the first weeks or months afterward, that weird sense that "this didn't happen" or "it's all a dream."

All this is going on in my mammalian brain, and the primitive response is so embedded that it cannot be altered by willpower alone. Throughout this process, I am learning a great respect for the brain, which works overtime to shield us from pain. My brain certainly doesn't want a repeat of that danger. By hanging on to those "clues"—which can be anything at all that reminds me of the crime or the criminal—it thinks it can make sure I'm never attacked again. It has not only circled the wagons but posted lookouts to watch for any sign of threat. The lookouts are always on duty.

The problem is, I no longer need that fight-or-flight response, that pumped-up dose of adrenaline. My brain served me well during the crisis. But it is continuing to produce chemically based reactions that are excruciating to live with. It will take months of therapy and learning before I begin to manage my monsters.

•••

INTERESTINGLY, it is exposure therapy, where I consciously revisit the trauma and feel the fear, that helps put the fear to rest. The theory is deceptively simple. By reliving the event in a safe environment (like a therapist's office), I demystify it. I retell the trauma until it loses its power and potency. During the exposure I also practice relaxation techniques, controlling every aspect of what Dr. Faude calls my "physiological arousal," including breathing, voice, and posture. This, too, helps me remember what happened without being disabled by it.

Dr. Dancu gives me "homework." I'm required to make audiotapes of everything that happened to me in Flagg's house. And she means *everything*. Because, she says, it may not be the big things—like handcuffs or ropes or guns—that will switch on my brain's fear mechanism. It might be an offhand phrase (I shudder when I hear anyone say the words, "Let's do this"—the killer's words before he first raped me). It could be a color (his sheets were forest green). It could be the smell of ribs, the main course of what might have been my last supper.

Then I have to rate, from one to five, my reaction to each memory. What makes me angry? Scared? Depressed?

Sometimes during this assignment I clutch the minirecorder so hard I'm afraid I'll break it. But within a few weeks I really do feel a growing command of the situation and myself in relation to it. At last I'm taking back the power he stole from me.

I am rewriting the story as I tell it to myself. A good example is the way I remember Thursday night, one of the most frightening times of all for me. "Tell me," says Dr. Dancu, "about that next-to-last night. The night you sat up in bed and he screamed at you."

At first the story comes out as I first experienced it: with panic and dread and humiliation. "I had to beg for forgiveness," I tell her. The memory makes me want to crawl under my chair. "I hated him, but I had to do what he said. He was my ruler. I was no better than a dog."

But by the fourth time I talk about it, and the fifth and sixth and tenth, I notice the telling has changed. Now I am placing the blame where it belongs. "He was such a bully, such a coward," I say, and I hear the heat in my voice. "What kind of man does this to a woman?" I feel contemptuous, and it is a good, strong feeling. "He wasn't powerful at all. He couldn't rule me. He couldn't even rule himself."

Dr. Dancu is pleased. I am pleased. I understand all at once that by continuing to fear the asshole, I am showing him the kind of respect one opponent shows another. Well, I won't do that.

BUT I HAVE not yet faced the hardest part of my exposure therapy. I know we are working up to it, and the day it happens I feel as if I am starting at the beginning all over again.

"Debbie," says Dr. Dancu, "you will have to practice saying his name."

"I can't. I don't want to." I'm being stubborn today, like the little kid who believes if she protests strongly enough, she will be let off the hook and allowed to postpone some particularly odious chore. I am quite literally afraid to say the name of my husband's killer. I shape my mouth in the right way and take a breath, but the sound lodges somewhere in my throat, refusing to be acknowledged. I look at Dr. Dancu pleadingly, as if to say, Have pity. Don't make me. She gazes back steadily, waiting.

"Oh, God. I don't know why, but it's harder to say his name than to look at his face."

Dr. Dancu is, as always, comforting, a gentle persuader. "I do understand, Debbie. But I want you to try it once. Take it slowly, as slowly as you need to."

But I still can't get that name out, and she adds, "You cannot go into court calling him 'the asshole,' no matter how richly you feel he deserves it."

I laugh at the unexpectedness of hearing this refined lady saying asshole, but in the middle of laughing, out of nowhere, I begin crying.

She leans over, places her hand on mine, wary of my scars, and presses it briefly. "I know this is so, so hard. But you have come so far. Take the next step. Begin by looking at him and saying his name."

"Okay." I drag my eyes to the mug shot and stare at him, eye to eye, and practically spit out the name, a word at a time. "Donald. Flagg. Donald. Flagg. Donald. Flagg." Then, the addendum: "Also known as the asshole."

Dr. Dancu chuckles softly, and leans back into her chair. "All right. That was good. Now, let's do it again."

13

NINO'S GRAVE STILL awaits a headstone. All that marks the site at Saint Patrick's is a typewritten plastic card with his name and date of death. Jay Beeson has told me the ground has to settle for about a year before it can support a heavy stone, but I go ahead and order one anyway, gray marble with an etching of Nino's boat on one side and musical notes on the other—the things he loved best in life. And beneath these, the words, "Beloved husband and father."

It is the first week in September, and after my weekly visit with Dr. Dancu—when I always feel at once drained and stronger—I've stopped by the cemetery for my weekly visit, a bunch of supermarket daisies in hand. I'm relieved to see that the ground above him, once a heap of fresh, dark earth, has softened till it blends almost completely with the natural slope of the hill. Grass has begun to grow, too, along with some clover. It doesn't look so much like a grave now.

Sometimes I come here with the kids—Michael especially, since he still lives around the corner—but I really prefer to come alone. That way, I can putter around and pull weeds and, if I want to, cry without upsetting anyone else.

It's good to cry, exhausting but good. I'm getting the hang of it. After months of nothingness, I have finally found my reservoir of tears, rivers and cascades of them. But I prefer to cry them by myself. If Mel or Michael accompanies me to the cemetery, I stifle the tears, for their sake, and I suspect they do the same for me. We still protect each other so much. So I come alone, sometimes with a cup of take-out coffee and a cigarette. I sit on the grass and smoke a Winston Light, Nino's brand. It's an offbeat tribute, I guess, but I know it would have made him smile. And sometimes, if the ground is dry, I stretch full out on the grave and lie there for a while, as if my husband and I were taking an afternoon nap.

It's warm today, like summer. The sun is glowing all around, and bees and butterflies float above the meadowy churchyard. After making sure no one else is around, I lie down and wrap my arms around the slightly raised mound of Nino's grave and try to hug it. "I'm here, honey."

This, for me, is the pinnacle of emptiness. God, Nino, I miss being held by you. I miss your physicalness, your skin, the stubble of your beard, every laugh line and mole. I don't know how I will do without love for the rest of my life.

EMOTIONS, stopped up for so long, continue to break the surface. I am fearful, jumpy, looking for peril around each corner. And—this is so awful—I've started wondering who will die next. Compulsively I go down the list of people I love, trying to decide who is most likely to pass. When it happens, I ask myself, will I be able to stand it? The answer, always, is no. Please, God. Not one more person must leave me.

But others do not understand this dread. People seem to believe, and they tell me quite unself-consciously, "Debbie, only good things are going to happen to you now."

It's as if they think in this life it's one lightning bolt per customer. More times than I can count, someone will suggest that because this crime happened to me and mine we've had our full measure of bad times. We're paid in full. And from here on out, we get a lifetime pass—a smooth ride, with no stop signs and no tolls.

"From now on, everything is going to be okay." Because lightning never strikes twice.

It makes me crazy. I want to say, No, no. You fools. I am not immune, I feel more frightened than ever. A sudden noise, the clatter of a branch against the window, is all it takes. You don't understand. These woods are filled with wolves. Look out! They're everywhere. But no one can see them but me and the kids.

Michael, for his part, visits me at home more often, prowling the place like a sentinel. Keeping watch. Mel's this way, too, from afar. When someone she loves is out of sight, she gets it in her head that they are, or could be, in danger. Her counselor tries to reassure her, but she finds justification for her fears in every ghastly news report, which confirm that, yes, people do die suddenly, in new and hideous ways. She makes Jeremy keep his cell phone on at all times. And out of the blue, at odd hours, she will phone me from Greenville, just to make sure I still exist.

The worst part for all of us is when people say, as they invariably do, "This was all in God's plan. We cannot see the purpose right now, but one day . . ." This I cannot bear. This makes Michael angry and makes Melissa question the validity of her own grief. God's will? Then it must be okay. So I must be all wrong to feel this way.

Occasionally I hear, "Nino's in a better place." But Nino didn't want a better place. He didn't want heaven, not yet. And how could some ethereal heaven improve on life here, with his children, his music, his Chesapeake? Nino's version of heaven was a long-distance call from Melissa or a Sunday on the bay or an afternoon cheering his son at the races.

I don't say it. How I would love to just blurt it out. Don't you dare tell me my husband is better-off dead. And that heaven stuff—to hell with it. It reduces this tragedy and wreckage to the level of a sympathy card, where all needs are answered in a few lines of syrupy verse. Yet how can I be angry? People are so well-intentioned. They want only to offer comfort, and I love their thoughtfulness. But I can't stand to hear them say there's a reason for all this or that somehow God's greater good had to include the murder of my husband. The idea is abhorrent to me, and when they say it to my kids, I want to explode.

Through all my years in nursing, from the intensive care unit to hospice, I've never bought into the attitude that there is something redemptive or holy about a tragic death. How easy it would be if I could think that way. But I refuse to believe there is a good enough cosmic reason for a child to die of cancer or for a young man like Keith to waste away with AIDS. What kind of God would construct that kind of universe? Not my kind.

When people say there is a reason for this, it's as if I'm being told not only to make sense of Nino's murder but to find the good in it.

Never. Don't tell me to be okay with this.

On this point, Dr. Dancu says my instincts are good. Diminishing the impact of the death is not a real-world response. Emotion that is deliberately stuffed down, pain that is forbidden expression, doesn't subside. It grows inside like a cancer, unseen but malignant. "Refusing to acknowledge your grief and anger just prolongs it. People invest as much energy in avoiding emotion as in taking it on and working it through. And no one," she says, "has the right to advise you to find purpose in this."

She reminds me, as does Dr. Faude, that neither the kids nor I can rush to healing. There is an old saying bandied about in lots of recovery groups: "It takes what it takes as long as it takes." When I grow impatient with my progress, I repeat this saying, and it helps me trudge through the next ten minutes, into the next hour, into the next day, when I can take up the battle again.

So I try, every day, to get better—dealing with the crime is at the top of my to-do list. As the weeks pass I conclude physical therapy but know that I will continue counseling for a long time; both are designed to put me together again.

PT, at least, has been successful: Dr. Sowa says I may never lose the scars around my wrists, but they are fading, till they look like a little girl's pink ribbons. I now have full function in both hands. That means it's back to work full time, and I long for that—it symbolizes for me a return to life, to normalcy, and to usefulness. But I know I can't help anyone else if I'm still fragile, and the thought of going back to work spurs me to work even harder on my emotional recovery.

My nursing supervisor, Shirley Brogley, is surprised that I am returning so quickly. Many of my nurse friends are surprised that I will continue on at all, particularly because it means regular exposure to the dying.

"But I loved my work; that hasn't changed," I tell Shirley. "Besides, this is a must for me financially." I ask for just one special consideration. "On my name tag, could you put, not Debra Puglisi but just Debbie? I don't want people recognizing me."

They recognize me anyway. When I enter a house, invariably there is one member of the family who will look twice, then three times, then say tentatively, "Are you Debbie Puglisi?" The condolences follow, and I accept them with gratitude, but I'm quick to redirect their focus.

"Thank you. I'm well. Let's talk about how your mom's doing."

I MOVE FROM hope to despair and back—hope that I will not be hardened by this, despair that these crimes, committed so blithely, will turn me hard, wary, cynical. I don't want that. I still aspire to be just like my grandmother, my Nana, who was the lovingest and deliberately happiest person in the whole world.

Nana, how do I do that now?

Like everyone else, I spent much of my life, especially my young years, figuring out a way to be in the world, a way that made sense and worked most of the time. Nana was the main influence for me, a woman who never walked into a room, even in the grouchy early morning, without a smile and a gentle word.

I loved her so much and saw how she was loved by others and decided, yes, that's the way to be.

For the longest time, it had worked. Up till April 20, I could have told you what I believed in, easily. My list was Nana's list. It included hard work and responsibility, kindness and respect, hopefulness and faith. I had long ago filled in the blanks about what I believed. Despite all evidence to the contrary—the nightly news about all the crime and hunger and treachery in this world—I was happiest letting my inner Pollyanna rule.

Not surprisingly, that outlook caused some friction in my marriage. I was a classic cockeyed optimist; Nino, a devout pessimist. Each of us thought our way was best: Nino, cautious in business and overly prudent about money, thought he was protecting himself and his family from the slings, arrows, and predators that beset every life. I figured it was just as legitimate, probably easier and a lot more fun, to stop and smell the roses.

But now that old way of being is gone. It didn't fade away or wear out gradually, from the little disappointments that accumulate over a lifetime. It was ripped away, in minutes, leaving a wound that is still open and raw.

Are the pessimists right?

At least Nino was. Nino was finally, fatally right.

Now I have to make up a whole new way to live, think, and be. The principles I always lived by, the things I thought I knew for sure, no longer make sense to me. Notions of trust and security seem like concepts or theories—very good ideas that have little to do with the life I lead.

As the numbness continues to wear off and I am flooded with unwelcome feelings, I discover I am mourning not just my husband and home but my point of view. And how I mourn it. The sweet ideals of trust, kindness, and openness—they were in the marrow of my bones. I loved them, defended them, and depended on them for more than forty years. Each and every day I made decisions based on them. Now they seem comically simple, and dangerously naive.

I miss a sense of security, the certain notion that when I walk into my home and close the door, the barrier I've placed between myself and others will not be breached. I miss the conviction that most people act pretty decently most of the time; and if they decide to do something wrong, they go into it with three things: a good enough reason, a measure of reluctance, and remorse. I miss my natural, unquestioning faith, the faith that says God creates good people who are bound by humanity to act in a decent, trusting manner. And I miss my confidence—the feeling that because I am a nice person among nice people, I will probably be treated pretty fairly in this world.

Nino was a nice person.

NOW WHAT? What in God's name do I think about things for the rest of my life?

And what to think of God? I continue to pray—I pray more than ever. But my prayers have taken on an accusatory tone, as if I am addressing an errant parent: Why did you let it happen to us, God? To me, to the kids, to Nino? Don't you love us anymore? If not, why not? What did we ever do to you?

I am no longer grateful to you, God. I am ashamed about that and sad, but defiant. I don't understand why you let us be hurt, God. I want an explanation.

Sometimes I fear my anger and newfound doubt will make God move even further from our lives. Maybe he'll send another lightning bolt down to punish us even more. Then I think, No. That was my husband's God, the one who tripped you up on Wednesday if you missed Mass on Sunday. I can't believe God would be like that. But the question still remains, what do I believe?

Right now, I don't know for sure. All I know is that I see what was invisible before: wanton, meaningless evil, the kind that can't be explained away.

BUT THEN THERE are the letters. When I am tempted to surrender to rage or give up on goodness, they're there. They come

from strangers, from people all over the country. They come
from people who knew Nino and me as kids, back in grade
school and high school. Some are from relatives of my former
patients or from Nino's clients of years ago.

For a while, during my retreats to Florida and then to Long
Beach Island, Gene and Karen took in my mail. They set the
obvious sympathy cards and personal letters aside from bills and
flyers and junk. Then suddenly they present me with a daunting
heap of cards and envelopes of all sizes.

At first I dread taking on this task, reading all these messages
from even more well-meaning people. Frankly I expect the worst.
I don't want to get another bellyful of "You will find the good in
this." I ignore the cards for almost two months. Then one week-
day afternoon curiosity overtakes me. I grab a few from the top
of the pile, retreat to the study, and begin.

Many of them begin with some variation of "You don't know
me, but . . ."

"I have never felt I should write to an 'unknown victim' in the
news, [but] I felt led to write to you. . . . I guess there'll never be
an answer to the 'why' question, but I feel things will be much
better for you with time. You're in my prayers."

"Although I have never met you, I felt compelled to let you
know how deeply sorry I am about the recent tragic events which
have befallen your family. . . . Please do not lose faith in humanity. There are many people who do care."

"Our sincere prayers to you and your family . . . We cannot
imagine how you're all handling this act of violence, but pray you
will find strength in each other. . . ."

"You won't remember me, but you were my mom's nurse
before she died. . . ."

"You don't know me, but I am remembering you and your
family in prayer. . . ."

Actually, they know me well. As much as I resist it and continue for months to argue with these kind people in my head,
this is what I need to hear, because this is what I want to believe.
As the months pass and I read on, I can feel the apprehension ebb

away. Sometimes I try to snatch it back—skepticism and distrust are my protectors. But I know in my heart I don't need to be scared of what these people have to say.

So often I want to scar over, to harden myself against people and the evil that people do. These letters, hundreds of them, which I continue to read for years, won't let me do it. These people—like the lady who includes three sticks of Wrigley's gum, one each for me and my children, as a sign of her good wishes— won't let me go under.

Some letters stand out more than others. "Dear Mrs. Puglisi, you don't know me, but I'm a crime victim, too. . . ." "It happened to me, I was raped by an intruder. . . ." "I know how it feels to be so afraid . . . It happened to me once. . . ." Though most of them preface it with "It was nothing like what happened to you," I'm not sure I agree. There is a shared disillusionment here, a shared reaching back to hope.

Women are writing to me, saying, Me, too. Me, too. I know what it's like. I've felt that way, too. But hold on. Hold on, because it will get better. Keep going. Stay strong.

I could not then know how important the community of victims would become in my life.

But my faith is still so deep-down shaken. I remain frustrated by the inability of my family to let me talk about the crime. Hearing from people—friends, acquaintances, and total strangers—is like talking about it. It helps me find my place in a story that still seems as if it happened to someone else.

Most of all, thanks in part to these letters, I am starting to recognize myself in the woman people have been talking about all these months. That brave and strong woman. The letters tell me what happened to that poor woman and how she strove to free herself. I think I can grow to admire that woman.

It's the beginning of pride in myself. One day, after my daily dose of letters, I go to the bathroom, wash my hands and face, and look at my image in the mirror. "I am breakable," I tell myself, then pull in a good long breath. "I am *un*breakable."

Wednesdays in Dr. Dancu's office I continue staring down photos of Donald Flagg and repeating his name—exercises designed to make me feel that I'm regaining control over my life. It is becoming easier and easier. Repeated exposure is helping me face him—or at least his picture—with the kind of calm determination I will need at the trial.

And I want that. More than anything, I promise myself that next spring, when the trial of my husband's killer is scheduled to begin, I will go there strong. The asshole, the coward who killed Nino, will not see a tear or a moment of fear from me. I will not go there still acting like a victim, trembling in fright at his presence. I won't give him the satisfaction.

Just as Dr. Dancu said, I vanquish the asshole every time I tell this story without falling apart. I am beginning to treasure my newfound sense of mastery over this situation. I am beginning to think, with amazement, that what they all said is true, after all: I really am a brave woman. I really do have courage. I can feel it in me now, straightening my spine, helping me hold my head high.

I notice that I have begun to be able to take pleasure in life without having to flog myself later. I also know that the indestructible optimist inside is asserting itself again. I try to shut it up. I tell myself I will never let my guard down again.

But when I am not trying too hard to stay wary, I can hear a little voice from inside that insists, Don't be afraid, Debbie. You can come out now.

14

THE FIRST SIX MONTHS have passed in a kind of weird fog. Through most of it I felt like a disembodied spirit, drifting above myself, watching my own actions without directing them or really even caring about them. Now I'm back in my body, fixing my feet to the ground, and it's October. It's hard to comprehend that we are halfway around the calendar year from that standstill time in April.

For the most part, I've resumed my everyday life or a replica of it. I work, shop, go to lunch with friends. I even do fun things— a ballgame, a Jimmy Buffett concert—without feeling guilty or disloyal to my husband. All the things that others do, I do.

It feels fine but still a little peculiar to be living. I'm like one who has to relearn a basic skill like walking. I'm wobbly and uncertain doing the ordinary stuff of life.

Yet I'm capable of enjoying, even savoring, the humdrum things, like cuddling with the cats or leafing through a catalog, scrubbing the bathroom sink or watching *All My Children*. Sometimes I ask myself if these are worthwhile uses of my time; in the asshole's house, I pledged that if I ever got out of there, I would fill every minute to bursting with intense and vibrant life. Aren't there better things to do?

Maybe not. It's true that sunrises are lovelier and sunsets more coral-colored and rain clouds are friendlier and bluer. I have taken to kissing and hugging more, and when I hug, I hold on longer than I once did. But I also love doing my dishes and sweeping the corners for dust bunnies. I do these things at a slow pace, loving the house sounds: a broom against bare wood, the rumble of a clothes dryer from the first-floor laundry room. I call Michael sometimes and remind him to bring his laundry home on weekends. I still like to fluff and fold. I have made it a personal quest to learn to fold fitted sheets so they're square, and with practice I get better and better. These little tasks give me inexpressible comfort. They're so normal yet so poignant. All the life I was sure I had lost—mornings and evenings, midnights and midafternoons—has been given back to me, and I'm glad. More than ever I want that life.

But these little chores, though pleasant, are solitary, and they remind me of how lonely I am. A few years ago I became very emotional when the kids went off to college—the empty nest syndrome. This is so much greater. Now, with no one here in the house but me, I feel I've been left behind. When Melissa and Michael left, Nino and I were two instead of four. I am one now, no longer one of two, and it's an unnatural state for me, just as it was for Stu Ross, Nino's friend who lost his first wife suddenly after a long, loving marriage.

I'm meant to be a partner.

I have literally never lived alone; I went from Dad's house in Jersey to Mom's house in Delaware to my first home as a married woman. And though I congratulate myself on being a capable head of household (wonder of wonders, the little woman *can* take care of business), I still despise it when I have to fill out any form or document that requires marital status. More than once I've had to check the "widow" box. Depressing as hell. I don't like being in this new category. One time as I'm checking the box I press down so hard the pencil point snaps.

But what's hardest is falling asleep in our big bed without Nino there. None of my old fall-asleep remedies help. I can't read at all anymore; I scan the same page forever. So these days I make it a habit to take long, hot baths, complete with scented candles—aromatherapy and hydrotherapy combined. It usually works. When it doesn't, I do what Melissa does to avoid her nightmares: force myself to stay up long past bedtime, until I'm so dog-tired I can't help but conk out when I hit the pillow.

But the last thing on my mind, every night, is what happened to Nino and where *he* sleeps now. And it's still the first thing I think about when I wake up.

Six months is a pivotal time in the aftermath of a death, sudden or not. In hospice, our interdisciplinary team of nurses and social workers includes a bereavement counselor, who contacts surviving family members at intervals—four weeks, eight weeks, three months, six—after the patient dies. This can continue until the first anniversary of loss. Because despite the relentless onward march of time, mourning is not something you ever really finish, and active mourning certainly takes a year at least.

By six months all the obligatory pomp and formality that surrounded Nino's death have concluded, and the initial shock is starting to wear off. The grief process is now really beginning. Our loved one is still gone, and the permanency of it all is hitting hard. But there are still a thousand things in the environment to bring him back to life, if just for the moment—socks in a hamper, a razor, a favorite cereal that no one else eats, favorite compact discs (like Steely Dan).

Though I've given away most of his clothes, there are some things I just can't part with: his ties, which go into a Wal-Mart bag for Michael. A goofy blue T-shirt that our Elkton neighbors, the Gormans, gave him years ago, with the word RELAX emblazoned on the front. Those old beat-up boat shoes, which ultimately end up in Karen Nygaard's back yard, as part of a rustic garden display. All kinds of notes with his neat, ultra-Catholic, Palmer method backhand. That was Nino—he never kept a pen or pad with him, so when the phone rang, he had to grab whatever scrap was at hand. And they're everywhere: envelopes, matchbooks.

If Nino scrawled on it, it's no longer a matchbook. It's a memento. It's a keeper. It's something I'll pass on to one of our children.

He is everywhere, my husband, but he is also nowhere. At six months I realize that when I try to call to mind a certain tone of voice or a familiar gesture, it's a little harder than it used to be. I cannot call his laugh to mind. I lost him so quickly in April. I am losing him now, very slowly.

Unfortunately, it is in the period from six months to a year after the death that the bereaved person is most alone. The compassionate neighbors who brought warm messages and casseroles and companionship have moved on. The coworkers who were attentive at first don't tolerate as easily the symptoms of fresh grief: the lethargy, the quick tears, and the naked sorrow. The implicit message is: let's put this thing away. Time to mend or pretend to mend. Protracted grief is unseemly.

Though I am beginning to revive (and though my own coworkers at Delaware Hospice continue to be exceedingly thoughtful, even tender, in their treatment of me), Dr. Dancu warns me that I have a long walk ahead of me, especially since the preparations for a trial can be just as distracting as the planning of a funeral. No way can I put this past me until the man who created this havoc is tried for his crimes and judged, sentenced, and jailed. On death row.

About the death penalty, Michael and I vehemently disagree. He is disappointed that I want capital punishment for Flagg. We don't discuss it at length—let's not have fights in the family about this, of all things—but he makes it clear that in his view the state should not take a life in retribution, no matter how treacherous the offender. I know better than to try to dissuade him. My Michael, as always, is stalwart in his views. He will not veer from them, even when we're talking about his father's killer.

Melissa agrees with me, at least for now. Unlike her brother, she's not guarded in her grief; it's right out there, a beast she wrestles every day. It's such a heartbreaking time for her. She's in love and, for the first time, thinking of marriage. But her happiness—the dewy, luminous happiness of a girl who's found her true love—has been shattered. She misses her dad with a singular passion, and she's distraught to think that he will not be there to give her away, will not be there to hand out cigars when her first child is born. He will miss every wonderful thing in her life as an adult. "Mom," she says, her pretty face wracked with pain, "it's that man's fault. And now all my memories of my dad will be childhood memories."

She is laid low by grief and as deeply angry, and as vengeful as I am.

IN APRIL, in the hospital, I was tested for HIV as well as other sexually transmitted diseases. All the tests came up negative. The asshole was tested in jail; he, too, was negative. But they were irrelevant negatives, as the virus that causes AIDS has a six-month incubation period. Now I can take the HIV test again and trust its reliability.

As a drug user and a man who is said to have consorted with prostitutes, Donald Flagg is at high risk for the disease, and the prospect of waiting for further test results is literally sickening. At odd times during the day—I could be doing anything—the reality intrudes: I could die of this. And I've seen death from AIDS. I know what it looks like, what it smells like. I've seen the way viruses and infection attack a person with a compromised immune system; I've seen the leisurely deterioration. In the worst moments, I imagine my blood laced with poison, with pestilence. All these months, I've managed to keep thoughts of possible infection at bay: I have become very adept at managing my emotions a step at a time, taking each day as it comes. Just like my old heroine, Scarlett O'Hara. "I'll think about it tomorrow." If I was given to cross-stitching, I'd put it on a sampler.

But now it's time. Each day I make a mental note to drive up to Christiana Hospital and get it over with. One vial of blood will do it, and the results come in two or three days. It seems an insurmountable task. I put it off and put it off and put it off. With so much going on—the sale of my house, getting ready to move, ongoing preparations for the trial—I don't think I can take on one more big thing. Certainly not this one, when I could learn that I did not survive after all.

IT'S SAD TO finally see a FOR SALE sign on the lawn at Arizona State Drive. It was our happily-ever-after house, and I don't want to lose it. But with my income more than cut in half, I can no longer afford it. And I know that the kids, Melissa in particular, would have a hard time coming home to the place where their dad was shot.

At first I worry that it won't sell. Buyers shy away from a home where a murder has taken place, and though Delaware law doesn't require that I disclose the house's history to potential buyers, I tell my realtor, "Make sure whoever looks at the house knows what happened. I don't want anyone to find out later and be sorry." I feel that the house deserves a happy family and that that family deserves to make an informed choice. Despite the murder, the house does sell and quickly. I've found a pretty town house not too far away. It's just big enough for me and the twins, and I can afford it. Though the move is still a month away, it's time to start packing.

I put this off, too, until some of my coworkers—those wonderful women who baby-sat me for weeks after my return—organize a packing party. Over pizza, beer, and soda we get everything ready for the movers. The only thing I won't do is pack up the basement. Try as I might, I cannot muster the strength to go down there, where the killer first raped me. This fear is a new one, and it stays with me. From now on I avoid basements. From now on I don't like anything underground.

●●●

WHAT IS IT that compels me to go to the nightclub that afternoon in October? Try as I might, I can't recall, even though that
decision ultimately proves momentous. All I know is that I am
visiting our family attorney, Bruce Hudson, at his office in
Wilmington, where we're discussing the trial. Or are we? More
likely we're discussing the move and my still-uncertain financial
situation. A recent community benefit for the Anthony Puglisi
Memorial Fund will go a long way toward getting the kids
through college, Nino's greatest dream. And the union workers at
Chrysler, of all places, got together during a shift change and
raised money for them, too: with matching funds from the company, it came to exactly $5,555.

But it will still be a challenge for us to get by, Bruce cautions.
He represented me during my dental malpractice suit twelve
years ago and has remained a wonderful counselor as well as a
good friend of the family. He was invaluable to the kids during
the week of April 20, standing by to handle powers of attorney
and the disposition of funds should I turn up dead. Whenever I
have a legal question or need practical advice, I call him first.

But today I don't want to hear what he has to say. Perhaps in
his candor he is painting a bleaker picture of my economic future
than I'm willing to accept, and possibly he's reminding me, as
Jim Ropp has, that the outcome of next spring's trial will not be
as simple and clear-cut as I hope. Whatever. All I know is, when
I leave Bruce's high-rise and walk out into the sunshine, I'm
upset and scared for us—the kids and me.

A quick wind whistles through the corridors between tall
buildings. I walk into it, head down, fists clenched, my coat flying out behind me. I head for my car, but in my agitation I walk
several blocks before I realize I've gone right past the parking lot.
Shit!

I double back, fumble for my keys, hand the attendant a wad
of crumpled bills and drive, aimlessly. Downtown Wilmington is
mostly one-way streets, and soon I'm going in circles. I am very
close to tears. I am also close—aren't I?—to the nightclub that
Bill Sharp owns. Isn't it near here? Then I see the street, and luck-

ily I'm going the right direction. I make the turn, and there's
Bill's car, a black Cadillac with his personal license plate: 212.

In the past few months, Bill has called at least twice to say hi,
how are you holding up, and to ask, in an almost paternal way,
what he can do to help me.

I've always come back with my stock answer: "Oh, nothing,
thanks anyway, we're getting along okay." But he's never let me
get away with it. "Good try, Debbie," he'd say, almost sternly.
"Listen, we've been friends for years. If there's anything I can
do—help you out with financial or legal issues—would you just
let me? I'm a businessman. I know my way around those things,
and if I don't know something, I can find someone who does.
Jesus, don't be alone in this."

In one motion, with no more hesitation, I pull into the lot,
turn off the key, walk up to the door, and ring the bell.

The door opens, and there he is. He looks at me and smiles.
Startled. Curious. "Hey there!" But when he sees my expression,
the smile fades. He grasps my elbow and steers me to a corner,
out of earshot of the deliveryman. "Debbie, hi. Are you all
right?"

I can't find an answer. He shepherds me to his office, sits me
down, then says, "Stay here. Let me handle this delivery, then I'll
take you to lunch. You need to talk."

WE DRIVE TO Kid Shelleen's, a neighborhood pub, and find a
table for two tucked into a dark corner. I'm grateful for the seclu-
sion. If I have to cry—and I'm right on the verge—people might
look at me. If they look, someone is bound to recognize me.
Then the whispers will start. There's the woman in all the papers.
The raped woman, the wife of the dead man. By now I've grown
tired of having my misery on display. I hate how strangers gasp to
see the broad, raised scars on my wrists and the way my tragedy
seems to excite them, even as they offer their regrets.

Bill looks at my wrists, too, and he winces, but with him, I
don't care. He was Nino's friend and mine. And though I haven't

seen him more than once or twice in twenty-five years—I saw him at a gas station a few times—I've always thought fondly of Bill. He was part of a wonderful growing-up time in my life.

I've forgotten how kind and attentive he can be. As we talk—about insignificant things first—his very presence is comforting somehow: familiar, stable, assured. He's concerned, too, in the tenderest way. How am I coping with it all? Not just what happened to Nino but all the rest of it, the sale of the house, the upcoming trial. And how are the kids? Do they need any help? He reminds me more than once that he's just a phone call away if I ever need help. Since he went into the bar business, he says, people are always turning to him for advice: he dispenses as much therapy as a psychiatrist for the cost of a couple beers. "The women call me Papa Bear," he says, and I laugh. Bill is a big guy with a beard, the Grizzly Adams type, and the name suits him.

He's been married and divorced twice, has a daughter he adores, likes owning a bar but aspires to a better location, something on the water. But we don't talk a lot about him—this is a selfish time for me, and with Bill's urging I allow myself to pour it all out, all the things no one else has been willing to hear: the rage, the frustration, the separation I feel from everyone I love. I tell him how the values I've held dear for a lifetime were disproved, one by one; how I'm working so hard to find evidence that they still matter. Bill listens without comment for nearly an hour and a half. He doesn't shrink from the worst of it. He doesn't have this need to protect himself or me from what has happened. Here is someone who's unafraid of the details.

I talk on and on about my husband, about his life and his death. Soon I find it necessary—therapeutic, even—to say the forbidden words: kidnapping, rape, murder.

Kidnapping. Rape. Murder.

Murder.

Strangely, it feels good. I talk and talk and talk some more, like lancing a wound just to let it bleed. Bill has a way of defusing my anger. His manner—nonjudgmental, sympathetic, accepting of every hideous thing I feel—is therapeutic.

And of course he knew Nino, had known him even longer than I had. The three of us were kids together so Bill shares the same history, the same old memories, and the same cast of characters. After a while we segue out of talk about the crime and get to talking about old times—riding in his white Corvette around Hoopes Dam, hanging out at Gino's Hamburgers, double-dating with my best friend, Kathy Manlove, and Bill's buddy Mark Clark.

We find a lot to laugh about.

I really need to laugh, to make sure I still know how.

Two days later, I turn forty-seven. Nancy Banis, my mom's best friend and a big sister to me since Mom's death, is taking me to the Hotel du Pont in Wilmington for dinner. It's the grandest place in the city, and we share an opulent meal in the Green Room. Nancy orders wine, and we lift our glasses in a toast. "I'm glad you're here," she says simply, and I know she means here on earth. We clink crystal.

Afterward, I'm to meet two girlfriends for drinks at Tarabico's, a place on Union Street. Bill had recommended it. We are not there an hour when he strolls in. "Not exactly the long arm of coincidence," he says, laughing. "Can I buy you ladies a round?"

We're having such a good time that we don't want the night to end. Someone asks where we can hear some good music. "I know a place up in Kennett Square," he says. "Let's take my car."

Kennett Square, just over the state line in Pennsylvania, is a small town surrounded by a sprawling agricultural community; the chief product is mushrooms, so if you drive through it at the wrong time of year, all you can smell is manure. The four of us jam into Bill's car and drive through the dark night. It's made darker because we're far from the city; the sky is starry as a Van Gogh. I roll down my window to let in the night air. Good. No manure smell tonight.

I twist in my seat to talk to the girls. "Hey, the Anvil Inn was once out here—the place we used to go when we were just out of high school. I met Nino there." I launch into a lengthy explanation of how Bill and I once dated and how I met Nino. Bill interrupts to add, "Yeah. I introduced them."

I turn to him, look at his profile against the window. "Bill, you didn't. Nino introduced himself."

He glances over. "Nino never told you? He came up to me at the bar and asked me if I knew a girl—how'd he put it?—a girl 'nice enough to take home.' That's when I pointed you out."

I lean back, staring at the fluorescent yellow line that splits the road.

"There's the club," says Bill.

We pull in and go inside, where a popular rock band called Jelly Roll is playing. Only the girls dance; Bill sits it out, laughing at us from our table. We have cocktails and stay till closing.

As we head back to Delaware, I feel nostalgic and light-headed. Extraordinary. I wonder at the serendipity of it all. Here we are back in Kennett Square, as if we've rewound a tape and gone back more than twenty-five years in time, to our youth, before any of our histories were written, when all our hopes were still intact.

I never knew that Bill Sharp, my first love, introduced me to Nino Puglisi, the man I felt certain would be my last.

Not until later, much later, does it occur to me that in a curious way, Nino has repaid the favor. He has reintroduced me to Bill.

15

WITH NINO GONE, it falls to me to complete one of his last, unfinished tasks: the kids' student loan applications. I scrawl the word "loans" on Post-it notes, on the calendar, and at the bottom of my to-do list, but it takes more than a week before I am ready to take on the hated task. I can't help remembering Nino's admonition, "If something happened to me, you wouldn't know what to do." When I finally sit down to it, armed with a pencil and fortified with a cup of tea, I find the process far less painful than Nino indicated. After half a dozen phone calls, my pencil is pretty chewed up, but the loans are secured.

Nino, I think, addressing him in my mind, what was all the fuss about? And why did everyone think I was incapable of handling this?

The house is now a warren of cardboard boxes, packed up and almost ready for the movers. I've been preoccupied with moving—deliberately so. Like giant-size loads of laundry, like second and third glasses of chardonnay, this is another thing that enables me to avoid what I prefer to avoid. But Bill is wise to me. A few weeks into November he calls, and as we chat, I can tell he's working up to something. Finally he says, "By the way, have you scheduled that test?"

I fall silent.

He sighs, loudly. "I guess that means no. Debbie, if you need me to do it, I will, I'll call the hospital right now and make an appointment for you. But you can't let this thing hang over you anymore."

"All right," I say, then pause. "But you don't have to call. I'll do it."

"Good. Do it right now. I'm going to call back and see if you followed through, okay?"

Okay okay okay.

I guess there's no getting away from this. Bill will pester me till I go through with it, and though I'm grateful for his goading, I would willingly put it off forever. But dutifully I call Christiana Hospital and ask to schedule a blood test. I'm told I don't need an appointment: "Just come on in." I do and wait in a sterile lounge for nearly an hour, reading old issues of *Time* and *People* until they call my name. The test itself is just one needle stick, one vial of blood. As the lab tech releases the plunger, I cross my fingers and mutter a prayer. "God, please."

Thankfully, it only takes a few days to get the results (the doctor, knowing my circumstances, has rushed things along). But they are days fraught with anxiety, the kind that makes you bolt up in bed nights. I try to persuade myself that the odds of getting the virus are minimal. People can have sex with an infected partner for years without contracting it: Rock Hudson's last lover never got it. And some people marry people with AIDS and don't get infected. When I need backup reassurance, I think of Magic Johnson: years and years with the virus, and he remains healthier than most of us. But no matter how I work it, the odds don't come out in my favor. The reason is that single time, the second rape on the first day in the asshole's house, when he bullied me down the hallway, shoved me face-first onto that mattress, and did it anally. I know the HIV virus is chiefly introduced through tiny tears in the skin. And that act—so brutal, so scream-out-loud painful—tore me up inside.

I tell no one—not Darlene, not Jane, not Bill or Sue, certainly not the twins—how out-and-out scared I am. I don't admit it even to myself, and whenever the paralyzing thoughts come up at odd, idle moments, I shove them forcibly from my mind. For the next two days my pulse quickens each time the phone rings. When I finally get the call, I jump, literally, for joy. But after I hang up, I go weak. I sag against the kitchen counter, knees buckling.

Then I call Bill. Our conversation is brief.

"Hi."

"Hi yourself."

"It's negative. I'm HIV-negative."

"Oh, thank God. Thank God."

I'll call back later, I tell him. I have to sit down for a while.

I DON'T KNOW when I start to think that Bill loves me. I do know that I'm startled. What is this? I have not been admired in this way—by a suitor—for twenty-five years, and it seems just a little absurd. In one way I'm pleased. Flattered. I had thought men would be repelled by me now, would think of me as damaged. I have confessed as much to Dr. Dancu, saying, "No one will ever want me as I am. I've been raped and raped and raped. It's like I'm disfigured, not a woman anymore."

Of course she disagrees, vehemently, saying the things I dearly want to believe: that my integrity and worth as a woman has not been and could never be destroyed by the crimes committed against me. And hadn't I told myself the same thing, during all those terrible assaults? I remember thinking distinctly, "He is raping my body only. He cannot defile me." But I know that to some people I will always be tainted because I have been raped.

So when Bill's interest in me becomes evident, I resist. He doesn't know what he's asking for. And truly, who would willingly take on a woman with my history? Besides, it's too soon, too sudden. I had loved Nino for a lifetime, and I love him still. To even

think about making a new life with a new man is unseemly, a betrayal of my husband. How can I hurt Nino that way?

Yet Bill is not someone new. He's an old friend, and for some
reason, that makes it feel more like changing dance partners. As a
young man, more than twenty-five years ago, Bill pointed me out
on the dance floor at the Anvil Inn, and for twenty-five years, I
danced only with Nino. Now Nino is gone, and just as I turn to
leave the floor forever, here is Bill, holding out his arms.

But I do not rush into them. Loyalty to Nino holds me back,
and there are other considerations. Bill's past. Two marriages.
Two divorces. A reputation—well-earned, he later confesses—as
a ladies' man. I have no desire to be the latest in a long line. But
the more we talk it out, the more I find that Bill in middle age
has changed, is chastened. His days as cock of the walk are long
past. He was faithful in both his marriages, he says; he had not
wanted them to end, and their failure was a great disappointment
to him. And like me, he dreads the prospect of living the rest of
his days alone.

It sounds reassuring, but I make no move toward a serious
involvement. For the moment I just enjoy our friendship. I enjoy
talking with Bill each day, enjoy his strength, his good humor, his
easy, laid-back manner. He's good for me. He has the wonderful
ability to calm me when I'm upset, make me laugh when I'm
angry or tempted to feel sorry for myself. As far as I'm concerned,
I'm still not looking for a close relationship. Just the opposite—
I'm trying to learn how to live without one.

And of course there are the twins. I can't even consider dating
without imagining how they will react. Without a doubt, Melissa
and Michael think of me still, and only, and always, as Daddy's
wife and widow, consecrated now to his memory. I'm very afraid
that if I begin a new relationship, it will hurt them deeply. Am I
willing to put my happiness before theirs? Right now I have no
answer. I simply do not know.

Even as I try to decide, I continue to grow fonder of Bill,
almost without thinking about it; the thing has a momentum of
its own, like a song that moves from overture to chorus so easily

you don't notice the progression. And this song sounds very sweet and natural to me.

A turning point is a getaway to Annapolis with a gang of the hospice girls. We drive down Friday night for a mental-health weekend. Because ours is such a stressful job, a few of us make it a practice to take off as a group from time to time to relax and recoup. After all, who else can understand our profession, with its daily exposure to death? Sometimes we do two and three deaths in one shift. We deal with people at their most vulnerable, their most sorrowful, sometimes at their angriest. Over the years it has bonded us as a group—these are really foxhole friendships—and every once in a while we get together to blow off steam, rant about the workload, dish like any other bunch of colleagues dish when they're outside the workplace. It's always great fun and restorative.

But this weekend something is different for me, so much so that the other girls recognize it and tease me openly. As we stroll the old cobblestone streets and shop the boutiques and meander along the waterfront with its fleet of fabulous boats, I realize that a full day has passed without talking to Bill. And I realize that I miss him.

And this is the start. When I return home Sunday afternoon, just in time for my four o'clock shift, I call him. After we chat about our respective weekends—the bar has been busy, he reports, so he's pleased; how was my trip with the girls?—he says that he missed me, too.

"Do you want to get together this week?" he asks.

"How about Wednesday? I don't work that night."

"I'll pick you up then. Is seven-thirty okay?"

On Wednesday, when I open the door, there he is, smiling that easy smile, and I can't suppress the feeling. Happiness. Relief. A feeling that maybe this is as it should be, that God has given me this wonderful gift. Maybe I don't have to feel it's more honorable to refuse it. Would I really honor Nino by living a lonely life for the rest of my days?

Bill kisses me, and—a bolt from the blue—says, "I think I'm

falling in love with you." I don't say a word. I just gape at him, thunderstruck. He steps back, laughs, adds hastily, "I didn't know I was going to say that." Then he turns away, flustered, and runs his hand through his thick gray hair. When he turns back, he says, "Deb, listen, I don't want to scare you off. I know this is fast. I'm willing to not talk about it for a while, for a long time, even. I want to give you all the time you need."

I continue to stare at him.

"We'll take it really slow," he says. "And if you decide you don't want to have me in your life that way, I'm just going to be glad we have a good friendship. Because we do. But I hope that won't have to be enough." He pauses, spreads his hands, smiles helplessly. "I don't know. I love you."

If he wants an immediate answer, I disappoint him. I wonder later if it was awful for him, to say I love you and get nothing in reply. But I am suddenly lost in thoughts of Stu Ross, Nino's friend who was widowed so young. And it was Nino who said six months later, "Stu, it's time to pick yourself up and get on with it." Now, less than a year later, I feel that with those words Nino's saying the same to me, giving me his permission and his consent to continue my life without him.

Silently, I thank him. Nino, I will take you with me, wherever I go, for as long as I live. But yes, I need to get on with it.

I won't make up my mind right away, but I will consider accepting this invitation to what is certainly the last dance. If it's right, I will allow myself to love again.

I look up at Bill, stand on tiptoe, and kiss him.

SO WHAT WILL it be like to love Bill Sharp back? Will that be okay with everybody, will the kids go for it, and, most important, am I allowed this second chance?

Answers: no, no, yes.

I try again, wanting better answers. No. Hopefully, in time. Yes.

I try again. Yes, everyone will ultimately be okay with this. Yes, as time goes on Michael and Melissa will understand and be glad.

The only thing that never changes is the answer to the third question. Am I allowed? Yes, God damn it. Yes. With time the ones I love will allow me and I will allow myself to welcome love back into my life.

Over the next few months, as our relationship becomes plain to everyone, I suspect—I know—there are those who think I'm the proverbial fool, rushing in, careering toward a great big disappointment. I hear them as certainly as if they're speaking to my face: She's on the rebound. She's in the grip of unresolved grief. She's afraid to be alone after everything that's happened.

I can't think of a way to answer things nobody says out loud. I continue to ask myself if I'm doing this for all the wrong, weak reasons.

But all these months I've been trying on the word "widow," trying to fit myself to the word, alternately rejecting it and trying to grow resigned to it. But resignation isn't coming easy to me. It's as if I've forgotten the meaning of the word.

Some people would get it, I think: this growing conviction I have about living as much as I can. I need to gulp up life, grab it, spend time as if it were currency that can't be saved for even a day. I guess people who have survived plane crashes and auto accidents would know this, or people who have drowned and been resuscitated, or people who have had heart attacks or lived through cancer.

I start to think sometimes I'm part of an elite group, a Mensa Club for highly evolved live-in-the-moment types, most of whom got to this place through something unspeakably bad.

Who would choose this enlightenment? I for one was dragged, kicking and screaming, to the knowledge of the value of every swift movement of the second hand. It's a lesson that once learned can't be unlearned. I find myself seeing and feeling life with such acuity it's painful. It vibrates.

But, predictably, it's tough on the kids. Every once in a while, when I'd talk with them by phone, I wondered if I should slip this into the conversation: "Oh by the way, Michael, by the way Mel, your mom is dating again."

Perhaps, I thought, I should make it a little more vague: "Your mom is seeing someone."

I also rehearsed this line: "Kids, I've been thinking I may start to have a little more of a social life."

But I never said any of those things. Perhaps it was cowardly, perhaps compassionate (I do not want to hurt these kids!). Perhaps it's both. Many times I would lie awake nights and pray on it, wondering if I should let Bill go for their sake. But as much as I agonize, I know I won't do it. I can't live a half-life, trapped in my loss like a fly in amber. Not now. They have to know.

We plan to spend Thanksgiving at the new place, our little town house a few miles from the old house. I have just enough time to get everything unpacked and create a semblance of normalcy—curtains up, books on the shelves—when Michael and Melissa, my stepmother Sue, and Darlene and her son (my godson) Jordan all show up. It's a daylong marathon of cooking and baking that starts in midmorning and continues nonstop. The smell of roasting turkey does wonders to make the new house seem homelike. Sue peels, cooks, and mashes potatoes. Darlene makes the cole slaw, using an old recipe of our mom's. My job is the stuffing, the only thing I really do well. It, too, is a family recipe—passed from Nana to my mother then to me—with lots of celery and onions, simple but fabulous. For dessert, we'll have store-bought pie.

In the kitchen Dar and I crack open a bottle of merlot, which makes kitchen patrol a little merrier.

At the table, we say grace. While no one offers additional prayers of thanksgiving, I know we're all thinking how glad we are to be together, still. This year could have ended much differently. Then we dig in. I watch the door a bit nervously, knowing that Bill plans to stop by after having dinner with his daughter, Dorian.

When he arrives, an hour or so later, I make introductions all around. Sue and Darlene greet him warmly. Melissa is polite but

reserved, Michael terse. Trying to leaven the atmosphere, I break
out the pies—cherry and pumpkin—along with coffee spiked
with Bailey's Irish Cream.

Over our coffee cups Bill and I regard each other with raised
brows, as if to ask, Is this going well?

As well as can be expected. Later, as I see him to the door, he
pecks me on the cheek and says, "Well, we knew it would take
time."

"I know. Good night."

THROUGHOUT MY MARRIED life we always divvied up the
holidays, spending one with my folks, the next with Nino's family; and sometimes we'd have everyone over to our place. But one
thing never changed: on Christmas Eve, we'd always go to early
mass then head to Nino's sister's house, where all the Puglisis
would gather: Dolores and Rick and their families and Nino's
mom, Angela. Dolores would always serve a nice buffet, with
ham and potato salad, and because December 24 was Angela's
birthday, there would always be a cake with candles. Afterward
we exchanged gifts. Nino usually bought his mother a jug of port
wine. She would give the kids envelopes with cash. It was not an
extravagant celebration, but the kids enjoyed it and looked forward to it. Over the river and through the woods. It was tradition.

This year it's not an option. We have not heard from most of
Nino's family since the funeral, eight months earlier; Melissa and
I last saw Dolores at that bleak twenty-fifth anniversary lunch at
Schaefer's Canal House. She sent a Christmas card, I sent one to
her, but there were no overtures, no "Let's get together." I knew
they were grieving, as we were, and I realized that it was their
choice to do so privately. If I've learned nothing else, it's that
tragedy does not magically bring families together. In some cases
it only exaggerates whatever enmity existed before. And murder
does not kill just victims. It kills families. I try to understand and
accept the new distance between me and my in-laws, but I am

stung, particularly for the twins. I find I cannot reach out to the Puglisis, either. Maybe someday, I think.

So this year we devise a makeshift holiday. On Christmas Eve, when the kids arrive at the town house, we drive together to the cemetery, where we place a bundle of fresh greens, tied up with a bright red ribbon, on Nino's grave.

Michael looks on, ever taciturn, as his sister and I clear twigs and leaves and fallen acorns from the gravesite. He believes, I guess rightly, that Nino does not occupy this place ("It's not like he's here, Mom") and observes this homage with us more from duty than anything else. Melissa takes it more personally. She kneels on the hard ground, whispers, "Hi, Daddy."

Afterward we walk down the slope of the hill to visit Nino's dad, who is buried in the same churchyard. When I realize we have not brought a wreath for him, I break a few boughs from Nino's and lay it at the base of his stone.

Then we head for New Jersey. We will stay at Dad's little house on the lagoon, where we spent that chaotic summer following the crime. But this time there's no wrangling, no turbulence. We're all being a little gentler with each other these days. I've come to see that my style of coping is not necessarily my kids' style—Michael still takes his problems, his thoughts, his quiet grief, on the road, for long runs, and I no longer press him to confide in me. Melissa is more like me, needing to talk, but I know she is better able to do this with Jeremy than with me. Once I found this hurtful; why would she turn to someone other than her mother? Now I know a mother's love isn't always the right prescription. I'm just grateful Jeremy is there to console my girl.

So grief is a solitary thing after all. This surprises me. We move in circles that sometimes interlock, but there is no denying that while we are not alone with this great pain, we can never fully share it. I once attempted to take the kids' grief onto myself, to wrest that weight from them—it was so hard for me as a mother to witness the sorrow of my children, and I would have done anything to spare them. Now I recognize that it's theirs alone. It's the cost of their love for Nino.

But each time Melissa calls from college, crying because she misses her dad, I damn the man who took him from her. Each time Michael talks about an upcoming race and I hear that despondent note in his voice because Nino will not be there, I ache to avenge all of us in court. And it's coming fast. The prosecutor, Jim Ropp, did not steer me wrong. The trial is slated to begin in April, almost exactly a year after the murder.

On New Year's Eve, Bill stops by the town house, and together we watch the ball drop on TV. I make no resolutions—I stopped doing that years ago—but when midnight comes, after we make a toast, I send up a little prayer of thanks that 1998 is finally over. Here comes 1999, and I have just one goal: to get justice for my family.

THE TOWN HOUSE is nice enough, but it doesn't feel like home. It's more an in-between place, a place to stay till I find out what comes next. Every once in a while I find myself driving in the vicinity of Academy Hill, and once there it's not hard to make the turn from Otts Chapel Road to Oklahoma Drive, from Oklahoma to Arizona State. It's weird to come as a visitor, strange to check out my old house; there are different cars in the driveway, and my bright yellow kitchen curtains have been replaced by something with checks. By spring the new occupants will have gotten rid of the herb garden, and then, even the rose bushes will go. Well, I can't blame them: nothing ever seemed to grow right in that ground.

I stop in to see Gene and Karen, and we munch on leftover Christmas cookies with coffee. They ask after Bill, but I'm still shy to talk about him; I fear anyone who loved Nino will resent Bill. Not Gene and Karen. "You're happy again, it's all over your face," says Karen. "How can we be less than happy for you?"

Maybe I'm not giving people enough credit. So far, no one— from the people I work with to my sisters to Nino's and my friends—has done anything but wish us well. It won't be long before Michael, the most reticent about my new relationship, will say, "Mom, I'm glad he's around you. Now I don't have to worry about you when I'm at school." And Bill's daughter, Dorian, has approved from the start.

What a relief. When I started dating Bill, I expected lots of arguments: I had already begun to rehearse what I would say back, all the reasons why I wanted to be happy again, and why everybody was just going to have to get used to it. Before anyone said a word, I was defensive. But I'm not getting the flak I had expected. People are happy for me, for both of us. The serendipitous way we came together has already made me feel that God wanted us to find each other. Now we have the assent of our loved ones. We are twice blessed.

16

ONE TIME LAST YEAR I thought of moving out of Delaware altogether. Newark is full of memories I'd now gladly live without—on every street, around every corner. There was the Olive Garden, where Nino and I would go Friday nights for pasta. And a club called Hunter's Den, where his band, Encore, played most weekends. The first year anniversary is almost here—and along with it, trial time—but these memories have not lost their poignancy. Each time I pass by the places that recall our life together, I have to brace myself, hold my breath, then let it out in small gentle puffs.

I go out of my way to avoid the saddest landmarks. What were once the happiest places are now, by direct inversion, the most sorrowful. So I find or devise shortcuts or longcuts to keep me away from them, but I make mistakes, and one wrong turn brings me head-on with the past.

But there's no getting away from it, at least not now; my employment is here, my son is here, and in just a few weeks, the trial will take place in Wilmington, less than twenty minutes from Newark.

I tell myself that afterward maybe I'll go away to New Jersey, where I can be close to Darlene and Jane and Robert and their families. It would be fun to live over the backyard fence, and I can do nursing anywhere. Or maybe I'll head down South, where Dad and Barb now stay most of the year. I could live on Florida oranges and the catch of the day and have that carefree beach-comber life Nino and I used to dream of. Even if the kids aren't close by, it's for sure they'll visit a lot. People always visit a little more when you live at the beach. And if it turns out that Bill and I stay together, maybe he'll go with me. But for now, this is where I must stay.

The first week of April jury selection begins. Now it is getting real, and I feel myself hunker down inside, get quiet, for the fight to come.

All these months Dr. Dancu has encouraged me to stand before the things I fear and look at them square. One thing I have continued to avoid is the community of Wellington Woods in Bear. Then I have a nightmare that compels me to return.

Unlike Melissa, I have not been cursed with nightmares till now. This recurring dream is all I will ever need to know of ter-ror. With the trial just days away, the asshole returns to me in my dreams. Or rather and, to me, far worse I go to him. In the dream, I am behind the wheel of a dark car, riding down a dark-ened road. I hold the steering wheel in a near-death grip, so hard I can feel the pain in my thumbs and knuckles. I am going faster than I usually go, taking curves with such speed that I can hear the squeal of the tires. I remember thinking, Careful, girl. The cops'll be on your tail any minute.

But I don't slow, not until I am there in his neighborhood, careering toward his street. I am racing back to my hell, and I cannot stop or even slow up. I pull into Hampton Court and stop at the dead end. He is outside mowing his lawn, back and forth, back and forth, until the mowed rows look like a green rug that has been meticulously vacuumed.

When I wake—thrashing under bedsheets that feel like wind-ing sheets—it takes almost an hour before my breathing returns to normal.

I've got to go there, to Wellington Woods, I decide. I have to see it.

Nino and I lived in Bear, in our first real house. In the midseventies, a few years before the twins were born, we bought the brick rancher on Rawlings Drive in Pigeon Run and felt just like the landed gentry. Amazing to me to have an excess of space. Real spare rooms! A whole acre of ground!

Back then Bear was as woodsy-sounding as its name, a still-rural village far removed from the big highways that were just beginning to flatten every blade of grass in New Castle County. There were no shopping centers (I would have loved to have had just one), and our corner had just one shop, B & J's Tires. Then along came multilane Route 40, and once it slammed down and sawed the community in two, shopping centers sprang up like weeds. Nowadays, the real weeds, the dandelions, thistles, and goldenrod, are long gone. It seems the actual town of Bear is secondary to the highway. Every corner is marked by strip malls, video stores, Burger Kings, you name it. It was so different in the seventies.

For me that first new house was near perfection. If asked our address, I would have answered, "Seventh heaven, cloud nine." And Nino loved it just as much; that first spring he bought a Sears rider mower and rode his range like a gentleman farmer. My domain was the inside. The chic decor back then included mushroom canisters in the kitchen (also from Sears), complete with all the accessories—salt and pepper shakers, napkin holder, coffee cups—till the mushroom motif took over the kitchen and spread through the rest of the house, like a—well, like a fungus. But I was twenty-four. I liked it. The kitchen was of the times: copper-colored appliances, a Litton microwave over the oven. All the latest gadgets.

But I did hate that carpeting. Dark red throughout, which meant I had to vacuum constantly (Nino thought this was a plus). And ugly red flocked wallpaper in the dining room. Flocked wallpaper must have been a staple in Bear.

When the twins arrived I decorated their nursery with a

Raggedy Ann and Andy theme, and before they turned a year old, Nino had to install a screen door to keep them from escaping. From the time Michael and Melissa could stand upright, they refused to stay in their cribs. They first went to school here, too, to the Commodore McDonough Elementary School. The school is still dear to my heart, because my kids went there. I still remember watching them board the big yellow bus, their matching plastic lunch boxes held tightly in chubby hands.

All of this, the sweet stuff recorded in old home movies and Polaroids so long ago, are what I used to think of when I thought about Bear. That's all changed now. I go out of my way to drive outside the town or alongside of it. Until one day I decide it's time to go and see it again.

The day is overcast, with clouds lowering in a pewter-colored sky; I feel I can reach up and poke my finger right through them. My car seems to drive itself off the main road into the warren of little developments behind Route 40, and I find myself wandering through cute little lanes with cute starter homes, little Cape Cods and bungalows with nice appointments like curving brick walkways and shutters that aren't meant to be used. Most of them are well cared for, sporting little wreaths on the doors, and distinctive mailboxes: this one in the shape of a dog, that one in the shape of a barn.

I stop at the stop sign just before Hampton Court. I linger there so long, a driver comes up behind me and sits on his horn. All right already. I turn left onto the street, pass a sign that says NO OUTLET, and pull alongside the curb about two doors down from the little house near the corner. I turn the ignition switch and the car engine dies. There is not a sound to be heard, not the wind, not the call of a bird. No one, absolutely no one, walks along the streets here. It's as if I have driven into a still photo and become a part of it.

It's just a little house, with a pitched roof and blue siding, obviously closed up now. Dark shades are drawn over each window, and weeds have taken over the front yard. The asshole would never have stood for that. The door is new, though—I guess the police made quick work of the old one. I marvel again how close it is to the house next door—less than a stone's throw—and wonder how so much went unnoticed and unheard. My screams that first night, my pleas: "Don't, don't." Those gunshots. The raucous rap music that pumped relentlessly from the radio, day after day, and sometimes at night.

There's the living room window, and if I close my eyes I can see it all again—how the living room led into the dining area, then the wallpapered hallway leading to the two bedrooms, then the kitchen where he cooked scrambled eggs on Wednesday morning.

Still no one around, though it is midday; no mail carrier, no one to see me as I sit here for fifteen, twenty minutes, looking expressionlessly at the sweet little house that was for me a prison and the place I might have died. And if he had killed me, as I'm certain he would as soon as he got his hands on some more drugs, what then? Would he have discarded me, buried me? Would he have carried me out to his garage, wrapped in the same pink flowered quilt, and loaded me up like a cord of wood? The thought makes my flesh crawl, alive and moving over muscle and bone.

And now *he* is in prison, at Gander Hill Prison—the name sounds so nice, like one of these developments—and I suppose I should wonder more about his experience there. Does he have regret, now that he is behind bars, facing trial for murder, facing the death penalty he was so quick to dispense? Is he afraid, like I was? Strangely, I don't care. I cannot occupy the mind of a killer, and I don't feel obligated to try to understand. Just as I don't feel it's my job to forgive. Let God understand. Let God forgive. Sorry, but I am not sufficiently evolved to care.

I care a lot more about what happened to his cats. After the arrest they were confiscated, either by the SPCA or the Delaware Humane Association—I saw the newspaper photo, where they were taken away in carriers. Poor things. I hope they went to the Humane Association, which has a no-kill policy. But about the asshole I am far less concerned. May he sweat out each night in his cell awaiting his fate, which I am certain will be the death penalty. I am not like the men in my family—Robert and Gary and Dad are so outraged they would gladly see the man raped in jail, and they don't mind saying so ("Let it happen to him the way it happened to you"). I cringe at the idea, but deep down, I don't know how strenuously I disagree.

How awful to hate. It feels powerful, like jet fuel, that strong; but it's foul and foreign. This is something I never had reason to feel, never expected to feel, and I resent the asshole for bringing this ugliness to my world, the world my kids live in. Even though I think of it less as personal hatred than as righteous anger, I do hate him, I do: I hate the way he prostituted me, made me barter with sex for my life. I hate the way he robbed my children and made them mourn before their time. I hate the casual cruelty of Nino's murder. But hate is an ugly thing, and I get no satisfaction from the feeling.

I hate him for making me feel it.

Though early April, it's so cold out. I realize I have been sitting here, hands on the steering wheel, for nearly half an hour now. I start the car, turn the heat on full blast, and get the hell out.

THE TRIAL WILL begin April 12. Because of school, the kids will not attend until I testify, but other family descends the night before, from points east and southeast—Robert drives over from Manahawkin, Sue catches a ride with Dad and Barb from Long Beach Island. Bill also drops in, and we cluster around the kitchen table, wondering out loud what it will be like tomorrow, our first day in court.

As always, Robert and Dad fret on my behalf. "Are you ready for this?" asks Robert. "How about when you see him walk into the courtroom? That could be a tough one."

I break a hot muffin and let the steam escape. "I appreciate you being one of my many mother hens, Robert"—I smile at my two stepmoms—"but please don't worry. I'm ready." I butter the muffin. "Pass that jelly."

A gaze passes between Robert and Dad; they are doubtful. Dad says, "Well, maybe it's not necessary for you to be there the whole time. Maybe you can take breaks, take a few days off when they go into certain things . . ."

Here we go again. For my family—surprisingly, it's the men who are most inclined to think this way—there are still unmentionables about what happened to Nino and to me. Don't they yet know that this trial, this day of reckoning, is as important to me as anything that ever happened in my life, good or bad? It's as important to me as my wedding day and the birthday of my children, as life-changing as the death of my mother and, of course, Nino's death. Avoid this significant event? I want every moment of it. It belongs to me.

God love my brother. Like a lot of cops he's a consummate caretaker, and this crime has weighed him down. Robert still feels guilty that he was not somehow magically there to protect me or rescue me. He wants to rescue me now. But does he really think that, after all I've been through, I'm going to buckle when I see Donald Flagg? It's just like the viewing, when all of them, Gary and Dad and Robert, kept urging me to sit down, Debbie, sit down. Use a wheelchair, Debbie. Take a break. Get out of the reception line. Rest. Finally I had to dig in my heels and say, "Please let me do this. These people came here to respect Nino and to see me. I won't sit it out." I had stood my ground then; I suspect I'll have to do so now.

They'll see tomorrow. They'll see I need to do this. And I really am fine. Only I know how rock-steady I feel inside.

Bill, who temporarily bows out of my life once the trial begins, has more trust in my resolve. Saying, "This is your fight, girl," he promises to be at arm's length for the duration (three to five weeks is Jim Ropp's guess) but feels he has no right to stand with Nino's family in this fight. Stepping aside is his way of respecting us all, especially the kids, who will be at court only sporadically, because of school. "But I'll be there every night," he adds, "to hash it all out and take you to dinner and give you a good-night kiss. But this—well, this is your time, Debbie. You're ready. You go do it."

It's getting on ten o'clock, and we have an early morning. Because I expect to be the last one up, I give my bedroom to Dad and Barb, assign Sue and Robert to the kids' rooms, and spread an afghan for myself on the pull-out couch downstairs. About eleven, when the lights go out, I fall asleep quickly, sleep soundly, and wake as alert as I have ever been.

Strange but nice, to have an almost full house again. Sue's in the kitchen, manning the coffeepot. I can hear Dad and Barb in the master bedroom, talking and getting ready. And when Robert and I collide in the hall, both on our way to the shower, it's like we're teenagers again. I laugh out loud. Robert defers to me— "Ladies first"—and I dash past him into the bathroom. Standing under the shower with the water at full blast, I feel as focused as the tip of a laser. I let the water run hot until the steam envelops me, then cold till I shiver. I jump out, brush my teeth, and dress quickly: dark blue suit, low-heeled shoes, and Nino's wide gold wedding band on a chain around my neck.

Sue pours coffee. On the table are cereals and fruits and Dad's favorite crumb cake. I open the doors to the deck, breathing in the cool morning air, staring up at the pale sky. It's after seven, but the moon still hangs up there, wearing its usual woebegone face.

Nino, it's time.

In the past twelve months, I've wondered a million times how this moment would feel, this morning. Starting today, I'll hear in detail everything that happened to Nino: the way he was shot and how he fell. The way his blood sprayed across the walls and how the killer dragged his body down the hall, to hide it from me. I'll learn about the police investigation and all the things that went wrong, the errors and mistaken assumptions that could have cost me my life.

Undoubtedly, I'll also hear that 911 tape. In the past year, especially since the gag order, I've heard it less and less and then only in bits and pieces. Usually, news shows play only the part when I start that ungodly, hysterical howling—the "good" part. Now I can expect to hear the tape again in its entirety. What will that be like? I certainly don't look forward to it. And yet—I do.

Let the jury, let everyone, see what that criminal did. Then let them decide if this series of dozens of calculated, cruel, and evil acts were the acts of a man out of his mind with illness.

I am confident they'll see through his posturing and the confabulations of his silver-haired, silver-tongued public defender.

"Everybody ready?" It's Robert, shrugging into his suit coat as he holds the front door open. We head out. What a beautiful, clear sky is up there, with the sun on one side and the moon on the other. Nino, be with me today. It's all for you, honey.

We climb into one car, the five of us barely fitting, with Robert at the wheel. I lean back into the headrest. As we jump on northbound I-95 toward Wilmington, I scrutinize my hands, joined loosely on my lap. There are the scars, so faint now; my left wrist is slightly, permanently disfigured. But these scars are no longer a deformity in my eyes. They are the measure of me, a barometer of what I am capable of enduring.

Who would have thought it? A year ago I hated this mutilation of my hands and tried without much success to hide the scars with long sleeves, with bracelets. Today I can't imagine myself without them, and I cannot imagine my life without this crime as the backdrop. It's as much a part of me as being right-handed or brown-eyed.

THE CITY OF Wilmington is not a metropolis. Like Delaware (state slogan: "Small Wonder"), it does not compare in size and scope with Philadelphia, on the same river twenty miles to the north. Not until you're in the heart of it does Wilmington start to seem like a real city, with luxurious hotels and hundred-year-old churches. Its downtown is all broad avenues and green plazas, mirror-clad office towers and splendid buildings, the most splendid of which may be on King Street. There a massive stone building takes up an entire city block. It houses both City Hall and the Daniel L. Herrmann Courthouse, where the trial will be held.

Robert drops us off at Rodney Square, across from the courthouse, then heads off to find a parking garage. As we cross the street, Barb nudges me and points straight ahead. It's a crowd of news vans, jammed into a parking area near the front door. Each one boasts a TV antenna, swathed in thick coils of colored wire, bending stiffly against the morning air. Is this for us? Crews scramble in and out, chomping doughnuts, hauling cables, and talking on cell phones. No reporters yet. We don't see them till later.

"Whoa," says Dad.

"Guess this is my welcoming committee," I mutter. I'm surprised. I didn't think there would be this much hubbub. I can feel a faint fluttering in my stomach. Thank goodness for Xanax—throughout the trial, it is my daily practice to take one in the morning, just to head off the anxiety.

Okay, so I'm not as cool as I want to be. But I don't need more than .25 milligrams of the tranquilizer, an infinitesimal dose, and as far as I'm concerned, that's an achievement.

First thing we do after Robert catches up is pass through a metal detector—its brand name, God help me, is Friskem—at the entry to the courthouse. As I load my keys and purse onto the scanner, the security officer, a kind-faced, just-graying man, leans in close.

"I knew Nino," he murmurs. "He was a good guy. I've prayed for you all." He waves us through to the lobby, nodding. "I knew Nino," he repeats. "Chin up now." It's a good way to start the day—an omen—and every morning from here on out, I look forward to seeing this nice man.

Our shoes click on the tile floor as we head to the Attorney General's Victims Office to meet the prosecutorial team (oddly enough, it's right across the hall from the Prisoner Release Office). Jim and his cocounsel Mark Conner brief us on what to expect this first day: opening statements by both prosecution and defense, in which each lays the groundwork for its case, and Flagg's videotaped confession, made shortly after his arrest. It won't be easy, we're told—not the tape and not Brendan O'Neill's opening appeal to the jury, when he will tell the jury his client is insane, therefore not guilty. It's all part of the game, and we mustn't worry. The state's case is compelling. Throughout, we're

warned, we must avoid shows of anger. It will be an ordeal, but
we have to stay cool.

"Well," says Mark, briskly rubbing his palms together, "are we
ready to go?"

Dad and Robert assume their positions, one on either side of
me. Sue and Barb fall in behind. We head to Courtroom 202,
where we are met by my sisters, Jane and Darlene.

Inside it's one solid mass of people. Standingroom only; this is
a tiny courtroom, just twelve or so rows of seats beneath a dome
of amber stained glass. God, we'll be so close to *him*.

When we enter, people crane their heads to watch as we take
our seats behind the prosecutors on the so-called bride's side. A
few rows up front are reserved for news media, including the
courtroom sketch artist, and the rest are for spectators—lots of
older women, I notice, some of whom seem to know each other.
These, I come to learn, are the regulars—trial junkies, who
attend every proceeding, big or small. This must be a treat for
them: a big, splashy murder trial.

To our right is the jury box, already filled with the twelve men
and women who will determine the fate of Donald Flagg, all
seated in straight-backed leather chairs. I glance at them, men
and women, black and white, young and middle-aged—a perfect
demographic composite.

Up front to our left is a long table with Brendan O'Neill—I'd
know that silver pompadour a block away—along with his
cocounsel, a plump black man named Kester I. H. Crosse. The
two confer over stacks of paper and file folders. Then a side door
opens, and there he is: a bulky male in a neat, light suit, escorted
on either side by armed guards. He stares at the floor, never rais-
ing his eyes.

It's him. It's him. My father lifts himself a quarter inch from
his seat and cranes his head to look harder; I can hear Jane's quick
intake of breath.

I note, with satisfaction if not pleasure, that the defendant is
handcuffed.

He and his guards squeeze through the doorway almost arm in

arm. Then one of the guards unlocks his cuffs, and I can actually hear them rattle. He greets his defenders, shakes O'Neill's hand. He then takes a seat alongside them. The guards stand nearby; they are never more than a few feet away.

Dr. Dancu, I can say the name now. Donald Flagg, Donald Flagg, Donald Flagg. I've forced myself to say it over and over until I could do it calmly. But to me, he will never be anything but the asshole, the coward who murdered my husband. I bore into him with my eyes, hoping, praying that he will look my way and see what he did not see those five days in April of last year: my defiance, my contempt, and my absolute lack of fear.

The bailiff announces the arrival of the judge. Everyone rises. The Honorable Norman A. Barron is a spare, balding man, thin but imperial-looking in his long black robes. He ascends the bench, sits, raps his gavel, and calls the room to order. Jim Ropp rises.

"Ladies and gentlemen of the jury, good morning. On April 20, 1998, at approximately three P.M. to three-thirty P.M. in the afternoon, Debra Puglisi was in the front yard of her home. It was a sunny day."

So begins the state's case against Prisoner 9804019233, the trial of Donald Flagg. He is charged with one count of intentional murder, one count of felony murder, one count of first-degree burglary, one count of first-degree kidnapping, one count of first-degree unlawful sexual penetration, one count of second-degree assault, five counts of possession of a firearm during a felony, and seven counts of first-degree unlawful sexual intercourse.

Jim opens with a straightforward recitation of fact. First he details for the jury Flagg's drive from Bear to Newark on April 20, 1998, and his determined search for a victim. "Donald Flagg—that man," he says, pointing at the defendant, "was driving around, cruising in his car, with a plan, with a gun, with a rope.

"He stated he picked Debra Puglisi because she was, in his words, a pretty woman." Jim describes how Flagg entered our home through an unlocked patio door, encountered Nino, and shot him dead with a Smith & Wesson .38 revolver. "After he had killed Anthony Puglisi Jr., he calmly reached into the refrigerator and took a Coors Light beer and drank it."

I close my eyes. Abominable. Sue's hand covers mine, and she squeezes gently.

Of my last brief chat with Nino, Jim says, "Debra Puglisi had no way of knowing that that was going to be the last conversation that she had with her husband, that that was the last time she was going to see him alive, and that the next contact she would have with her husband would be at the funeral.

"She had no way of knowing that when she entered the house and went into the kitchen that she would be immediately struck on the head by Donald Flagg, tied up, then taken to the basement and raped.

"She had no way of knowing that then she would be taken to his home at 8 Hampton Court and, over the course of the next week, be repeatedly raped until such time as she had the courage to loosen her bonds to get to a phone to dial 911."

The jury members listen attentively. Many hold notebooks, pens poised above them.

"Debbie Puglisi had no way of knowing during that ordeal that she would be unable to talk to her children to tell them she was alive.

"Debra Puglisi escaped 8 Hampton Court," says Jim, "and prevented what Donald Flagg had told her, at one point during her captivity, was perhaps 'the perfect crime.' Ladies and gentleman, my name is Jim Ropp and I'm a deputy attorney general."

Jim goes on to specify the who, where, and what of the crimes as they happened, from the early afternoon of April 20 to the night of April 24, 1998. "[Donald Flagg] took a rope, and he took a gun. His plan was to kidnap somebody."

He then goes into a point-by-point account of that terrible assault, or series of assaults, in our house—from the kitchen and that first blow to the head to the basement and the first rape to the moment Flagg pressed the knife to my throat before tossing me into the back of his car. I flinch only once, when he mentions the way Flagg wrapped me in the comforter so "no one would see him remove the body."

Jesus. The body. They're talking about me.

It is the responsibility of the state, says Jim, to prove its case against Flagg beyond a reasonable doubt. He promises to do so with an abundance of evidence—from testimony to physical evidence to Flagg's own jailhouse confession.

"In short," he says, "the state submits to you that the evidence points to one person and one person only—it's that man, Donald Flagg. As you will hear, Donald Flagg knew exactly what he was doing. He was not deterred when the unexpected murder occurred. You will hear that he took great pains to prevent his capture," including parking his car so no one could see it, hiding Nino's body, tying me up, then, at his house, gagging me and turning the radio up so no one could hear my screams. I follow what Jim's doing; he is starting now to preempt the defense claim that Flagg is crazy.

One of the jurors, a young, sandy-haired man, leans slightly forward in the jury box. The defense, Jim says, will claim that all of Flagg's acts—so obviously calculated, so carefully planned— were the acts of a deranged man. Don't believe it. Flagg was an armed man who knew what he wanted and devised a formula for getting it. Is he insane? Hardly. His acts that day were eminently sane, all "pieces of purposeful, planned conduct that are shown as a rational attempt to conduct the crime that he intended to commit," which was to hold me hostage in his home, "kept by him for the purpose of his sexual gratification."

In forty years Flagg had shown no evidence of insanity or mental illness. Until the crime, he maintained a job and a home; he had worked twenty years at Chrysler, where he had an exemplary employment record. By all accounts, he had led a "normal" life.

"The state anticipates that there may be evidence of a defense that Donald Flagg suffers from mental illness, a defect or condition which he will argue would render him not responsible for his crimes. If there is such testimony, the state asks you to use

your common sense to filter through this evidence." When
O'Neill and Crosse suggest that Flagg is insane, Jim says, the
state would ask the jury to consider several important points first:
Was Flagg ever diagnosed before his arrest? How was he diagnosed? Was his diagnosis based almost solely on his, Flagg's,
reporting of his symptoms? Had he ever been treated, medicated,
or hospitalized before?

Finally, Jim says, the women and men of the jury should ask
themselves "whether Donald Flagg would be capable of malin-
gering or faking any symptoms" to avoid responsibility for his
actions.

I nod. All he says sound like supreme good sense to me; who
can deny it? But next comes Brendan O'Neill, and almost immediately my confidence begins to falter.

I have warned myself about this, braced myself for it. I know
that what O'Neill will postulate before this jury is a collection of
half-truths, fabrications, and pseudopsychiatry, but it's evident
from the start: he's good at it. He is somehow capable of making
it all sound plausible. To my consternation O'Neill cuts a far
more dramatic figure on the courtroom stage than Jim Ropp. Of
the two, it's O'Neill who will prove the superior orator, and
where Jim gives a dry presentation of facts—horrible as those
facts are—O'Neill oozes passion and sweep. In short, he's the
better actor. It's frightening.

He begins by lamenting the terrible crimes against Nino and
me. He does so in a sad, sincere voice, as if there is no one in this
room who is sorrier for my family than he. He acknowledges that
we were victimized and brutalized. "This case is a very unusual
case, because the defense is going to contest very, very, very, very
little of what the state is presenting to you. Mr. Flagg is not going
to contest the fact that he entered into the Puglisi home. He is
not going to contest the fact that he kidnapped and raped Debra
Puglisi.

"You will hear, as Mr. Ropp outlined, evidence of a horrible
series of acts inflicted on these poor, innocent, undeserving people. Mr. Flagg does not deny any of that. Mr. Flagg acknowledges

that the state will meet its burden of proving its case beyond a reasonable doubt. He did those things.

"Mr. Flagg's defense is that under Delaware law, he is not guilty by reason of insanity. Because of his schizophrenia, he lacked the substantial capacity to understand the wrongfulness of his act."

Flagg is a victim himself, O'Neill continues, the survivor of childhood trauma that included repeated rape and molestation at the hands of an older cousin. The jury will hear testimony about his horrific youth, says O'Neill; this will be advanced as explanation, if not justification, for his crimes. And he is also seriously mentally ill. He is, says O'Neill, incapable of forming intent and unable to recognize the seriousness of his actions. If found not guilty by reason of insanity, Flagg will be committed to a state mental institution, possibly for life—though lifelong confinement cannot be guaranteed.

So here it is: the transformation of a rapist and murderer into a delusional man, driven by impulses beyond his control—a poor, sick, addled man, incapable of knowing right from wrong, who can beat and murder with no recognition of his own brutality.

I am sad and sickened but not quite surprised. Turning the aggressor into the victim is standard operating procedure, with mitigating circumstances supposed to excuse the most evil acts. As O'Neill preens and postures, playing to the crowd like a TV lawyer, I silently argue every word. You don't know, I think. You didn't see that man's rage and feel that man's fists as I did. You don't know. I'm relieved Melissa and Michael are not here for this speechifying.

About Flagg's seemingly normal lifestyle, which Jim says indicates he was sane, O'Neill says just the opposite. With paranoid schizophrenia, he says, "It's not that you're stark raving crazy lunatic mad where you have saliva coming out of your mouth and you're howling at the moon. Schizophrenia is a disease that affects people differently.

"In many, many circumstances, for most of their lives schizophrenics are able to function in a way that appears to be normal, even though they're very, very sick.

"In addition," says O'Neill, "they're adept at holding repetitive-type jobs. You'll hear evidence that Mr. Flagg worked at the Chrysler assembly plant here in Newark and that he held that job for twenty years. It's precisely the kind of job that a person with his disease can hold and appear to be normal nonetheless being extremely, extremely sick."

Although schizophrenics can go for years without an obviously disturbed episode, he says, they can be "torqued-out" by great stress: "for example, loss of a pet or loss of a relationship to people. People with schizophrenia are affected much, much more intensely" by such things.

"In the evidence in this case," he tells the jurors, "you'll learn that in the months before these events, Janet Pagan, his only friend in the world, his only love interest in the world, told him that they were finally through."

"But really, the primary witness for the defense is Dr. Carol Tavani. She's a psychiatrist, and she's licensed to practice here in Delaware. In fact, she's on the board of trustees at the Christiana Care Hospital. She's president of the medical staff at Christiana Hospital. She's a former president of the Delaware Medical Society and a former president of the Delaware Psychiatric Society."

Tavani, he says, will explain to the jury that schizophrenia is a "major mental health disease with a genetic origin. Dr. Tavani will tell you about the thousands of pages of documents she reviewed about Mr. Flagg's mother," a "profoundly ill woman" with "severe, severe schizophrenia."

Dr. Tavani diagnosed Flagg as a schizophrenic, too, says O'Neill. "She took a history from him," says O'Neill. "She formed an opinion, and based on her observations, her training, her experience, she formed a diagnosis. Paranoid schizophrenia. . . ."

When the jury hears her testimony, he assures them, they will have no choice but to find the defendant not guilty.

At the end of the day, I leave with my family to the sound of whirring TV cameras. Heading out, we huddle a little closer and walk a little slower than we did going in. Now that the first volleys have been fired, the exhilaration of finally going to trial has already dimmed a bit. I understand more fully that there are people in this world who will not only defend this killer but defend him with passion, zeal, and great persuasive power. I find this very depressing on a deep level. I cannot understand it. I never will.

17

THE SECOND DAY (a superstitious friend points out to me that it's April 13) brings the testimony of Assistant Medical Examiner Dr. Michael J. Caplan, and I am barred from hearing the testimony—in fact, I'm shunted out into the hallway, where I must pace back and forth for what seems like hours while he is on the stand.

To me this is not only patronizing but insulting. Again I am being infantilized—people believe I cannot handle it. I remind Mark and Jim, heatedly, that I'm a nurse and not unaccustomed to the kinds of things that would be discussed by an ME. But later on I wonder if they did me a service by excluding me. During a break friends who were inside tell me that although the proceedings were fairly clinical, I would not want to know each detail of the autopsy, the details of it, the "searing" of gunpowder imbedded in Nino's skin; once logged in my memory, those things would never go away. "And you don't want that, Debbie. Someday you're going to want to forget."

I'm not certain I agree. This is my husband they're talking about, the father of my children. I want to know what happened to him; it's my duty to Nino to know, to hear, to not hide from this. His pain is mine, "for better or worse"—I promised him that once, I meant it, I mean it still. But my arguments meet with firm refusal by Jim and Mark. While the medical examiner is testifying, I am not permitted in the courtroom.

At day's end I learn, also from friends, that Brendan O'Neill attempted to have all but two of the autopsy photos kept from the jury. Only four were to be admitted in the first place, O'Neill argued that two of those should be excluded—the two photos showing Nino's face—saying they would cause "unfair prejudice, confusion of issues, delay, waste of time, or needless cumulative evidence."

He wanted extreme close-ups only—photos of the gunshot wound, without Nino's face or features.

Confusion of issues? For God's sake, tell the truth, O'Neill. You don't want the jury to see that the victim has a face, an identity. You don't want them to see my husband as a human being, a real man, once living, now dead—murdered in his prime, now lying in a grave he should not have been put in for another thirty years. People thought I would be upset by Dr. Caplan's testimony. I am far more upset by this deceitful attempt to minimize my husband, to make him incidental to these proceedings. It is just the beginning.

But at home nights I'm always reminded there are lots of good people on our side; Kim, a labor and delivery nurse with Christiana Hospital, has created a cooking circle with the Neonatal Intensive Care Unit nurses that provides us with tons of casseroles and extravagant desserts—so much food that soon the freezer is fully stocked, and we start feeding the neighbors. I am bowled over. It helps so much to know there is good out there, good that strives every day to outweigh the evil. I have to cling to that.

Then there is Bill. He checks in nightly and sometimes accompanies the family to dinner. We go to McGlynn's, a local place with a Tuesday night burger special, or the Howard House in Elkton. A year ago that's where my dad wept into his salad when Robert told him I would probably not be found alive. A few hours later I was free.

Whenever Bill stops by, he always asks if it's okay that he's here. "Do you guys want it to be just family tonight? Just say the word, Debbie, and I'll disappear." His tenuousness is endearing. My answer is always the same: "Come in, Bill. Please don't disappear."

MY BROTHER GARY has come up from Virginia but can't stay long, which is probably a good thing: at trial, his anger simmers so near the surface, I'm scared he'll blow a blood vessel—or, worse right now, breach the tightly monitored decorum of the court.

As Jim said, we're not to get angry; and if we do, we're not to let it show. If we let it show, it could be deemed prejudicial and inflammatory. It is a cursedly difficult task to seem unmoved when underneath we are injured, outraged, and looking for a place to express it. We thought court was the place. No. Jim's instructions to me are more explicit: if I find I can no longer tolerate what is being said, he says, "Leave the courtroom. Just get up and go."

During the first week of trial a stream of witnesses take the stand, including many of our neighbors, past and present. Listening to their testimony is like reading one of my murder mysteries, but this mystery strains credulity. It is filled with the sort of plot turns and surprises that are so fantastic that they would have made me scoff if I read them in a novel. For one thing, in a neighborhood full of people at 4 P.M. on a Monday, why did everyone fail to see a kidnapping in progress? The answer comes first from our neighbor Joe Strykalski, who was walking his dog by our home that day and saw Flagg's car as it cruised slowly by then backed up to the front door.

Joe knew Nino, knew how obsessive he was about that lawn of his, and here was someone backing onto the grass, plowing ruts into the ground. According to Joe, he thought, "Nino's not going to like that." But when he turned the corner and saw Nino's Jeep out front, he shrugged it off. Obviously Nino was home. Whoever was in the car must be picking something up. Joe thought nothing more about it.

Another neighbor, Denise Lee, also walked by; she took her cue from Joe. When he seemed unconcerned, she figured there was nothing to worry about. If either of them had inquired, the murder mystery would have stopped midsentence. One deviation from the script and all our lives would have changed—or, more accurately, they would have hardly changed at all.

Shirley Brogley and Nanci Osner testify about coming to the house to look for me early that evening. With Gene Nygaard, they found Nino's body. Gene testifies as well. A year later he still struggles with the memory of Nino lying spread-eagled on the bedroom floor with a jacket over his head and blood staining his shirtfront. He is tearful on the stand, and I hurt for him. Such a good man, such a good friend. He, too, is a survivor and, just like everyone else in the family, carries his share of guilt, grief, and endless second guesses. Like the rest of us he wonders what he could have done to divert this heartbreak, make it just miss us instead of slamming us head-on.

GLEN BEACH, a ballistics expert for the Bureau of Alcohol, Tobacco and Firearms, takes the stand to attest that the bullet that struck Nino came from a gun found in Flagg's home. Beach describes the gun as a .38 caliber double-action revolver that cannot misfire or discharge accidentally—testimony that proves crucial as the trial progresses. As the gun is offered into evidence, I glance away then force myself to look back. I need to see what Nino saw.

"You have to want to fire this gun," says Beach. "You have to pull the hammer back and exert fourteen pounds of pressure to pull the trigger. It doesn't fire by itself."

I feel a jolt of fear and pain and tell myself, like I used to, that I have just canceled out some of Nino's pain. But the ritual no longer works—I no longer feel that through my own pain I can take on his. Still, it's strangely important to see and face it all, so I look at the gun until it is removed from the prosecutor's table, staring it down as if it is the asshole's face.

Every night the kids call me or I call them; sometimes Michael comes for dinner and sits and studies a while afterward. We don't avoid talk of the trial, but I am careful to edit events, leaving out awful stuff about the autopsy or details of the attacks on me, lest they get upset in advance. They'll find out soon enough what goes on. Both have taken time off from school to be there on the first day of my testimony—April 16, just four days before the anniversary of the crime.

But as always, I cannot protect them. The day before I testify, Melissa comes home. She is already apprehensive, and it's catching. Soon I'm glad to have my little cache of Xanax. Up till now I've congratulated myself on my composure, but I'm worried for her and worried, too, that O'Neill will try to—do what? He certainly can't impeach my credibility; I have told nothing but the truth. All the evidence supports that. But I've heard how the truth itself can be mangled, manipulated, obfuscated in the course of a criminal trial. So I'm afraid.

Jim and Mark tell me to relax. Though I have not developed a truly warm relationship with either one of them—of the two, Mark is far more accessible—they are wonderful in this: carefully preparing us, calming us, telling me the kinds of questions I will be asked, reviewing with me statements I made shortly after the crime, and assuring me that the defense would be foolish to attack me; harassing the victim would only undermine their case.

Relax, they say.

I have decided that on the day of my testimony I will carry a rose to court, a single, perfect, plum-colored rose. Jim frowns on this— perhaps he considers it a theatrical gesture—but this time, I won't hear his disapproval. I am resolved. For me, a rose has become a symbol of reclamation, of redemption. Let the killer see that my life goes on despite his best efforts to extinguish it. If he is the only one to see and understand my message, that is sufficient.

■ ■ ■

THE MORNING OF April 16, Michael and Melissa walk with
me arm in arm into court. Even more than usual I notice how the
roomful of spectators and reporters look our way, murmuring
softly, trying not to look like they're staring.

The kids take their seats, nervous but in control. After the
lawyers assemble up front and just before the killer enters, I grab
their hands to get them through the first few seconds of seeing
him. Then he walks in, escorted as always by guards. Everyone in
the courtroom turns to see the kids seeing him for the first time.
Melissa looks hard, pales, and turns her head into my shoulder.
Michael cranes his head and stares for a moment. Then he, too,
turns away. He is expressionless, but I notice that his hand grips
mine with greater force.

Today Domenick Gregory, the chief investigator, is the first to
testify. I like Domenick, who has a Marine's buzz cut, the shoulders of a linebacker, and such a kind manner. He's my idea of a
good cop, in the mold of my brother, Robert. Among my friends
I refer to him as Joe Friday. Strong and principled, one of the
good guys. After he is sworn in, he identifies himself to Mark
Conner as a detective in the "persons squad, which handles
crimes against persons—rapes, homicides, assaults, suspicious
deaths." Today he starts by explaining 911 Enhancement and
how the system works. He likens it to caller ID.

"If you have caller ID and someone phones your residence,
their name will appear and their number; however, no location."
With 911, however, "We get the exact location."

"Do you know if a 911 call was made in the evening of April
24, 1998, from 8 Hampton Court?"

"Yes."

"Do you know who made that call?"

"The person making the call was later identified as Debra
Puglisi."

"Whose voices are on that tape?"

"On that call is Debra Puglisi's as well as Steve Conrad's, the dispatcher. There is a call-taker on at the beginning. I don't know him; he's assigned a number."

"And is that 911 tape a fair and accurate copy of the call that was made?" asks Mark.

"Yes."

"Objection." This is O'Neill. "That would call for specula-tion."

I am already tense; this pushes me back in my seat, and Michael looks at me, mystified. What is there to object to?

"What's your objection," asks Judge Barron, "hearsay?"

"The objection is insufficient foundation," says O'Neill. "He wasn't part of that call. How does he know?"

Mark offers to get Steve Conrad to testify as to the "fairness and accuracy" of the tape. Only at that point does O'Neill with-draw his objection.

Now I am beginning to understand the fine art of arguing a case without foundation. Throughout the next two days, during my testimony and for the rest of the trial, O'Neill focuses on the little things—tiny deviations from the record, which he uses to try to make the state's case seem sloppy or unreliable. My imper-fect recall (under extreme duress), which he implies makes me a faulty or not wholly believable witness. He never says it out-right—that would make him the aggressor, and he must avoid that at all costs. He does it slyly, almost subliminally, until I find myself flustered and apologetic about my little errors.

Michael has to leave at halftime, after the noon recess, for a test at school. So he misses my testimony after all, but I cannot help feeling relieved as he hugs me and heads off across Rodney Square. As much as I love having him here, supporting me, I'm not sure I want my son to hear about my captivity and the rapes in what is bound to be excruciating detail. Mel remains, but that's different somehow. Just because she's a woman.

At quarter to two, court reassembles, and Judge Barron says, "The state may call its next witness."

"Thank you, your honor," Mark says. "The state calls Debra Puglisi."

Melissa gives me a final squeeze, an encouraging smile. As I walk to the witness box, I am aware most of all of my proximity to the defendant. So close that when I turn sideways to slip between the defense and prosecution tables, I can reach out and tap him on the shoulder.

Mark told me in advance that he will be as respectful as he can be, but there's no getting around it: he will ask me to recall in specific terms what happened to me a year ago when Donald Flagg took me from my home.

There is little preamble. We begin at the beginning and surge forward, covering everything from the last moments of my married life with Nino to the first attack in the kitchen and everything that happened thereafter. With the help of Dr. Dancu and Dr. Faude, I have prepared myself. I know I'm going to have to tell it all, even the most intimate abuses, and I have practiced it all, just as I practiced saying the killer's name.

"He was angry. . . . He pulled my pants down. . . .

"So I was face down on the bed. . . .

"He applied K-Y jelly to my rectum. . . .

"He raped me. . . .

"The ropes were untied. . . . I was going to hide it because I didn't want to be punished. . . .

"He raped me vaginally. . . .

"It was very painful, and I asked him to stop, and he would not. . . .

"He tied me very tightly. . . .

"I was hog-tied. . . . The cord is connected to the wrists and ankles. . . .

"Washcloth. . . .

"Duct tape . . .

"I also remember like a blindfold. . . .

"He asked if anyone was at my house. . . . I said no because I didn't want him to go back and hurt Nino. . . .

"I thought he had broken my nose—my head hit the ground pretty hard. . . .

"I remember the red rugs, urinating on the red rugs. . . .

"I spent the night in the bathroom, praying to my mother. . . .

"I could hear him coming in and out. I could hear a clicking and inhaling. . . .

"He later admitted to me that he does crack cocaine. . . .

"I heard him fire his gun twice. . . ."

"When you heard him fire the gun twice," Mark says, "what were you thinking?"

"That I was next."

I keep my eyes on Mark's face, but I'm very aware of movement and sounds in the courtroom. I hear a sigh out front that I'm sure is my father's; and Melissa is out there, hearing this all for the first time. This must be painful for them; here are all the facts, all laid out, all the little details they didn't want to know. I'm careful to keep my voice level, my expression passive. The emotion wells up from time to time, but I ball up my fists and press on. I don't want to make my family cry.

What happened on Tuesday morning, asks Mark? How did I learn of Nino's death? It was the radio, or TV, "and I remember hearing that Anthony Puglisi had been shot in the head. And that was the first time I learned of my husband's death."

"Did you then realize," Mark asks softly, "why Nino could not come to your rescue?"

"Then I realized." I glance over his head and scan our side of the courtroom, looking for Melissa. There she is, long hair spilling over her face, eyes downcast in an attitude that is almost prayerful. As grateful as I am that she's come, that she's willing to hear this, suddenly I want to put my hands over her ears and keep her from knowing it all.

"Were you able to grieve, or could you let the defendant know that you were—"

"I did not want to show this person any emotion," I reply. "I was afraid that if I displayed anger toward him for doing this, he would also hurt me."

"You were still obviously fearful."

"I was afraid for my life more."

"After hearing that Nino had been killed and the defendant stating, 'I'm sorry I had to kill your husband,' what drive kept you going at that point?"

I breathe deep, look down at Mark, press my lips together. For the first time I am on the threshold, teetering there, tears gathering in my eyes. Oh, God. The asshole is right there, watching. Waiting to see my sorrow. Will it please him?

I cannot allow that. I sit up straighter, gaze into Mark's eyes, and answer as calmly as I can, "My children." But despite my best efforts to remain composed, my voice breaks on the second word.

Painstakingly, through most of the morning, we cover the five days of captivity. Every sexual violation. Every conversation. His use of cocaine and the violence that went with it. The cessation of violence when he stopped. The defendant boasting that he was a "criminal by profession." His gleeful proclamation that he had committed "the perfect crime."

How, asks Mark, did I feel when he said that?

"Powerless. If he feels he's committed the perfect crime, there's no way he's going to let me go."

Mark leads me through the events of Thursday evening—eating soul food, watching *ER*, watching the nightly news. I hear someone gasp when I mention that Flagg suggested we watch his favorite movie *Fargo* on video—I still haven't learned it's about a woman who is kidnapped and murdered. Then Friday. The asshole left for work, came back to check on me, left again. The courtroom is very quiet, so much that I can hear the court reporter's fingers move swiftly over the keys.

"Now when you thought he left on Friday, what did you decide to do?"

"I had heard on the radio or on the news that my husband's viewing and his funeral were on Sunday. I wanted to be there to make my closure and say good-bye to him. I knew I would probably not get out of there alive. I needed to make a decision."

"What was that decision?"

"That night, April 24, I knew that I was either going to survive or die."

"What did you decide to do?"

Once again I look out at the bride's side, searching for my daughter's face. "Survive," I say.

I go on to describe my escape, the interminable minutes it took to release the hog tie, the walking into the closet, the panic, searching in the blackness for the portable phone I'd seen on the dining room table earlier that day. "And I shuffled to the table and it's dark, so I felt, and my hand went right on the phone."

"What were you thinking when you found the phone?"

"I couldn't believe it. That was the first time during that week that I actually believed I had a chance." I look down and realize for the first time that my hands are clenched so tightly, the fingernails have dug bright red arcs into my palm. As I describe the final moments of that torment and the elation of hearing the police kick down the door, I make a conscious, probably conspicuous effort to relax. Breathe in. breathe out. Zen-like. Lamaze-like.

"Your honor," Mark says, turning to address Judge Barron, "with the court's permission I would ask if I could play the 911 tape at this point."

Here we go. It takes a moment to rig up the recorder, during which a palpable tension fills the courtroom. Poor Mel. What a thing for her to hear. But before I have a chance to agonize, there is a squeal of microphone feedback, the clumsy whir of the tape, and then those voices—the call-taker asking, "What's going on there, ma'am?" then mine, whispering so low I can hardly distinguish the words. "This is Debbie Puglisi. Help me."

It is the first time I have heard it in its entirety. It goes on and on and is horrifying, the very vocal torment of this woman, but I feel a certain disconnect—a bizarre sense that this is someone else's story—right up until the portion of the tape where I ask for my children. Melissa presses her fists to her eyes and cries, and I cry for her. My glance goes to the asshole, emotionless and blank, and his attorneys, who are unruffled. I clasp the purple rose in my hand till it nearly breaks.

At the conclusion of the tape, Judge Barron says, "A good time to stop. Ladies and gentlemen of the jury, we're going to break for the day."

TESTIMONY CONTINUES Monday, April 19. It's a worrisome day for me, because this is the day I face O'Neill. But first Mark completes his direct examination. "I have just a few more questions—that's the good news," he jokes. "During that week [of captivity], how would you address the defendant?"

"I always called him sir."

Mark asks why.

"I worked very hard to gain the trust of this person. I wanted him to think I was his friend and I was on his side, and I would do everything I could for him not to hurt me."

Because the entire case hinges on the legal definition of insanity—a large element of which is knowing the difference between right and wrong—Mark then asks if the defendant knew that difference, could perceive it, acknowledged it.

"You indicated that as of Wednesday, he began to change somewhat."

"He changed because he was not doing the drugs. He knew—"

O'Neill rises from his seat. "Objection. That calls for speculation, Your Honor."

"He told me that," I protest—doesn't it matter what Donald Flagg himself said about his drug use and its consequences?

Judge Barron says, "I'm going to sustain that objection."

"I move to strike that response, please, Your Honor," says O'Neill.

"All right. I would ask the jury to ignore the answer to the last question."

O'Neill, again, is theatrical—a native Californian, he has an easy stride, a toothpaste smile, and that distinctive Ted Baxter hair. He is comfortable in the spotlight and seems to relish his role as standard-bearer for the accused. I dislike him intensely, yet I can't help wishing one of our guys had that kind of swagger. Jim is taciturn, stiff, almost rehearsed before the jury; Mark is only slightly more animated. Of course the truth doesn't change, but presentation matters. I know O'Neill is good, and that's the whole problem. He's good, and he's chosen to be on the wrong side.

As he advances toward me, I stiffen. He is polite to the point of being chivalrous. I distrust him from the start. "Good morning Mrs. Puglisi." I brace myself, gaze out at him, nod. "Good morning."

Like Mark, O'Neill takes me through the crime moment by moment, but his questioning makes me feel as if I am being lifted on a current and carried almost imperceptibly away from the truth. He selectively edits his client's brutality ("He raped you anally only once, is that right? Then he never forced you to have anal sex again, did he?") He then goes on to focus on what can be construed as Flagg's kindnesses—"He loosened up or took the ropes off your hands and off your feet, is that right? He brought you coffee, is that right? He asked you if you'd like to clean up. He got you Advil. He ran the bathtub for you. He gave you a new toothbrush. He gave you a change of clothes, and then he laundered your clothes. He cooked breakfast. He helped you, is that right?"

Because I must answer the questions as asked, without adding or subtracting, I soon sound as if I am extolling the virtues of my attacker.

"It's fair to say, isn't it, that the only time that Mr. Flagg ever hit you is when you came into the house—or into the kitchen, rather?"

"Yes."

"He didn't hit you again while you were at your house."

"He did not hit me."

"And he didn't hit you when you were in the car driving to his house?"

"No."

"And he didn't hit you after you got to his house, did he?"

"He didn't hit me."

"That's correct, isn't it?"

"That's correct."

But he also threw me to the floor twice, so hard I thought I had broken my nose. He threatened to kill me, hog-tied me, held a knife to my neck. He broke my toe. He left bruises all over my body. The assault nurses at Christiana counted forty-two separate injuries. But all the jury hears is, "He only hit you once, is that correct?" "That's correct."

O'Neill's next strategy: to seek out inconsistencies in my previous statements and broadcast them to the jury. One of the first: I told Domenick Gregory that the asshole had pressed the knife to my neck there in the foyer before throwing me into his car. I did not say this to the detectives at Christiana Hospital.

O'Neill asks that two transcribed interviews I taped with police on April 25, shortly after my escape, and a May 11 interview I did with Domenick be entered into evidence as Defense Exhibits One and Two. My own words.

"Mrs. Puglisi, I ask you to turn to page twenty of Defense One, and could you take a look at it?"

He directs me to a passage in which I said to Detective Mike Walsh, "I just remember lying on the floor and seeing a knife. He might have touched my neck with a knife; I don't know." I remembered it differently when I spoke to Domenick several weeks later. O'Neill takes this as evidence that either I am not reliable or the transcripts are inaccurate. But I know why my statements varied: after my release, I saw the scar on my neck, so I knew he must have pressed that knife into my skin. I tell O'Neill as much: "I have a scar there"—but he is not satisfied with my answer.

"Well, Mrs. Puglisi, my question is, when you spoke to the detective on April 25 in the early morning hours, what you said to him was what was transcribed here in this document, Defense One."

"Right."

"Those were the words you spoke."

"Those were the words I said that night."

"The words [you spoke] were 'he might have put the knife—he might have touched my neck with the knife,' and then it was 'I don't know.' "

"Those were the words that night."

"And if I recall correctly, when you testified a little while ago, what you were intending to do when speaking with the officer that night was to try to tell him everything while it was freshest in your mind."

Yes, but, my God, I had just escaped from five days tied up in that man's house. I was dehydrated, exhausted, sleep deprived, scared to death. Did he expect photographic recall? "But I couldn't tell him everything exactly—it was too much."

"I understand that, ma'am, but what I'm asking you is, is that what your intention was, is that you were trying to do?"

"That was my intention."

"And these in fact are the words that you did speak on that occasion."

"They must have been." I am suddenly flustered. Have I said something wrong? But I can't remember everything and certainly couldn't remember everything back then. I hadn't slept more than a few hours in those five days. Doesn't he understand that?

"You described Mr. Flagg as a cleaning fanatic."

"I wouldn't say that exactly."

Again O'Neill brandishes his copy of my statement and tells me to read aloud. " 'I drank a little bit of water, because I didn't really want too much. I didn't want to wet myself. In fact he did put a shower curtain underneath. He was a cleaning fanatic.' " I look at O'Neill, who is staring at me over the tops of his glasses. "So I must have said it."

"These are your words?" he demands.

"Those are my words."

"Now when you spoke to the police in interview number one, did you tell Detective Walsh that 'Basically everything I asked of him, he would get me?' Do you remember saying something like that?"

"I'd have to read it." He finds the passage in my statement, thrusts it at me, tells me to read it for the jury.

So I said it. Yes, I said it. No, I don't recall saying it. But I guess I said it. I am feeling more and more disconcerted. As the questioning progresses, this has become my litany: I don't recall. I don't remember. I can't honestly answer that. I don't recall everything.

I feel foolish, small.

Finally, O'Neill asks me to read the portion of my statement (page four, Defense Exhibit One) where I describe how I beguiled the defendant—deliberately and to save my life—into thinking I liked him.

" 'I told him I thought there was some goodness in him,' " I say, reading from the transcript, "and I said, 'I really, you know, don't think that you're a really bad person.' "

"Part of what you were doing is saying these things in an attempt to befriend Mr. Flagg."

"Exactly."

"So you would feel safer."

So he understands. "Exactly."

"Because your feeling was, 'If I'm going to survive this thing, maybe I can get this guy to like me. Then he won't kill me and he'll stop doing these horrible things to me.' "

"That's exactly right."

"And you made that judgment because to some degree you did see something about him like that, didn't you?"

I look at O'Neill, openmouthed. I am incapable of speech. He crosses his arms, waits. I shake my head. "This is painful for me, I'm sorry—it's hard for me to use the word 'goodness.' "

I cannot believe it. For some reason I am apologizing.

But the ultimate affront is yet to come. Next the defense attorney suggests that if I "put aside the big picture" in which these horrible things were being done to me—multiple rapes and death threats—would it be fair to say "Mr. Flagg did things that people who love each other do as a general courtesy and everyday social niceties?"

I move back as if I have been hit till my spine touches the straight back of the witness chair. Oh, that's it, O'Neill. I've had it. I'm so angry, I feel like the heat is rolling off the surface of my skin. I fix him in my sights and snap, "Can I have that question rephrased? I have a problem with that. I have a problem using the word love."

It reminds me of the days in the asshole's house when I endured and endured, put up with and put up with, until I was constitutionally incapable of taking another moment of assault. Now in court I am reaching the limits of my tolerance, and I wonder if I can continue to refrain from showing what I am not permitted to show.

That I am angry. I am angry, I am angry.

IT HAS BECOME our custom to start the day in a tiny café on the ground floor of the courthouse, an unglamorous place with chairs made of molded orange plastic, folding tables with an ersatz wood grain, and a menu that doesn't aspire beyond grilled cheese sandwiches and a soup of the day. Here Dad buys me eggs on toast and hot chocolate each morning—again, comfort food, designed to shore me up for the rigors of the day.

The Public Defender's Office is also down here on the ground floor, and I go out of my way to avoid Flagg's attorneys. If I see O'Neill and have time to duck, I duck; if I don't, I walk stoically past as he greets me, nodding and smiling, oh so polite.

And I think, How can you address me so easily, you who are concocting phony pleas for my husband's killer? How do you sleep at night? I say nothing.

On the afternoon of April 19 we are treated at last to the love story of Donald Flagg and Janet Pagan. It's the loss of this great love that the jury is asked to believe was the prime mover behind these crimes. The dissolution of this romance, says O'Neill, drove the asshole to kidnap and kill and rape.

A heavyset white woman with a crown of russet-colored curls, Pagan, too, is a longtime employee at Chrysler Corporation's Newark plant—like Flagg, she has racked up almost nineteen years. When they met in 1990 she was a welder just back from medical leave; Flagg had temporarily taken her place on the job. "It was watching him do the job with such a meticulous attitude that caused me to want to get to know him better," she says. They started to date and within six months had moved in together.

On the stand Pagan relates the sad saga of Donald Flagg: she tells of his ostracism at Chrysler, where he was criticized for dating a white woman and teased for "not fitting in." She shares the story of their failed romance, which ended for good in August 1997. She tells of his fundamental loneliness and how he filled some of that void with a love of nature and animals. In her soon-to-be-celebrated phrase, Flagg is a "bird with a broken wing," a pathetic creature who is more to be pitied than reviled. She is not dissuaded from her view by the fact that in February or March of 1998, Flagg broke into her own home at 5 A.M., demanding to know why she would no longer have sex with him.

What an appalling pattern: confronting women, seizing women, holding them. But, despite all she now knows of his violent behavior toward other women, from Rosetta Shepherd, the friend he held against her will in a hotel room, to Patricia Mann, the young mother he raped as her son slept nearby, to me (and who knows how many others) Pagan is endlessly forgiving of her former lover.

Pagan knew all too well about Flagg's drug-taking. When he failed to show up at work last April 20, she showed up at Wellington Woods to check up on him; and later that day, it was her voice I heard on his answering machine, saying, "Don? Are you coming in to work?"

Because he seldom missed work and because he tended to isolate himself when he was on a crack binge, she suspected that his absence, two days running—Saturday, when he would have been paid overtime, and Monday—meant he was using again.

"I was concerned," she says. "I wanted to remind him that he needed to get himself to work, that if he did not return my call I was going to call the police. I was concerned that he might overdose, and as usual there would be no way for me to get in to take care of the cats."

She finally did reach him that Tuesday and scolded him for missing work; Pagan admits she filled something of a mother role in Flagg's life, doing his taxes, helping him buy his house, and forcing him, just once and against his will, to see a counselor.

When she got him on the phone, says Pagan, "He said he just needed some R and R." The phrase makes me shudder. Rest and relaxation. This is the man who had just killed my husband, who as they spoke had me tied up on the floor of his bathroom, soaked by my own urine. "In fact," says Pagan, "he had just finished cutting the grass."

My father, shifting in the pew beside me, lets out a short, impatient breath. I reach out to hold his hand. Don't get mad, Dad. Let's just stay calm, like Jim and Mark said. But I know just what he's feeling: I cannot believe the inhumanity.

Jim now addresses Pagan's meeting with Flagg that week, in which he took her to a doctor's appointment. On Thursday, April 23, when Pagan needed a ride to the doctor's office, she called Flagg. She now calls it "the bizarre conversation of the week."

"In what way?"

"That was the conversation in which he attempted to tell me he had done something. Out of the blue, he said, 'I am scared. I've done something. I don't want to go to jail, oh, my God, not jail.'"

Pagan talks about Flagg's everyday existence: his ability to work and function, to handle his finances, to pay his bills and his mortgage, and to keep his home (he was an "excellent" housekeeper, she says).

The woman who was supposedly closest to Flagg for the longest time of his life has established that he led a seemingly normal life and that he was fully aware that he had done something wrong—in direct opposition to the defense claim that he was an "extremely sick" man who did not understand even the concepts of wrong and right. Now O'Neill emphasizes the latter by introducing a letter written by Flagg from jail to Janet Pagan. First the defendant decried the impact of his actions on his cats: "Poor Buddy and Butch. How could I do such a thing to put them in harm's way?"

As sad as I am for his cats—poor innocents, now most likely gone—I recoil from this expression of regret. So much worry for his animals. Not a word for Nino, who is dead by his hand, or for Nino's children, who will live with holes in their hearts and souls forever.

Flagg wrote, "Well, as we get closer to the trial and the finger gets pointed at me, what am I going to say?" He noted that September 30 is the cutoff date for making a plea of insanity.

In his letter he went on to contemplate the death penalty. It clearly frightened him. I take no joy in this—how I wish I could. I want Donald Flagg to die and feel certain the jury will agree, but the anticipation satisfies nothing in me. It only confirms what we all know, that death is indeed punishment, the harshest penalty, the very last sentence. All of us who love Nino—the kids and me in particular—have spent a year trying to reframe his death in its loveliest light, telling ourselves that it was his passage home to God.

Faith tells us to believe this. Though my own faith has taken a nasty hit these past twelve months, I do continue to believe, as do my children. But we know that this death was also a punishment, a punishment of the worst kind. Nino got the death penalty, and the man who meted it out without pausing for an instant now trembles to think of the same end.

"It's a hell of a thing," Flagg wrote, "to know the day of your death. If I had the choice, I would rather not know, and the way things are now, every day has that question in it." But my Nino knew the day of his death—Nino surely knew, if only for seconds, on that Monday afternoon that he was about to die. He knew he would never be able to say good-bye to his cherished son. He knew his uncanny premonition about Melissa, spoken just weeks before ("I'll never see her again"), was coming true. His family knows it, too, and the kids and I will have to reckon with that horror for a lifetime.

As for me, I died every day that week—every day was the day of my death. Asshole. The hate comes up like vitriol, flooding my system.

But on the outside I stay calm, just as I have been told to do.

18

THAT CALM NEARLY deserts me when Carol Tavani takes the stand April 22. She is the prison psychiatrist Brendan O'Neill promised would be the pivotal witness for the defense. He begins by asking her to enumerate her professional affiliations, a task that consumes almost ten minutes.

Dr. Tavani is executive director of Christiana Psychiatric Services, an independent contractor with Prison Health Services, and the elected president of the medical staff at Christiana Care—in her words, "at the helm of the leadership of 1,200 doctors."

She runs the physician's health committee for the Medical Society of Delaware, serves as a delegate to the American Medical Association, and is on the professional guidance committee of the Delaware Bar Association.

The list is impressive, as it is meant to be. Dr. Tavani is trim and petite in a peach-colored suit, and she assumes the stand with an air of authority and self-assurance.

O'Neill asks her first to explain the illness known as paranoid schizophrenia.

"Maybe a definition would be best stated by saying what

schizophrenia is not," says Tavani. "It isn't, first of all, a split personality. It doesn't mean you're demented or don't have your cognitive processes, like orientation.

"It doesn't mean you go around babbling, although certainly
severely psychotic people can be seen to do that." Schizophrenia,
she says, is a "brain disorder. The wiring of the brain—the hard
wiring—is abnormal." She reiterates what O'Neill said in his
opening statement: that schizophrenics thrive on routine and are
traumatized by breaks in routine.

O'Neill asks "Are people with paranoid schizophrenia capable
of keeping jobs?"

Indeed they are, says Tavani—they are particularly good at
"rote jobs" that involve "sameness, repetitive patterns, doing the
same thing over and over. That would be just about an ideal job
for someone with that symptom complex."

"For example," says O'Neill, peeking over the rim of his
glasses, "an assembly line job?"

"Yes," Tavani replies. "That would be one."

Schizophrenics, she goes on, suffer from delusions and hallucinations. "The most common delusion in schizophrenia is paranoia, or feeling that people are after you or watching you or out
to get you or something of that nature." Because schizophrenics
isolate themselves, she adds, they tend to have few social supports.

Now O'Neill lays the groundwork for his primary defense:
that Donald Flagg came unhinged when he lost the woman of his
dreams, his fellow welder Janet Pagan. "What is typically the
reaction of a paranoid schizophrenic who experiences the loss of
a relationship," he asks, "a personal relationship?"

"Of course, it's a major life change," says Tavani. "Your whole
life could be upended."

At O'Neill's urging, Tavani goes on to educate the jury on the
nature and manifestations of schizophrenia: it is largely genetic,
and it usually becomes evident in the late teens or early twenties. "It
tends to flare, often under stress of some sort," she says. But schizophrenics don't go back to a "baseline of absolutely Joe Normal."

"Can this disease be faked?" asks O'Neill, brows raised. "Can I pretend to be a schizophrenic?"

"I've seen people try to fake schizophrenia," says Tavani with an eye-rolling smirk. "It's usually pretty pathetic."

Her diagnosis of Donald Flagg was made on the basis of what she terms a "comprehensive initial evaluation." In Flagg's case, it consisted of a single sixty-minute interview at Gander Hill Prison in April 1998, shortly after his arrest. During the interview, she says, the prisoner complained of depression, which prompted her to ask him more.

"I always ask, how long has this depression been there, how far back does it go? And he said, 'I think it goes back to childhood. And so do the voices and the paranoia.'"

Dad shifts in the seat beside me, and his fingers drum rhythmically on the bench. He's a no-nonsense man with little tolerance for hubris, in others or in himself; as Tavani sets out her defense for Flagg, it is he who is most offended by it, he and my brothers, who are made of the same stuff. That they manage to check it here in court, where the justifications are heaped one atop the other without embarrassment, just makes me respect them more.

Donald Flagg had never spoken of voices to anyone until he committed murder. At least once, as we learn, he was admitted to a thirty-day drug rehab, where he had daily contact with therapists, and in 1994, at the behest of Chrysler and Janet Pagan, he saw a psychiatrist about his cocaine addiction.

But despite ample opportunity, he remained mute about any voices. After his arrest, however, there it was at every opportunity—voices, hallucinations, "shadows." I glance toward the jury, wonder how this will play for them. Are they going for it? Do they see through it? I can't tell. For the most part they are inscrutable, as I suppose they must be. Diligent, with their spiral-bound notebooks, and inscrutable. I avert my eyes. They can't possibly believe this, can they? If they do . . .

At least one juror—the foreman, a thirtyish man with wheat-colored hair—gives me cause to hope. When O'Neill launches a heart-tugging tale of Donald Flagg and his little dog, Diablo, he shakes his head incredulously.

The dog. If it were not so dreadful, it would be comical: a defense attorney and a psychiatrist attempting to mitigate murder this way, by blaming it on the death of a pet Chihuahua.

"Can you give us any opinion as to what effect the death of his dog would have had on him in early 1998?"

Robert leans in close and growls, "I can hear the string section tuning up."

"It sounded," says Dr. Tavani, solemnly, "as if it were very devastating."

Devastating. He lost his little dog. We are asked to feel pity for this loss, Melissa and Michael and I, who have lost Nino.

The judge calls a lunch recess, and I hurry with my family for the elevator. I have a sudden need to breathe the air out of doors.

WE USUALLY LUNCH at a cafeteria on the second floor of the Wilmington Trust Bank across the street. It has tall, wide windows and a pretty view of downtown Wilmington: Rodney Square with its statue of Caesar Rodney (a signer of the Declaration of Independence) the du Pont Hotel, and, in pleasant contrast, the perfect, tiny, stone spires of old church buildings. The food is quite good.

As a group we draw some stares (I'm becoming good at lipreading, and I can always tell when someone whispers, "Puglisi"), but no one imposes on us, for which I am very thankful. Let this be a time for just family.

We're careful not to talk about the proceedings. Before each break—either for lunch or at the end of the day—Judge Barron reminds jury members that they are not to discuss the case with each other or anyone else outside the courtroom; they must report anyone who tries to initiate conversation.

The judge hints that there is a considerable (if unspelled-out) penalty for breaking this rule. So we take it to heart, too, at least at lunchtime. We talk about the cafeteria's great salad bar and the daily special, and Dad remarks that they make a pretty decent cup of coffee.

Back in court it's Jim's turn to take on Dr. Tavani, and though his interrogatory style remains low-key, I'm glad to see him make some hay of this morning's testimony. He undercuts Tavani's assertion that Flagg does not understand the concept of wrong with Exhibit 191, a letter Flagg wrote her in the summer of 1998.

"Now," Jim says, "would you agree that at least portions of that letter suggest that Mr. Flagg is stating he's ashamed of what he had done?"

"Yes."

"Can you square that with someone who lacked the capacity to appreciate the wrong?"

Tavani tilts her head. "Well, when he wrote this, he was getting treatment," she says. "*Here* he is appreciating the wrongfulness."

How does remorse, Jim asks, coexist with active paranoid schizophrenia? "You said in August of 1998 he was still suffering from schizophrenia." In fact, she said much more: according to Tavani's clinical notes, that summer Flagg still had "very disturbed thinking, aggressive impulses." He was "entirely confused with relationship issues" and had "very bizarre thought disturbances."

"It would be clear, wouldn't it, that he knew the wrongfulness of his actions despite his schizophrenia?" asks Jim.

"When he wrote *this,* yes," says Tavani. "He was on medicine when he wrote this. For two months."

From my vantage point in the first row I can tell Jim is getting irritated, like a schoolteacher who cannot cow a smart-aleck student. "*Despite* the medicine," he presses, "you found him to be very disturbed."

"Well, yes," says Tavani, unperturbed. "Would you like me to explain?"

"If you think you can."

Dr. Tavani began her testimony with a rundown of her cur-

riculum vitae, which was lengthy and sounded quite distin-
guished. Now Jim points out some things she failed to mention:
that she is a consultant to the Delaware Public Defender's Office
but has no similar affiliation with prosecutorial agencies. That
she has testified as a forensic psychiatrist in just two cases, both
times for the defense.

Jim also makes sure to note that at an hourly rate of $350, Dr.
Tavani will make from fifteen to twenty thousand dollars for her
participation here (of approximately fifty hours spent on the case,
three were spent in the company of the defendant). Then he
moves on, asking how she made her initial diagnosis of schizophrenia. She says she relied on a medical history, personal observation, and "notes by a mental health worker."

"So is it fair to say, Doctor, that when you made your initial
diagnosis, everything you knew about Donald Flagg came from
Donald Flagg himself?"

"That's correct, and from my observation of him."

But according to the mental health worker, who also worked
with Prison Health Services, Donald Flagg was "alert and ori-
ented, appropriate in mood and affect, eye contact good, and
responsive to questions in a clear, sequential manner."

"That's right." Tavani nods, as if the contradiction does not
trouble her in the slightest.

How about the "blunted affect" that was so critical to Tavani's
diagnosis? asks Jim. The notes from PHS refute that altogether.

Dr. Tavani nods, and a tiny crinkle forms between her brows.
Yes, she concedes, "It misses it entirely."

Jim then asks if Dr. Tavani, in formulating her opinion, read
victim statements—my hospital interview with police and the
interview with Domenick Gregory conducted several weeks later.
Yes, she says, she did. Yet, Jim says, these were not given any
weight at all in her assessment, Jim remarks; in fact, they were
not even mentioned. "Is there some reason why you made no reference to Debra Puglisi's statements in your report?"

Tavani smiles, lifts her tiny shoulders in a half-shrug. "It was
just an omission on my part, to be honest."

"So ninety percent or more of what you included in the report is history given by Donald Flagg?"

"Which I later corroborated."

"And you knew at that time, did you not, that he had been charged with murder?"

"Yes."

"Is it clear to you that would be a motivation, perhaps, for him not to give you a fair and accurate history?"

She doesn't lose a beat. "It could be. But he appeared to me to present credibly. There were things he did not have to tell me that he volunteered rather spontaneously." Presumably about those voices. "I would have to say one gets a sense whether someone is trying to skew the facts."

TAVANI REMAINS ON the stand for a day and a half. She discusses the mental health history of Eliza Flagg, Donald Flagg's mother, even more than his. Apparently Eliza was a wretchedly ill woman, a genuine schizophrenic who was hospitalized some twenty times before finally being institutionalized. Her case included literally thousands of pages of documentation: treatments, hospitalization, schizophrenic episodes, more treatment, and on and on.

"How many pages of past psychiatric history did you have for Donald Flagg before he was arrested for murder?" Jim asks the doctor.

"I didn't have any," says Tavani. "Because he wasn't diagnosed or treated."

My question, which I hope is the question in the mind of every juror: How did this illness, which usually manifests in the teenage years, go without detection for more than two decades? How did Donald Flagg, who had supposedly heard voices since childhood, reach his fortieth year without being diagnosed?

The thrust and parry continues. Jim says, "Isn't it true that abusing certain drugs can give psychotic symptoms that sometimes mirror the diagnostic criteria for schizophrenia?"

"That's right," says Tavani. "That's why it was so important to me to determine that the schizophrenia came first."

Jim isn't having it. He reiterates that she made the diagnosis after a one-hour interview in May, when cocaine—which does not leave the body for about four weeks—was still in the defendant's system. He asserts that there are no laboratory tests for schizophrenia and reminds the court that Tavani's assessment was based largely on "the report of the patient." Donald Flagg *claimed* to hear voices, so he must hear voices.

LATER THAT DAY on the car ride home, I chip off another piece of a Xanax. Afterward, weary and puzzled beyond words, I check in with the twins at their respective schools—not to talk about the trial but just to hear the voices of those who mean the most. Later still, when Bill stops in, he must sense my agitation, because he gives me an extra-big hug that almost lifts me off the ground. "How'd it go today?"

"I guess okay. It's all these lies. What if people think they're true? The defense, they make it all sound true. The other day I'm the one who sounded like the liar."

"Okay, honey. It'll be okay."

"Oh, God, Bill. I won't be able to stand it if they don't send him to jail. He has to go there." Bill hugs me again and talks into the top of my head, so I don't quite hear what he's saying. But I think he says, "It'll all be over soon."

"Doctor, you talked yesterday about delusions." Jim, buttoned-down and buttoned-up as always, continues his cross-examination first thing in the morning. "I think you indicated that one of the most common delusions that you see with schizophrenia or paranoid schizophrenia is that people are out to get them or people are looking for them."

"That's correct."

"Well, in this particular case, Donald Flagg had a rational reason to believe that people were out looking for him, didn't he, during the time of the crime?"

"Yes."

"There were cops looking for him." Next to me, Robert nods sharply, as if to say, Now we're really making some sense.

"So this wasn't necessarily an irrational paranoia on his part," Jim says.

"That part, no, not at all."

He goes on to ask if she was aware that "he did certain things to conceal his crime and avoid detection by police"—among those, parking the car away from my house, entering it through a rear door, punching me "immediately" and dragging me to the basement, concealing me in the comforter and tying me up, driving his car into the garage to conceal it—was she aware of all that? Yes, says the doctor.

19

It's unnerving the effortless way Dr. Tavani explains away all Donald Flagg's brutal behavior, how easily she makes him a pitiful figure. By the time she concludes her testimony, it seems, even to me, as if it would be the height of cruelty not to feel compassion for this poor, sick man. Tavani is good, and my spirits have been knocked windless by her testimony. Worse, I can tell it's not just me who feels this way. When the psychiatrist steps down, Jane looks upset, Darlene angry. Robert rubs a hand over his eyes, tiredly. Dad is quietly fuming.

We drive home, not speaking.

I try to put it all out of mind, but her words resound again and again: Flagg (whom she always calls "Donald") is a tragic man, "devastated" by personal loss—he lost his girlfriend, he lost his Chihuahua. And on the scales of justice, this, *this,* compares to the death of my husband, the kids' dad.

I am learning that a criminal trial is like a shell game, a shadow show. A game of interpretation in which two sides can take the same facts and draw utterly different conclusions. If the players are skilled, both conclusions can seem plausible. How can this be? How can people turn my husband's murder into a game, a contest? But that is what is happening.

The minute we arrive home I phone Dr. Dancu. She is away at her beach house, but she left the number of her service, saying, "Debbie, call any time, and don't feel you're disrupting anything. Call." So I do, and within a half hour she calls back. By now the dam that contains my feelings is eggshell-thin, and the instant I hear her voice, I feel it begin to break.

"How can she do it?" I ask. "She's a woman, Dr. Tavani is. How could a woman—how could she get up there and say this man who killed my husband doesn't know right from wrong? Day after day I go in there and hear why it's okay my husband is dead, why it would have been okay if I turned up dead, too. It's because that asshole is so sick, so sick. It's okay for him to kill us." I start to cry, so hard I begin hiccupping, like I did when I was little. "He's a killer, Dr. Dancu. And it's okay with everybody."

"It's not okay with everybody. Debbie, I hear you. You feel violated and rightly so," says Dr. Dancu, softly, in that quiet, soothing voice. "But Dr. Tavani is a woman doing her job, as horrible as that seems to you right now. She needs to do it, and the system demands it."

I don't want to hear this; I don't want to be reasonable or fairminded. I went to court for justice; instead, I feel I am being raped again, murdered again. I want to scream.

Against my sputtering tears, Dr. Dancu talks on: the defendant is getting a fair trial, which is his right. A fair trial includes a defense. The jury is hearing the excuse; it is also hearing the truth. It's hard, but I must persevere; my fight is nearly done. And I have faced obstacles far worse than this. "Call on your strength, Debbie, as you've done in the past."

"I don't want to be strong. Why do I have to keep being strong?"

I'm curled up in an armchair, phone tucked in the crook of my shoulder, knees up to my chest. As soon as I'm done crying, I'm able to listen.

"Strong is not something you use, that you only bring out

when you need it," she says. "Strong is something you are. You've proven it."

I sigh out loud, laugh mirthlessly. "This is the worst."

"Not the worst," she says.

I pause, lift my eyes to the ceiling. "Oh, yeah. You're right. This isn't the worst."

THE PENDULUM SWINGS back on April 28 when the prosecution's psychiatrist, Dr. Robert Sadoff, takes the stand. He is the state's answer to Tavani—tall and grave, with glasses, sparse white hair, and a long, lined face. Sadoff boasts a vast professional résumé, having worked for both defense and prosecution in some nine thousand criminal trials, including three thousand murder cases in twenty states, several federal jurisdictions, and one or two foreign countries (Tavani, by contrast, has testified in three).

It is all overwhelming, but how good it sounds. The cavalry has arrived in a beautiful blaze of glory, and Sadoff is my version of John Wayne. Here is someone who can put the defense hypotheses about Donald Flagg to rest for good.

During Jim's direct examination, which lasts through the morning, Sadoff undoes Tavani's defense as handily as he might dismantle a Tinkertoy. First he makes it plain that the voices of schizophrenia—the genuine auditory illusions that must have filled the mind of Eliza Flagg—follow a very predictable pattern, beginning in childhood or adolescence; those who hear such voices almost always speak of them, so the phenomenon is easily corroborated.

By contrast, when someone starts talking about voices only in the wake of an arrest "and never prior to that," it signals he is probably trying to get himself out of a jam. Sadoff mentions a former patient who during an interview suddenly exclaimed, "Boy, that green monster just flew into the window."

"Well, there was no green monster," says Dr. Sadoff. "He was trying to con me."

My palms are suddenly damp, as if a fever has just broken. I am elated and so relieved. All I want is to hear the sound of honest words in this court, and I am hearing them now, from someone the jury must see is absolutely credible.

Sadoff examined the defendant twice. During their first jailhouse interview in January, Flagg was distracted, vague. "When I get this kind of thing in a person whom others have diagnosed as schizophrenic, I usually ask, 'Is something coming to you, are you talking to somebody else, is there any other stimuli coming in besides my voice?'

"He said he was starting to hear the voices."

The voices Flagg described were very explicit. They said "bad things" to him. They told him, "Find someone to rape." Flagg told Dr. Sadoff that when he first raped me, he ejaculated prematurely, so the voices told him, "Well, you haven't really raped her. You have to take her to your home, and you have to rape her there." Later the voices told him, "Yes, keep Mrs. Puglisi because she's a good companion, and she's sexually available to you."

Why, asks Jim, did Flagg reveal none of this to Dr. Tavani, his own psychiatrist?

It's easily explained, says Sadoff. Embellishment is a common feature of deceit; over time the liar refines his story, adding detail in the mistaken belief that it adds credibility. "He's thinking more and more about what he's doing, and the version he gives me is the least incriminating."

Flagg's account of the crime is certainly a work in progress. Over time my kidnapping has become the result of a sickness, a mania. His version of Nino's death has also changed with the telling. When he confessed, Flagg said, "I was in the dining room; he came through and I shot him." To Tavani, he framed it differently, as if he were defending himself, saying, "He charged me and I shot him." To Sadoff, Flagg said, "I hit him, and the gun accidentally discharged." Now it's all an accident. I want to rise up, speak out, call him the liar he is. But I must sit here, quiet and demure, like I'm in church.

His plans for me have now also evolved into something far more benign. Before I escaped, Flagg told me that if he freed me,

his life would be over. The night of his arrest, he told Domenick
Gregory he knew if he let me go, his life was "fucked." But by
January, when he talked to Dr. Sadoff, his story had changed: he
claimed he had always planned to let me go eventually.

I am seething. Asshole. Liar. You know you were going to kill
me. You were going to kill me and put me out with the trash or
dump me on the roadside or in the river, and to hell with my
kids. Let them wonder forever what happened to their mom.

He sits at the defense table, unmoving, with shoulders
hunched and head slightly bent. He seems passive, almost meek.
Is he is on drugs? Maybe. Oh, God, just once, I wish he would
show everyone gathered here the monster I met in my kitchen
that April afternoon. But as in most criminal trials, the monster
has been dressed up, quieted down, made respectable, made
remorseful for public consumption. No one here will be introduced to the monster I knew. Perhaps they wonder if it even
exists.

Maybe it doesn't. Without the fuel of cocaine—not schizophrenia, damn it, but crack cocaine—the monster inside Flagg
may no longer exist, or exist only in a dormant state. The monster in embryo. But it existed for Nino, for me, for poor Patricia
Mann, and perhaps for other victims we'll never know about.

But now, at least, the fabrications are becoming more transparent. That afternoon at lunch my folks and I manage to relax a
bit, even laugh. I hate to think of the trial in terms of winning—
this is a matter of justice, which hopefully follows truth—but I've
learned that truth has many formidable opponents. During the
defense testimony I felt the truth was being obscured; it frightened me. Now, at least, our team is ahead.

Back in court, it's almost entertaining to watch O'Neill and
Sadoff go head to head. By now, it's like watching a runt try to
bring down a linebacker. O'Neill takes potshots at the doctor's
professional credentials ("You're not licensed in Delaware, are
you? You haven't treated patients for twenty years, have you?
You've never treated Mr. Flagg, have you?"), but Sadoff is unperturbed. O'Neill pulls out his old trick of attacking the witness's

recall, asking Sadoff, inanely, if there were windows in the prison interview room and insinuating that because he cannot remember, his credibility as a whole must be called into question. Such tactics worked well with me, but Dr. Sadoff seems almost amused.

He concedes that Flagg is an unstable man. Who would deny that? In Sadoff's opinion, Flagg has a "personality disorder with schizoid and antisocial features." But, he adds, his instability would not have become homicidal mania without the excessive, compulsive ingestion of crack cocaine. Drug-taking is voluntary. Therefore, the defendant does not meet the medical standard for insanity, or the state's. Full stop.

OF THE REMAINING witnesses, two stand out for me, for very different reasons. First is Brian Northrop, a convicted felon who roomed with Flagg at Gander Hill Prison last November. He wears a prison-issue bright orange jumpsuit and, once on the stand, willingly admits to a criminal career that includes petty theft, robbery, and parole violation. Northrop testifies that in prison, he and Donald Flagg became confidants. Flagg confided many details of the crime, which Northrop now discloses. Flagg also told him he was so concerned about a conviction and possible death sentence that he planned to "act crazy" in court, adding, "You have to be sane for them to kill you."

O'Neill blasts Northrop as a snitch who will sell out fellow prisoners to improve his own chances for parole. He accuses him of learning all he knows about Flagg from the newspapers, copies of which are placed in evidence, and adds that Northrop got his idea from an article in which a cell mate of the accused murderer Tom Capano cut a deal with prosecutors in exchange for parole.

Northrop, though admitting he wishes the state could do something to improve his situation, says he has been promised nothing in return. If anything, he says, his status in prison has been hampered by his testimony here. And when it comes to the newspaper, he looks directly at the jury and says, "Ladies and gentlemen, this is the first time I'm seeing these articles."

Amazingly, Brian Northrop is credible. He does not pretend to be other than he is; he freely admits his past addiction and his former transgressions. He says he is coming forth because he is "sad" about what happened to my family. When he steps down, he passes a folded piece of paper to Jim Ropp, which Jim later gives to me. It is a scrawled note from Prisoner 308697.

> Dear Ms. Puglisi, I am writing this Letter to tell you I salute you for your courage and determination to survive the ordeal that you went through. It's because of you that your husband did not die in vain for you reflect everything that he believed in, and that's Love standing strong and Brave through the worst of times. So keep your head up high so god can see his child being bless with the greatest reward that is important and that's justice for you and your husband. And even though you don't know me as a Person, I want you to know my deepest Prayers go out to you and your children everyday; for it's because of you that every Person viewing this case including myself will know the Meaning of courage and Determination.
>
> Again I salute you and pray that God will Plant the Flowers Back in your life that Donald Flagg has Destroyed.
>
> Your Friend Always, Brian

Carefully, I press his note between the pages of a book in my purse. When I get home, I place it in one of the cardboard boxes of letters I plan to keep, the letters that helped me come back to life.

THE NEXT WITNESS almost moves me to tears. Patricia Mann is a timid, sweet-faced young girl with brown hair that curls softly on her shoulders. She cannot be more than twenty-three or twenty-four, just a few years older than Melissa, a single mom of limited means who lives on a not-too-nice block of apartments in New Castle that had become run-down over the years. Just a struggling girl with few advantages. And she is the young woman Donald Flagg raped last April 17, three days before he came to Academy Hill.

On the stand, Patricia is wide-eyed and tremulous, tensed up as if at any moment she will turn and flee. She is plainly uncomfortable being here before strangers, talking about the sins committed against her. Watching her tearfully relate her story—Flagg broke into her little apartment through a sliding door, found her asleep on the couch with the TV on, woke her, and attempted to sodomize her, as her toddler son slept in the next room—I feel two things: regret for her and renewed fury at Flagg.

Patty Mann doesn't have many defenses—not the calluses of age and experience and, I daresay, not the kind of support and professional help I was fortunate to find. She is an innocent who had every right to remain so. Now look at her. She has fear she shouldn't have and memories she will have a hard time getting rid of. What's going to happen to this poor girl? She doesn't have my resources, and I don't think she has my anger or resilience. From what I can see, all she has is hurt and fear.

O'Neill doesn't go after her. It would be like striking a child.

WHEN I USED to read murder mysteries—before I lost the capacity to read them—I was always tempted to peek at the ending; I'd have to force myself to keep from turning to the last page. I feel that way now; it has been three weeks, closing arguments are due May 3, and for me and all the members of my family, the suspense is exhausting. Throughout the trial, the jury has not lost its impenetrable face; we do not know what the jurors are thinking. We can only trust they will see the truth and arrive at the right, just conclusion.

We have made friends here: the "good morning man" at the Friskem machine; many of the reporters, who despite their on-air impartiality have made it clear they are on our side; some of the courtroom regulars; the cook and cashier in the ground floor café. I will never see most of them again, and I feel a pang of regret at the thought. But I know it will pass. Of necessity these alliances have been brief but intense; they begin and end like the relationships I share with most of my hospice families. I will never forget these kind people, and I will always bless them for their support.

But soon it will be time to go home, back to my life, a life I now know I will share with Bill Sharp.

I guess we knew it as early as last fall: that more than likely we were going to stay together. It was Bill who officially broached the subject, but he didn't quite propose; it was more like, "Where's this all going, this thing with us? I want you to stay here, in my life, with me. Will you?" It was all I needed to hear. From that point on we knew we would marry but kept it to ourselves for a while. I was still so afraid of the kids' reaction. I wanted them to grow accustomed to this new man in my life. If they accepted him there, maybe they would invite him into their own lives. I could only wait, hope, and pray.

MARK CONNER BEGINS closing arguments by asking, as Jim Ropp did the first day of the trial, that the jurors use their common sense. "If you do that," says Mark, "the state is confident you will return a true and correct verdict of guilty on each and every count."

He says this case, which started as a "true whodunit," will now end with every question answered. He recaps the testimony of each witness—our neighbors and friends, the police and detectives, the medical examiner, the ballistics expert, Dr. Sowa and his assistant, Kathy Rainey of the sexual assault nurse team, the psychiatrists, Patricia Mann—and weighs it all against the testimony of the sole witness for the defense, Dr. Carol Tavani.

He describes the charges against Flagg and asserts that the state has "proven the facts of each and every one." He discusses the state standard for a verdict of not guilty by reason of insanity and reminds the jury the defendant cannot claim mental illness if the "proximate cause" of his illness was excessive, deliberate use of crack cocaine.

Mark also reminds them that Dr. Tavani arrived at her diagnosis of paranoid schizophrenia after a one-hour session, with no evidence before her but the defendant's own "self-serving, self-reported hallucinations and delusions." He scrolls down the list of people closest to Donald Flagg who for all the years they knew him never heard a thing about voices: his friend, his former girlfriend, his brother.

"These are the facts, ladies and gentlemen, and they are completely inconsistent with a verdict of not guilty by reason of insanity."

Dr. Tavani's convoluted testimony is next. Against all reason and every shred of evidence, she insisted that the defendant did not understand the wrongfulness of his actions. Mark cites Flagg's daily, methodical, exhaustive efforts to conceal the crime as proof that he did. Donald Flagg feared capture and did all he could to avoid it.

He also knew he had harmed me and my family, Mark says. He cites Flagg's own words to me the morning after Nino died: "I'm sorry I had to kill your husband."

"What is sorry?" asks Mark. "Sorry is remorse. You can't show remorse unless you know you did something wrong." He goes on to criticize Tavani's dual role of treating psychiatrist and forensic psychiatrist. "You can't be a treating psychiatrist then go in and render a forensic opinion on the same person," he argues. "It doesn't work. You have to be impartial."

He talks about the testimony of Brian Northrop, Flagg's cellmate. According to Northrop, Flagg confided he was going to "act crazy" in court.

Finally he tells the jury Donald Flagg cannot avoid responsibility for his crimes because he committed them under the influence. "You cannot claim to be mentally ill if the mental illness was caused by crack cocaine. That's not how it works in

Delaware. Essentially, if you smoke crack cocaine, you're responsible for your actions."

"Ladies and gentlemen," says Mark, "this 'bird with a broken wing' was able and willing to take the life of Anthony Puglisi and forever change the lives of Debbie Puglisi and her family. The state asks that you return a verdict of guilty to each and every charge."

O'Neill begins his closing after a short recess. He addresses the jury in a warm, confidential tone, as if his time with them in court has bonded them in a common cause: the pursuit of truth as O'Neill sees it. "This part of the case, when the lawyers do all the talking, is what is commonly referred to as a closing argument," he says, smiling easily. "I personally like to refer to it as a discussion. We're all done arguing."

Again he waxes sentimental about my family and our losses, which I find unbearably galling and patronizing. "Nothing can bring Mr. Puglisi back, and nothing can make Mrs. Puglisi whole again."

This was a "series of horrible, horrible crimes," he says. "It's understandable that you would want to automatically convict Mr. Flagg, send him on his way, vote for a death sentence. That's the automatic human reaction. Find him guilty, get it over with.

"Not only is this court system unable to do that, but that cannot be the basis for any decision that you reach at this time. Each and every one of you has to overcome that immediate, natural reaction. Each and every one of you took an oath as a juror to decide this case according to the law."

Though the testifying doctors do not agree on a diagnosis, says O'Neill, all of them agree that Donald Flagg is disturbed. The fact that he took drugs does not ameliorate his crimes, "and nobody on our defense team is saying that drugs are an excuse." But the symptoms of Flagg's mental illness, he claims, predate his drug use. "And drugs in a mentally ill person . . ." O'Neill shrugs. Quite another story.

"The key thing is that Mr. Flagg just doesn't get it. He just doesn't appreciate what he was doing to this poor woman. And the reason he doesn't get it is because he's mentally ill. He's sick. He has or he had no real appreciation for the harm he was inflicting on this poor woman. How can that be? Because he's mentally ill, that's how."

O'Neill has altered his approach somewhat; he has abandoned the professorial demeanor in favor of a good-sense, guy-next-door approach. His language has become very colloquial, as if he's chatting with sensible, like-minded folks at the local diner. And they agree with him, don't they, that when you come right down to it, the poor guy's got to be crazy. And if that's true, well, give him a break.

But you don't need to let him off the hook to do that. At this point the defense attorney makes a remarkable, unexpected departure from his original plea—it is so sudden I am momentarily disoriented. Without preamble, O'Neill now begins to argue for a verdict of guilty but mentally ill. Somewhere along the way he must have recognized he could not successfully argue for not guilty. This jury has heard in lurid detail the cruel way Flagg treated his victims. They could not have been unmoved by Patricia Mann's tearful recounting of being forced to crawl on the floor of her apartment, of having the clothes cut from her body with a knife, of having to find some hand lotion so it would be easier for her rapist to rape her.

So that's it. O'Neill believes a verdict of guilty but mentally ill will be more palatable for the jury.

He goes on to defend his defense psychiatrist (Dr. Tavani is a "treating psychiatrist with no agenda") and slam her opponent (Dr. Sadoff, he sneers, is a "professional witness"). Then he takes on the issue of Donald Flagg's changing story of the crime as he remembered it (or reinvented it). Interestingly to me, who bore O'Neill's scathing attack on my faulty memory, he now goes on to explain why Donald Flagg's story differed so much on different occasions.

"Any person who's attempting to recount an event that

occurred in April of 1998 is going to tell it differently in May. If he recounts it again in August or September it may be a little different, too, and in January, some eight months later, there are going to be some differences. These are not inconsistencies. He's not lying."

No, O'Neill thunders, Flagg did not report the voices in his head to Domenick Gregory the night he was arrested, and why? Domenick never asked! "Mr. Flagg responded truthfully, right down the line, to the questions asked by Detective Gregory," he says. But Domenick never asked him about his psychological state, says O'Neill, "and that's why it was not on the tape." All these are "red herring issues."

I wrap my hands under the edge of my seat and just hold on. Oh, God. How can he twist these things so silkily, so easily?

Now it's back to Dr. Sadoff. O'Neill quotes Mark Twain, who once said, "An expert is a guy from out of town." I am offended. It's a funny line but insulting to Dr. Sadoff, who deserves at least professional respect.

About Brian Northrop, O'Neill reminds us that he is a felon with multiple convictions. "He is the ultimate con man. He would sell his own mother for a buck and then complain he didn't get enough money for the sale." O'Neill says Northrop was just trying to improve his own situation by ratting on a fellow prisoner, and his testimony "really puts into question the quality of the state's evidence as a whole."

He walks away from the jury box then turns back dramatically, like a lawyer in a soap opera. "Is Mr. Flagg guilty?" he asks. "Yeah. Is Mr. Flagg mentally ill? Yeah. As a result of his mental illness was his thinking, feeling, or behavior substantially affected? Yeah."

He pauses then resumes in a softer tone. "I have to go back to what we said in the beginning. The natural reaction of each and every one of us when we heard what happened to Mrs. Puglisi, when we heard the 911 tape, was to convict Mr. Flagg and lock him up. But we can't just do that. He is guilty, but he is mentally ill. . . . "

A rush, an about-to-be-sick feeling, comes up from my toes into my stomach. I am suddenly light-headed. Oh, Lord, I cannot take this. Get me out of here. I place my feet square on the floor so they will support my weight and push with my hands till I'm upright. Then I walk. I walk, seeing nothing, to the end of our row, then left, then toward the door, which looks like it's a mile away till I barge into it and it swings open. I keep going, down a hall, through another door and another, moving until I can follow the windows to the exit. There are the flowering trees of Rodney Square, trees and sky and a grassy green that I want to fall onto. I can't. I need a hiding place, and I stagger like someone who has been punched to our bank cafeteria, where I collapse into a chair.

Soon someone—someone who followed me from court—comes to sit beside me and hold my hand. I don't know who she is—I am too upset to tell—but she is a sister of mine.

Darlene is petite and fair, with long, dark hair. Jane is tall and tan with short, curly hair. They do not look at all alike. Yet I cannot tell who it is, sitting here beside me.

THE NEXT DAY, Saturday, Jim Ropp calls me at home. Because of my dramatic exit, he tells me, Judge Barron is considering barring me from the courtroom for the rest of the trial. We must go to his quarters Monday morning to find out his decision.

I replace the phone in its cradle, slide into the nearest chair, and bend down so my forehead touches my knees.

Sue's there, and she comes and kneels and puts her face close to mine. "What is it?" she whispers.

"They might not let me back in. I got mad. I wasn't allowed to do that."

20

LATER ON I tell the kids it was for all the world like a trip to the principal's office. First thing Monday morning, we walk to the anteroom of Judge Barron's quarters. Jim, the hall monitor, and me, the student who misbehaved. It is a magnificent place, like a judge's room should be: dark walls lined with leather-bound books, a broad, gleaming desk, oil paintings in massive gilded frames. I am impressed. I am thoroughly intimidated.

But the moment Judge Barron enters, I know it will be all right. In a suit and tie, without those magisterial robes, he is less imposing, more human—he even seems a bit frail. Close up, I notice that he wears a hearing aid. To my relief, the judge, though stern, is not unkind.

"I understand your feelings about these proceedings, Mrs. Puglisi, and I can only imagine how difficult it is for you," he says. "But I must warn you against emotional outbursts in the court. It cannot happen again. If it does, you will be removed."

"It won't happen again, Your Honor. I promise."

I have been scolded. I have learned my lesson. As Jim and I return to Courtroom 202, I mentally draw a drape over my feelings about all that has transpired here and all that may yet take place. I have waited too long not to see this through to the end, and I will behave.

WHEN JIM ROPP delivers his closing argument that morning, he does so with words that are deliberate and damning and blunt, and as he speaks I want to nod, say yes, say amen.

"This is a case," he says, "about the facts. This case is about cocaine use and lust. This case is about planned, purposeful, intentional criminal conduct."

Where Mark challenged the defense contention that Flagg is insane or so mentally ill that his thinking and actions were substantially disturbed during the crimes, Jim presents the defendant as not only guilty but crafty—a murderous man who is using a lie of insanity to justify his crimes and buy back his life. He quotes Flagg's letter to Janet Pagan, in which he asked, "What am I going to say when the finger gets pointed at me?"

"What do you think he's doing while he's sitting in jail?" Jim asks the jury. "He's running it through his head. 'What am I going to say? Alibi? Oops, that's not going to work—I already told police I did it. Let's see. Not enough evidence? No, that's not going to work. Somebody else did it? No, can't use that one—I already confessed.'

"What's left?" he asks. "Insanity."

If Donald Flagg did not know the difference between right and wrong, between innocence and guilt, Jim says, why did he act like a guilty man? Why did he engage in stealth and concealment? Why did he hide me, bind me, gag me? If, as the defense contends, he did not recognize the broad line between good and evil, why did he tell me he was sorry for killing Nino? Why did he tell Janet Pagan he had done something that he feared would land him in jail? Why did he talk about fleeing the country? "Does this show a person who does not understand the nature and consequences of his actions?" asks Jim.

He reviews Dr. Tavani's written report on Donald Flagg, in

which she wrote that her patient "demonstrated the cognizance of illegality." But once on the stand, says Jim, Dr. Tavani "backed off that. She kept using the term 'illicit.' But what does illicit mean? It means illegal. To support her conclusion, Dr. Tavani had to twist the legal standard in her definition of wrongfulness."

Also according to Tavani, Flagg harbored "grossly delusional" thoughts about me—I was less a hostage than a budding friend and lover. He indicated he was "having a real relationship" with me, he described our time together as "normal, everyday life, except she couldn't leave."

But these were not delusions at all, Jim insists; they were strategy, my strategy.

"Debra Puglisi was trying to save her life!" says Jim. "She *was* nice to him. She flattered him. She said things like, 'I see the good in you.' Why did she do that?" asks Jim. "Why would anybody? She had been bound, gagged, raped, and her husband had been shot. Isn't she going to want to try to keep the same fate from happening to her? This was *not* a delusion."

Jim gets it. He is making it easy for the jury to get it. God, I thank you for this day. My justice is here, it's happening in this moment. In this same moment I see the truth about myself: that I saved myself, that I was a hero to myself. It was so hard to accept at first, but it's true: I did this, and for all the asshole's manipulations and all the terror he visited on me and all the extraordinary luck he encountered in stealing me and keeping me hidden, I am the one who changed it all. I am the one who changed his luck, once and for all. I am at once proud and humble. God gave me this blessing—a seed of courage that bloomed to full flower in my hand the very instant I needed it—and now he is enabling me to appreciate it.

Now onto the mantra of the defense, the words of Janet Pagan and the most lyrical way I have ever heard to explain away murder. "Donald Flagg, you heard, is a 'bird with a broken wing,' " Jim says. "What's that mean? It means you have a helpless thing that can't defend itself. Was it a bird with a broken wing that shot Anthony Puglisi between the eyes and with a .38 caliber revolver?

Was it a bird with a broken wing that punched Debra Puglisi so hard she went down in a pool of her own blood? Is it a bird with a broken wing that dragged her down to her basement, dropped her on a concrete floor and raped her, tied her up, drove her to his house and repeatedly raped her over the next week? Is that a bird with a broken wing?"

Donald Flagg, says Jim, was hardly a bird with a broken wing, nor was he legally insane before, during, or after the crimes. Donald Flagg, says Jim, " gets into trouble only when he's using cocaine." He points out that Flagg's 1989 imprisonment of Rosetta Shepherd, the April 1998 rape of Patty Mann, and the subsequent crimes against Nino and me took place during binge states, when he was stoked-up on crack.

"If the illness is caused by the cocaine, then he's not entitled to the defense. He doesn't get the benefit of not guilty by reason of insanity or guilty but mentally ill."

Jim also takes on the testimony of Brian Northrop, which Brendan O'Neill denounced as self-serving and opportunistic. "Brian Northrop is no angel," Jim says. "He has a record, but what do you think, they have nuns in those cells?" But the facts remain: Northrop had information he could not have come by but through Donald Flagg, and he got no guarantee of leniency in his own case.

The defense claimed a paranoid, chronically isolated person like Donald Flagg would never have confided in a prisoner he had known for only a few weeks. But Northrop, Jim points out, knew many details that were never published in the papers. "He knew the nature and manner of the death of Anthony Puglisi. He knew details about Flagg's brother, where he worked. He knew about the premature ejaculation, the anal sex. . . . Do you believe these things were actually in the *News Journal?*"

Jim asks the jury to look at "the entirety of the defendant's acts and deeds. Basically, ladies and gentlemen, Donald Flagg talked about committing the perfect crime. The only question is, Did he feign mental illness?"

Finally, says Jim, the defense would have the jury believe that

Dr. Tavani is the truest observer of Flagg's character. She is the one who best understands him and his motivations. She sees behind his actions to the troubled man inside. But, Jim says, there is someone else who knows Donald Flagg far better than Carol Tavani or Janet Pagan. Someone who saw the defendant up close and unguarded, who learned through his own words and actions what he is made of and what he is capable of.

That person, says Jim, is Debra Puglisi.

With that, the state rests its case.

I BOUGHT THE SUIT at Macy's about three weeks before sentencing, and when I showed it around ("Do you like it? Don't you love it?") the reaction was less than enthusiastic.

"Well, it's nice and simple, good lines," said Jane.

"A good color for you," said Darlene.

"Debbie, it may not be quite the right thing to wear to sentencing," said Kathy Manlove.

"Well, everybody better get used to it, because I won't go there in black. In fact," I said, "I may never wear black again. I don't think I like black anymore."

When I meet Jim Ropp in court on May 11, I look to see if his eyes open wider than usual. They don't. But I must say, I look emphatic, like an exclamation point. I may be the only person here dressed all in red.

The jury foreman, I soon learn, is a thirty-one-year-old geologist from the small historic town of Odessa, Delaware. His name is Dave Caulfield. Of all the jurors, his is the face I have watched most often, I think because it was safest to watch. He was never overtly expressive, but he seemed skeptical when the defense rolled out its many and various pleas for sympathy. Whenever my gaze passed over the jury box, whenever I felt I simply had to look there, for affirmation or to try and gauge what they were thinking, I always looked to him, because somehow I felt certain that he cared.

Now it is Dave Caulfield's task to read the jury's verdict. He does so, repeating the same words for every count, beginning with first-degree felony murder and continuing eighteen times: "Guilty as charged." The first time, it feels like I've breathed in pure oxygen or helium; I am woozy. I can feel my head fall back, my shoulders push back—this is pure exaltation. Hands grab mine, I feel my family get close, gathering in.

Nino, we did it. Are you watching?

On the count of first-degree burglary: "Guilty as charged."

On the count of first-degree kidnapping: "Guilty as charged."

On the count of first-degree unlawful sexual penetration: "Guilty as charged."

It goes on and on, without deviation: "Guilty as charged," says the foreman. He cannot say it often enough for me.

I look to the left, to the defense table. Donald Flagg, convicted murderer, is still, emotionless. His defenders are impassive.

Then I look around me to see other faces. I see strangers who are glad for me and people I love who are dazed and smiling. Robert reaches into his breast pocket, pulls out a big cigar, and sticks it between his teeth. He glances sidewise at me, grins, and blows an imaginary smoke ring.

We exit the courthouse to a mob of news cameras and photographers and clamoring voices all shouting questions. But the gag order is still in place till after the penalty phase. Until then, I have no voice. But soon. Soon.

BETWEEN CONVICTION and penalty in a criminal trial comes a pause, an intermission, when the lawyers step back and allow others—the wrongdoer, and the wronged—to speak without fetters to the jury. First comes Donald Flagg, no longer defendant or accused or doer of alleged crimes. He is now a convicted killer, and though he chose not to speak on his own behalf during the trial, he may now rise up and say his final peace before the sentence is handed down.

Flagg stands. His voice is low and slow, not the explosive sound I remember. "I wrote something down here to try to explain some of what I did and to apologize for my actions and try to plead for my life, doing something that was pretty horrible. Here it goes."

Each word of his "apology" is an affront. At the front of the courtroom, eyes on the paper in his hand, he reads, stumbling over his words. He attempts to sound both penitent and pathetic. He is regretful at first for our sakes ("It was me who caused such sorrow to your family by an act of selfishness") then quickly veers into an account of his own misery ("I needed help but I was too proud to admit it"). He is wronged and wrongdoer, all at once. But he spends far more time talking about his own problems: his childhood with a mother who "stopped coping," the harassment he experienced at work.

"The life I knew as a free man will never come again, and the harm I caused can never be undone," he says. "I'd like to ask the ladies and gentlemen of the jury to please spare my life."

Then it is time for the families of the victim. Though Jim Ropp has implored Nino's relatives to speak out for their brother and son, they have refused; indeed, they have not come to court a single day. So it is up to Melissa, Nino's only daughter, to tell the jury the impact of the crime on her.

Melissa is not a public speaker; in school she was always terrified of giving presentations in class. This day she is nervous but determined. "Mom, I'm going to do this for Dad," she says, "for justice. I'm going to tell that man exactly what he took away from me." She ascends to the witness box, where she is poised and eloquent. Jim is there to guide her, asking her questions, but I know she could have done it on her own.

"In the past year without my father, I have experienced many different emotions; the one that is most prominent lately is a feeling of being cheated—cheated out of an adult relationship with my dad. My dad will not see me graduate. That was his big dream for me and my brother; all he worked for in life was to send his children to college. I've been cheated out of having my dad give me away on my wedding day. That was my own dream." She talks about her dad as a person and as a father; at one point, we look at each other and lock eyes for a moment till my image of her blurs around the edges. I have never been so proud of my daughter.

"For the rest of my life, for as long as I live, I will never know what my relationship with my dad could have been," says Melissa. "I will never be able to call him at the end of a long day and talk about work; I'll never be able to come home to visit and give him a big hug, because home is gone and so is Dad. And I can never have it back, because my dad, who I loved and who loved me, will never be here again."

Life stopped last April 20, abruptly. It was a Monday. Our life was shattered, and our plans, too, and any thinking and feeling about ordinary things. All of these things stopped, all have been in pieces this whole long while.

What now? I still believe Nino deserves the ultimate retribution, and I console myself by remembering that this is a death-qualified jury. During jury selection, they all pledged that they could recommend capital punishment if the crime warranted. They have already discounted Donald Flagg's insanity defense. I'm sure they will agree that the gravity of his crimes outweigh the mitigating circumstances: his childhood, his personal problems, his work problems.

But the jury does not make the final decision in this case; under Delaware law, the jury in a death penalty case can only recommend a sentence. Even though the judge must give that recommendation great weight, the ultimate decision rests with him. At the same time, no Delaware judge has ever overridden a jury's decision in favor of life imprisonment.

On Friday, May 14, back in Courtroom 202, we find out how the jury feels.

It goes quickly. The members of the jury file in shortly after 10 A.M. Their decision, written on a piece of paper, is handed to the judge, who unfolds it and looks down. Just before he opens his mouth to speak, I cast a quick look at the jury box. The foreman is shaking his head slowly from side to side, his lips pressed together in a thin line.

I think I gasp before I hear the words. Then I close my eyes, fast.

It's life. The jury has voted, seven to five, for life for Donald Flagg.

When I open my eyes, Flagg is smiling and shaking hands with Brendan O'Neill. O'Neill rolls his shoulders, flexes, punches air, like a fighter who has just emerged from the ring. My brother Robert sits bolt upright, fists on his knees, glaring straight ahead. Somewhere behind me I hear someone whisper, "Next time I kill someone, get me O'Neill."

For the defense, it is a qualified victory but a victory nonetheless. O'Neill acknowledges as much when he speaks to reporters outside the courthouse. He says he is "very gratified" by the "favorable sentence."

Jim is reconciled. "The jury is the conscience of the community," he says. "We accept their verdict."

Hugged on all sides by family, I trudge from the courthouse to the front steps, where a throng of reporters waits. Now, at long last, if I choose, I can speak. But there are no words adequate to the occasion. It is useless to express my disappointment, because it will not change any minds.

This must be how soldiers feel when they leave the battlefield. Sad and fatigued. Even if the jury had recommended death, it would still have been no cause for triumph. Suddenly, all I want is to go home. But the news people want a statement, and I suppose it's right that I do that much. I walk into the circle of their microphones. Dozens of camera shutters begin to snap and whir.

"I believe in the justice system," I begin, faltering. I don't want to cry. Behind me, slightly to my right, is my father; I feel his hand cup my elbow, and I shift some of my weight to him. Then I stand up a little straighter. "I know the jury struggled with this. Every day Donald Flagg spends in prison, he'll get his justice. I am a faithful person, and I believe God will be the judge."

AND NOW, with the gag order lifted, the jurors may speak as well, and I finally learn how some of them came to their decision. It seems Brendan O'Neill really did score a lot of points with his claim of insanity. Jackie Pilla, a pretty blonde who, I learn, is the reigning Miss Delaware, sums it up. Pilla—who also works with prisoners—is vocal in her concern for Flagg. "I actually felt a little sorry for Donald. I couldn't imagine how difficult it must be to know that in a few seconds he could be sentenced to death."

A newspaper account notes that some of the jurors criticized what they perceived as my "lack of emotion" during the trial.

So they wanted emotion after all. I struggled so mightily every day to contain my emotions, for many reasons—for the sake of my kids and because I did not want the killer to feel he had won; also because I was explicitly ordered to leave my emotions at home.

Sometimes it all lives deep inside. The horror, the misery, the fear, the sadness. The anger. The Spartan's fox.

All I wanted was to go to court strong, no longer a victim.

ON JUNE 11 FRIENDS and family members accompany me to the final sentencing by Judge Barron in a third-floor courtroom that is far more imposing than our little 202. Each of us wears a button depicting the Puglisi family as it once was: Nino and me and the kids, happy, arm in arm. Taken on our very last Christmas together, it's one of my favorite photographs, with Nino looking as if he is just about to laugh.

When Judge Barron enters the courtroom, we brace ourselves. Will he put aside the jury's recommendation?

He gazes out over the filled rows, nods almost imperceptibly in my direction, and begins.

"Debra Puglisi went though an indescribable ordeal," says Barron. "Words cannot convey the horror, debasement, and agony she suffered at the hands of Donald Flagg. Indeed, Donald Flagg personifies every woman's worst nightmare. Nothing can be more cruel than being made to sleep, side by side, next to the murderer of one's spouse.

"The subjugation to which Debra Puglisi was exposed for more than one hundred hours marks one of the most horrifying experiences ever recounted in my courtroom. The physical and mental scars that Debra Puglisi suffered as a result of the murder of her husband and her own captivity will remain with her for the rest of her life. She is to be admired for her courage, her strength, her will to survive, and her resolve to move forward for the sake of her children and her own well-being." He pauses then looks in Flagg's direction. When he resumes, his voice takes on an icy tone.

"Donald Flagg's crimes against Anthony and Debra Puglisi sent panic throughout our state. Fear gripped the citizens of Delaware, as well as the cities of surrounding states, all of whom came to realize that no one is truly safe, even at home. In my view, a crack addict's random rampage of murder and lust is no less heinous than the deeds of a cold-blooded assassin."

I stare up at the judge, but I don't see him. I only hear. His words are consummate fury. I am beginning to believe it—he is preparing to set aside the jury's recommendation. He is going to impose a death sentence. If he does, this whole room could erupt.

"No juror who sat on this case was opposed to the death penalty," says the judge. "Each juror swore that he or she could recommend a sentence of death if the facts and evidence so warranted."

The entire courtroom strains for the next word.

"Though Donald Flagg is a pathetic human being, the evidence showed that his early upbringing was by any standards abysmal. He was reared in an abusive and dysfunctional environment; his early years were chaotic and totally devoid of nurturing care and affection. Further, Flagg was and continues to be by the accounts of all medical experts who testified at trial mentally ill. . . ."

I slump back. He is going that way after all.

"I agree that his mental condition must be given due consideration in the sentencing equation. And Donald Flagg has shown remorse. . . ."

"For the murder of Anthony Puglisi, Donald Flagg shall

receive a life sentence without benefit of probation or parole or any other reduction," says Judge Barron.

The tension that's kept me upright in this seat all morning drains away, and I sag like a rag doll against my father. The judge continues to speak; I cannot comprehend more words. When I look back at the bench, I can see his lips moving, but there is a roar in my ears, like ocean waves, blotting out the sound. But Dad is nodding approvingly, and I strain to hear Barron go on to impose a total of eight life sentences plus 166 years. With his options limited by the jury, he has done all he can to insure that Flagg will never walk free. In a nod to me, he has also ordered that every year for the first ten years of his incarceration, Flagg will spend five days in solitary confinement. From April 20 through April 24.

"The life sentence which this court will now impose is, in a very real sense, a death sentence," he concludes. "It will simply take longer than the usual eight years to carry out. For those who fear that Donald Flagg will be released from incarceration at some point in the future, let me offer some reassurance.

"When Donald Flagg leaves prison, he will be in a prone position, lying in a wooden box, his arms folded across his chest."

WE EXIT TO the usual throng of reporters, some of whom now seem like friends. I make conciliatory noises: "I know the jury worked hard and acted according to their consciences. I accept their decision. I accept it."

Privately I believe that many people, perhaps some seated on this death-qualified jury, simply do not believe in the presence of evil in this world. For their own comfort they must explain it away with illness and childhood neglect. And as horrible as those things are, as much as I regret that people experience them, I have learned that they do not disqualify evil as a cause of murder.

Evil isn't always personified by a monster like Ted Bundy or Jeffrey Dahmer. Sometimes evil walks beside you on the street, works alongside you in the office, waves to you from the yard next door. To kill Nino and do it for no reason other than lust, convenience, and cowardice—I call that evil.

I don't think the majority of jurors in the trial of Donald Flagg saw it that way. Instead, they felt sorry for him. Yes, I accept it. I have no choice. But I do ask people to consider the existence of evil—self-serving, self-pitying evil.

As Robert pulls away from the curb, I watch in the rearview mirror as reporters pack up their cameras, tuck away their notebooks, and slowly disperse on to the next big story. At the corner, we turn left and head for the interstate on-ramp. Heading home.

Robert turns to me, nods. "So it's over."

"Yup."

"How you feeling?"

"Relieved, I guess. Maybe that's not the right word."

Relieved is what I think I should feel. Maybe later it'll hit me—the feeling of completion, a sense of justice won. But now I am vaguely dissatisfied. Yes, we did what we came here to do. The result was not as good as I had hoped, but if I try hard enough, I know I can make it be enough. Still, the word relief implies an end to the pain. There is none of that for me. I rest my head on the window and stare out at cars speeding by, at drivers distracted, pissed off, yammering on cell phones. My eyes wander up to billboards touting car dealerships, furniture warehouses, radio stations playing all the hits. Above them there is sky and fast-moving clouds and a lone bird banking, with wings spread against the wind.

"Now," says Robert, nodding, "you can just get on with your life."

I lift my head, smile sidewise at my brother. "That'll be good."

Dad leans from the back seat into the front and briskly rubs my shoulder. "Forget this past year," he says. "It's history."

"Yes. It's all over now."

A WEEK LATER, on June 18, in a small first-floor hearing room at the Herrmann Courthouse, Flagg pleads guilty to the rape of

Patricia Mann, this after a DNA test overwhelmingly indicated that he was the likely attacker. After that, his guilty plea is voluntary.

I sit behind Patty, reaching out from time to time to squeeze her shoulder. I reflect that if I had not been in my garden on April 20, Flagg would have moved on. I would have been spared, but he would have continued hunting until he found another woman, perhaps one as young and vulnerable as this one. Or he might have taken a teenager, just a few years younger than my Melissa.

Well, better it was me. I was tough enough—or got tough enough—to take it.

But I worry about Patty. She's damaged, maybe for keeps. The lessons Donald Flagg taught her about disillusionment and distrust could grow in her until she's unable to love freely, sleep easily, or walk the street without looking over her shoulder. He destroyed something in her, and she may never retrieve it.

This time, with no possibility of a death penalty and minimal media presence, Flagg has no apologies for his victim. When questioned, he is defiant, even angry.

Judge Barron hands down two additional life sentences plus forty-three years—an extraordinary penalty for rape and one that assures that even if the jury conviction is overturned, Flagg will never be released from prison.

Then, with barely controlled wrath, Barron sees fit to further explain his sentence in the first trial, for which I will always be grateful.

Had the jury not recommended life, he says, the outcome would have been far different. But, Barron adds, he knows that defying the jury would have resulted in years of appeals. A death sentence would most likely have been overturned in the end.

He notes that such appeals "take on a life of their own" and prevent victims from getting on with their lives. Ultimately, he concludes, it would have led to greater pain and disappointment for my family.

"But I will go to my grave," says Barron, gazing out at me

from the bench, "wondering if I made the right decision by following the jury's recommendation. It was without a doubt the most difficult decision I have ever made."

At these words, my composure is gone. I guess I could cry forever. But this time, only a handful of spectators—not hordes of photographers or a jury of Donald Flagg's peers—are there to see it.

Before the trial ended, Dr. Dancu warned me there might be a letdown ahead. "This trial has kept you very preoccupied, very busy, directed toward a specific goal for more than a year," she said. "When all this hullabaloo is over, you might not feel the sense of completion you expect."

As always, she knew. When Donald Flagg, in prison jumpsuit and shackles, is taken away for good, I wait for the flood of feeling, the sense of victory I have expected for so very long. It doesn't come. All I have is emptiness, a void where victory is supposed to be. It's like I was hungry and have eaten but remain unfilled.

I leave the courtroom and the courthouse and head for home.

21

THE DAYS SINCE the trial feel like years, unnaturally long, with stretches of hours I can't seem to fill. Busy work helped once, so I try again. Just like last summer, I'm the compulsive cleaner, vanquisher of cobwebs, a builder of tall piles of clean bath towels and blue jeans and underwear. When that's done, I make up new tasks to fill the day. Reread my condolence notes and sort and box them. Buy scrapbooks and fill them with family photos once stuffed in desk drawers or shoe boxes.

Through the photos I relive so many moments, special ones, ordinary ones—birthdays, holidays, vacations, and odd ones where I can't recall the occasion. The best ones are those with Nino and the kids. The best ones are the hardest.

When I'm finished with photos, I wonder, What's next? Keep busy. Keep moving and doing. Every lull brings thinking, and with thinking comes everything I can't stand to feel again, to feel still: fury and a bad case of the blues. With the trial done, there's no place to put that stuff anymore. With the trial done, the hours are endless and empty. I have to fill them with something besides the trial.

It's over. How can it be over? We haven't won anything.

Melissa feels it, too. One night not long after the sentencing hearing, she calls from East Carolina U. "Mom," she says, "I feel really crummy lately. The stupid trial is over. Aren't we supposed to be better now?"

I STILL SEE Dr. Dancu weekly or biweekly, and also Dr. Faude. The first time I see her after the trial, she says, "Up till now, Michael, Melissa, and you haven't really been able to feel the full impact of Nino's death. Now your grief can begin in earnest."

Not what I hoped to hear. We have grieved long and hard already and want no more of it. We want this thing called closure, the closure we expected after the funeral, after the trial, after conviction, and certainly after the sentencing. It's not happening like that.

Aren't we supposed to be better now?

The fight's over; the consensus is that we've won. Case closed.

It's over for everyone else. Nino Puglisi's murder has been avenged, in the courteous, civil fashion proscribed by our culture. But we—Michael, Melissa, and I—are still the losers.

During this past year real grief was respectful and remained at arm's length. Now it comes to envelop us. Before summer it will seem like the only thing we feel.

MELISSA CRASHES ALMOST immediately. The panic attacks that came on sporadically last year are back with a vengeance, so bad she's afraid she'll have a heart attack. Her doctor at school puts her on the antidepressant Zoloft, which should help—Michael takes it, too—but I guess Melissa's anxiety is beyond control. One night she calls, so late I think it's a hospice call. Barely above a whisper, she says, "Mom? I feel pretty strange."

"What's up, sweetie?"

"I feel scared again." She pauses, tries to compose herself. I hear long, hard gulps. "Mom, these panic attacks. I wake up, and half the time I can't breathe. I think I'm going crazy."

Oh, Jesus. And here I am, hundreds of miles away. Helpless to do much else, I act like a nurse. "Are you taking your meds?" I ask. "Do you think you might need to up the dosage?"

"Mom, I don't know. Yes, I'm taking my pills. I just want to come home." With that she lapses into sobs.

I talk loudly, to reach her through the tears. "Honey, now listen, you come home. Come home right now."

Within the week she's in Delaware, and at last I'm able to mother and care for her as I could not that awful first summer after Nino died. She needs to collapse. Let her. She has good reason. I comfort and cater to her, just as Dad did for me last summer. I surround her, maybe even more than she wants, and find it helps me feel less restless. One afternoon, in between soap operas, we curl up on the couch to talk about it.

"So how long has this been going on with you?"

"A little while. A few months, maybe, since just before the trial. I was afraid to tell you."

"For goodness' sake, Mel. Why in the world?"

"Because you've got your own stuff going on. I thought I was just partying too much. Then I stopped that, and it didn't go away." I watch her face, so pretty, so pale, and think of the killer.

See what you've done to my daughter, asshole?

"Well, Melissa, you stay here with me for a while. Relax." She doesn't quite. Before long, she's picked up a few classes at Delaware and a part-time job at the mall. That's okay. It seems to help her just to be home, close to Michael and me, talking. All these months she's relied on her boyfriend, Jeremy, to take care of her. He has, wonderfully. But Jeremy, in his final year at ECU, has school commitments that demand much of his time. Besides, I doubt if anyone outside the little circle of Michael, Mel, and me can fully appreciate how this crime has demolished us as a family and how hard it still is to put our pieces back together. It's good that she's home, if only for a while.

"Just don't try to keep it in," I tell her; these words are becoming my credo. "That never works."

Michael, too, is paying a steep physical price. It began before the trial, when he complained of a low-grade fever, runny nose, and other seemingly insignificant symptoms. None of us was concerned, because he was running better than ever. Relentless training had paid off, and in January, he was nearly unbeatable on the track, breaking records every time he ran. I caught a Saturday race and watched in awe as he skimmed past his competitors.

"Michael," I told him, "you're like a gazelle."

"Oh, Mom, not a gazelle," he said. "The world's swiftest animal is the cheetah."

In his first meet of the year he beat his best 3,000-meter record by a full ten seconds. Next time out, he ran his fastest 5,000-meter race, by twenty-two seconds. By midseason he was running almost effortlessly. "Dad would be loving this," he said.

He ran just one more great race. A day later he became dizzy and felt a strange heaviness in his limbs. His joints were hurting. He stopped by the house, flopped into a recliner, and threw his head back. "Jeez, I feel like I've been hit with a ton of bricks. What's going on?"

After a few days off, he was not replenished. His next race, he reported, was "a disaster." He took a week off but still didn't improve on the track.

"Michael," I said, gently, because I knew he would resist the idea, "maybe it's the stress of everything that's gone on this year. We've all endured so much. It's got to take a toll on your body."

He shook his head abruptly. "That makes no sense. I was doing fine up until now."

"But sometimes these things hit when you least expect it. You don't even connect it to what's behind it."

He looked at me, eyes narrowed. "Mom. I've been running great all along." Like his father, he was unlikely to concede that emotional trauma could upend his physical training. At that moment, he looked exactly like his father.

It will take months and many inconclusive tests before Michael is finally diagnosed with a so-called stealth virus called human parvovirus B19. It's a rare disorder that typically strikes people with compromised immunity, like HIV patients or those who have had organ transplants. Parvo causes severe anemia and according to one website poster "makes you feel like you're ninety-nine years old, overnight."

And overnight, parvo B19 puts an end to Michael's running career. "I'm not sleepy-tired," he says. "It's my body. It feels like it's made of boulders." He is unable to run and so exhausted he doesn't want to get out of bed. Mike and Steve, his roommates, start calling him "Grandpop." And at last Michael succumbs to depression. Running was his last, closest link to his father, whom he still calls his "greatest fan."

Michael will never make the link between sudden illness and the sudden death of his dad, and by now I know better than to force my view on him. He knows what I think.

Me, I have lots of somatic symptoms that were occasional before the crime and are now chronic. Headaches. Irritable bowel. A spastic colon and what I describe to my doctor, delicately, as very productive bouts of diarrhea. Lovely stuff. It's stress. Since the crime and especially the trial, Mylanta has become my cocktail of choice.

It no longer surprises me. We are all one thing, one being; mind and body and spirit. All are intertwined. Post-traumatic stress disorder affects all three points of that trinity, and for some, the body manifests what the mind refuses to acknowledge.

I'm hearing the same kinds of things from other crime victims. There's the woman who responded to stranger rape by gaining seventy pounds in six months. The woman who, beaten and robbed, went from social drinker to a daily half-pint of rum within a year. The abused wife who developed a peculiar condition called trichotillomania, in which stressed, depressed people literally start pulling out their hair, including eyelashes and pubic hair.

The body tells the story.

There's the thirty-year-old single mother who got crippling headaches after seeing her rapist for the first time at a preliminary hearing. She had never seen him during the attack, because he said if she looked at him, he would kill her. It was six months since the crime, and all that time, she had barely thought about the crime.

"I'd read about this so-called brutal rape in the papers, and I felt no emotional involvement in it," she told me. "I thought I was a pretty tough cookie. Then I saw him. Can you believe it? I did not cry about the crime until that instant."

Yet like many with PTSD, she did not make the connection between the events and her physical response—the headaches— until an ER doctor asked her if she was under undue stress.

"No," she replied. "Just this rape trial." At that moment, the lightbulb flickered on.

She and other victims have begun to find me. In grocery stores. On the street. In restaurants. They approach with their "me-too" stories, and I am astonished to learn how much we all share. It's like a fraternity or sorority—you wouldn't line up to join, but once a member, it really helps to meet others in the club. Most of us share the isolation and disillusionment that follows violent crime. Many of us have had our run-in with the criminal justice system, which can be a uniquely disillusioning experience. If they are still hurting I tell them, Look, it happened to me, too. I know how much it hurts and how furious you are and how scared and betrayed. I really get it. So do you have people to talk to?

What I hear most is some variation of this: "Well, it's been a couple of years now. Nobody wants to hear about it anymore."

SAME HERE. Even now, long after the crime, with the trial over and Flagg in jail forever, few people ask me what went on during those five days. I know they're curious, so I have to conclude that they avoid the subject out of respect for me. What they don't realize is that even years after a crime, many victims find it therapeutic to talk about the experience. As for me, if someone is willing to listen, I'll never shut up. It still helps me.

Take my high school reunion. Actually, it's just girls, about twenty of us from Burlington Township High's class of '69. We meet at an Italian restaurant in South Jersey, and we have a blast; we eat and laugh for hours, then five of us, including my best girlfriends from school, Connie and Deb, head back to our hotel for a pajama party. There things get so giddy that at one point, Deb actually flashes her boobs—she'd always been a little flat-chested, and she wants to show how much she's grown.

As we share our stories, I find that one of the women, Natalie, has not heard about what happened to me. She starts to question me pointedly, without reservation; I'm surprised until I find out she's married to a policeman. As I explain what happened, Deb starts to pace. Within minutes, she becomes very upset and through tears demands that Natalie stop questioning me.

"I wouldn't dream of asking things like that," she says hotly. The chatty mood is broken.

I appreciate Deb's concern and later talk to Natalie alone. But this avoidance is pervasive. People cannot stand to hear the details. What they don't understand is how much crime victims yearn to tell and tell again and tell yet again—to hear people get scared for them and mad for them and angry on their behalf. It helps so much, like balm on a wound. It heals.

When it happened to me and for a long time afterward, all I wanted was someone to say, as Bill said that day at Kid Shelleen's, "Tell me everything."

Then I could finally say the words out loud. Kidnapping. Rape. Murder.

SOMETIMES IT DOESN'T seem so long since that spring and the perfectly blue April day that went so wrong. Easter had just passed, the kids were on their way back to school, and Nino was preparing to put the boat in the water. I was complaining, as I did each spring, about being the neglected wife of a sailor. He reminded me, with pretend annoyance, that he was not a sailor but a seaman.

The bickering was routine. Truth to tell, though I enjoyed the occasional boat ride, I didn't mind being left behind. It was nice to have a little time just for me, to see friends, shop, laze around. It was better than battling mosquitoes and baiting hooks and sleeping in those cramped quarters below decks. I was too fond of plain comforts to love that life. And Nino was content to leave me on my own. As first mate, I'd never been very seaworthy, and he'd just as soon leave this landlubber ashore.

So I planned to stick around Academy Hill, hang some pictures that were still packed up, maybe read a good murder mystery. A few days earlier Gene had promised me a few new rose bushes, and I needed to find a good place to plant them, too.

Less than two years ago—not that long at all—this is what was going on.

Now I am out of the new home into one even newer. Nino, too. After all this time, he must be getting used to heaven.

I try to know for sure. I look for signs—something to tell me he is still near and with us and at peace. There are none yet, but every day I send out thoughts, like radio signals that may or may not be received. Maybe we are on different frequencies now. Or maybe it takes more time for messages to pass between heaven and earth.

The kids miss you, hon.

Don't ever worry about us.

Now, when everything about my life with Nino is retrospective, it's easy to wish I'd never stayed home on those Chesapeake weekends. Thinking it makes me feel like a liar, because I know that if Nino were still here, I still wouldn't go very much.

But I wish it still and tell him so.

Nino, I'd give years of my life to go with you, just once more.

How did time go by so fast?

I feel as if I live with a foot in two dimensions, past and present. Sometimes when I'm out shopping, I'll still toss a package of baloney in the cart for fried baloney. Other times I struggle to recall Nino as he was in life—a man, not a tragic figure, symbol, statistic, or victim. I don't want to deify him, but the temptation is irresistible. By airbrushing his memory, editing out all his miserable, cranky, unreasonable traits, I feel like I'm making up for the horrible way he died.

I do it until I catch myself. Bad enough that he's dead without me trying to turn him into a marble statue. He'd hate that. In my thoughts—my radio messages—I ask him to forgive me.

Love you, honey.

Honey, sometimes you could be a real pain in the ass. I'll remember that, too.

For the first time since that springtime of such loss, I can almost hear him laugh.

Epilogue

There's so much more embracing
Still to be done, and time is racing
—*Comden and Green*
"Some Other Time"

I DON'T KNOW who to ask for advice about the dress. What do you wear to your second wedding when your first husband is in the ground and the man who introduced you is about to take his place? There's no etiquette that applies, but I care only a little bit; I'll just go with what I like.

I have to match Bill, who's going very casual and islandy, in khaki shorts and a white open-neck shirt. I find it at an outlet store in Rehoboth Beach: a confection of a dress, pale and pink as the underside of a rose petal, with a fitted waist, tiny straps, and matching jacket. The instant I try it on—smiling and spinning in front of the dressing room mirror—I know it's perfect. Sleek, modest, but so pretty. I almost feel like a girl in this dress. But I'm glad I'm not. This time around, both bride and groom have lived full, sometimes difficult lives. We're old enough to know who we are and what we want in a mate; we've been leavened by time and, occasionally, by tragedy. We're still here, and we figure whatever life remains for us, let's spend it together.

The night before my wedding, Darlene and our friend Lori and I loll on the beach at Sixth Street in Ship Bottom, New Jersey, eating ice cream cones and staring at the evening sky, where a massive, orange-colored moon has lifted out of the horizon. For the longest time it hovers there, right above the ocean, as if it is too heavy to gain much altitude; and all around us, people stop midstroll to gape at this big smiling pumpkin of a moon.

"Just look at it."

"Look at all the people looking at it."

"It's so close. It's like you could reach up and grab on to it."

"So is it a harvest moon? A blue moon? A new moon? Just what kind of a moon is that?"

"It's a giant-size mother of a moon."

I lean back on the cool sand, wiggling my butt around so it makes a nice place to lie, and the three of us—me and my kid sister and our pal—giggle like girls and talk about boys: why we love them, why they make us nuts, why we get married to them. In an hour or so, the moon pushes higher, up and up, and turns from orange to sparkly diamond-white.

If I were not so eager for morning, this night would be a perfect place to linger. But tomorrow on this same beach, Bill Sharp and I will marry; tomorrow, I get to be a wife again. The world starts over, new and better and more cherished than ever before.

It took a long time for Michael and Melissa to accept Bill, longer still before they embraced him. But he has won their trust and affection at last, and we will take our vows happily, knowing they're happy for us.

The ice cream is done, and the moon has taken its usual place far up in the sky. We walk back to our car and drive away. Once in bed I take a long time to fall asleep, and when I do, it's lightly. A few times in the night, I wake up just to know how happy I am.

We're keeping it simple, with just our families. Though dear Judge Barron offered to marry us, we decided to do this in Jersey, so our friend Pastor Jeff, a Lutheran minister, will officiate.

The next morning, Bill—who was first and is now last—waits for me at the edge of the surf. As I walk down the beach to meet him, escorted by my father and son, I see rose petals, cascades of them, all red and pink, strewn across the sand.

I send a kiss up into the blue sky. From the moment I met him and for twenty-five years afterward, Nino Puglisi had my heart. I'll carry him there for the rest of my life.

But today I get to be a wife again, and I have a feeling it's okay with him.

Afterword

When evil functions to reveal good, it becomes good itself.
— *Buddhist principle*

APRIL CONTINUES to test me. I always hesitate before turning the calendar to April 20, the anniversary of Nino's death. The crime has left its remains. Like the marks on my body, the emotional scars have grown faint, but they will not disappear.

At the end of the trial, well-intentioned friends and family were quick to say, "Now you can just move on with your life." "Just forget about all those horrible things that happened." "It's over, Debbie, put it in the past." But it's never completely over, and each and every one of us carries our past into the present and future; I will continue to be a crime victim as long as I live. But I made the decision long ago to find the benefit in this, the gold in the straw, the lesson that's worth the pain. I decided, too, that if I could not find it, I would create it. It has become my mission to help other crime victims, to share with them all I've learned about trauma, survival, and putting together the pieces of my life.

To that end, I talk about it to anyone who will listen—as a national speaker, in classrooms, and now as the author of this book. In the past year I've become a consultant for The ETC Group (ethics, training, community), an organization that educates the array of professionals who serve victims of violence, including law enforcement and health professionals.

In April of 2000 I was invited to be the keynote speaker at the thirteenth annual Crime Victims' Rights Week seminar in Atlantic City. I later learned from the Victim Witness Coordinator that more than 450 crime victims, social service providers, and law enforcement personnel "sat in stunned silence as they listened to the 911 call and your speech. . . . The audience hung on your every word, awed by your strength and composure, with many moved to tears."

It was then that I decided to continue my speaking. I have spoken many times before the Middle Atlantic–Great Lakes Organized Crime Law Enforcement Network (MAGLOCLEN) whose training law enforcement coordinator, James Boylan Jr., contacted me in the fall of 2000 after hearing about my first speech at its third annual Sex Crimes Conference in Egg Harbor, New Jersey.

Since then I've taken my story all over the country, to Chicago, New York, Seattle, Houston, talking about the pain, anger, grief, and despair that is the legacy of violent crime.

I was invited back as a guest to the Victims' Rights Seminar in Atlantic City, where I was privileged to meet the keynote speaker, Darryl Scott, whose beautiful young daughter, Rachel, was murdered at Columbine High School on April 20, 1999. When I approached Darryl, saying, "That's a hard day for me, too," we bonded at once. This is a community, and it's growing. On September 11, 2001, America became a nation of survivors.

How tragic to see how many are still traumatized years later. For them, the experience is certainly not "over," it cannot be "put behind them." What will happen to them, the women, men, and children who haven't had appropriate counseling, who have no one to listen, understand, and reassure? This is not a minor problem: 30 million Americans become victims of violent crime every year. If we as a nation disregard or undertreat them, we risk the health, happiness, and productivity of a significant segment of our society.

The first thing I tell these groups and individuals is that it's vital to understand, anticipate, and treat post-traumatic stress disorder. Trauma is sometimes slow to begin (this is shock); it can wear a cloak of normalcy and adjustment for months or sometimes years. It is even slower to recede; PTSD needs confronting and counseling, because its effects are far-reaching and long-standing.

Here's an example from my own life. It was October 2000. All in all, I felt wonderful: happily remarried and excited at the prospect of decorating my new house with Bill, just a few miles from that other dream house in Academy Hill. Our life was beautiful now.

One sunny day Bill was out, and I was busy around the house. Later I ran out for groceries then came back, walked into the garage, and entered the house from the laundry room. Because my senses are much more acute these days—my awareness is almost annoying—when I passed the powder room, I saw the toilet seat was up. Now I knew my Bill hadn't left it that way; he just doesn't do that. Though I tried to shrug it off, the fear was there, fast as fingers snapping: "Oh, no. Oh, my God. Not again."

When I walked back to the car and saw our cat, Bandit, stretching out in the driveway, I froze. We never let our cats out; we were especially careful then because of all the construction going on in our new neighborhood.

I grabbed Bandit, pushed him and the groceries inside the front door, slammed it, and ran into the street, where I stood at the curb, staring at the house and shaking. I noticed a neighbor three doors down. I ran to him. "Please help me," I said. "I think there's somebody in my house."

He saw my panic; he was instantly concerned. "Okay, okay, Debbie. Let me go in and check it out for you."

"No!" I clutched at his shirtsleeve. "Oh, God, no. Please, can't we call 911?"

As it turned out—after the police were summoned and multiple phone calls were made—the incident was easily explained.

Our electrician had done some work inside that morning; he had left the seat up. Later, very apologetically, he said he must have let the cat out when he left for his next job. For me the episode was so troubling that I had to return to Xanax for a time. And to this day Bill has to announce himself whenever he comes home. Otherwise, I'd freak out every time the front door opened.

Other triggers are likely to set me off. Bill has learned never to use the words, "Let's do this." Those were the words of the killer just before he raped me for the first time. I cannot hear them without feeling a physical sensation of illness, of revulsion. And in bed, I cannot bear it if Bill wraps his arm around my chest. As safe as I feel with my husband, that gesture—the killer's—is unendurable to me.

It does not end there. It took more than two years before I could pick up a good murder mystery, once a bedside staple. I still can't watch movies or television shows with violence. And the casual use of violent imagery in language still unnerves me. For example, I cannot hear people say things like "I could shoot you for saying that" or "I would kill for that dress." (Ironically, I'll say things like "I'm tied up at the moment" without blinking. No wonder people look at me like I'm deranged. How could I, of all people, say such a thing? I don't really know.)

I tell my audiences, "Find the triggers, watch out for them. Respect the victim's ongoing fear. And for goodness' sake, let them talk about it as long as they need to. Please. Let them talk till they're done."

When I speak to victims, I advise them to work hard every day at getting better. I tell them that it takes as long as it takes, that they cannot rush to the end of grief or to the acceptance of what has happened to them.

I tell them they will grieve until they stop, that they will become functional a lot faster than they will become happy. And if they have lost a loved one to crime, they may feel bad on the day they start to feel happy—as if being happy is a betrayal of their loved one. This is uncomfortable and painful but also very normal. Most of all, I urge them to learn about PTSD, so they can understand what's going on inside. It's such slow going. They'll visit all the textbook "stages," but these are not graved in stone; they may linger in one stage indefinitely and revisit others from time to time. Again, normal.

But for most victims, the aftermath still remains a mystery. PTSD is routinely diagnosed but seldom treated adequately. We must make it our goal on local, state and federal levels to save these damaged lives, for their sakes and for our own.

I consider myself an exceptional survivor, thanks to Dr. Dancu. But I knew—because she warned me—that my journey to wholeness did not end with the trial. Nor was I immune thereafter to hard times. That proved true very quickly. Last year Bill was diagnosed with colon cancer.

Like Nino, Bill was always afraid of dying young. He had partied hard and hearty for years. He had never taken care of himself. He was overweight. Now, cancer. We were devastated. My husband—the big, tough, gutsy guy, whose broad shoulder was my pillow—was scared, far more than he let on. More than anything, he told friends, he was afraid of making me a widow again.

My first thought: Dr. Dancu. Call Dr. Dancu. She had been my stronghold, my sounding board for so long; my reliance on her had become like an umbilical cord, and my unstinting trust in her had deepened into a deep, essential, almost mother-child relationship. But this time I could not call her. Several months before, she had informed me that she was ill and would be taking a five-month leave of absence.

Dr. Dancu, too, had cancer. She told me she'd see me in the fall, but it never happened. She failed rapidly. With her husband's permission, I visited her at home (thankfully, she was in hospice care), but by now she was unconscious. I stood at her bedside and told her how much I cared for her. I told her she had changed my life and the lives of so many in the community. I told her that thanks to her, I would be okay. She had given me the tools to move on with my life, to battle the terrors that would certainly arise from time to time. I held her hand and felt her life slip slowly away. I would never see her again. Dr. Constance

Dancu. She was my teacher, my friend, my heroine—a remarkable woman who had lived her life with grace, professionalism, and compassion and helped me save my own life.

Eight days before Bill's surgery, Dr. Dancu died.

Though it seems insignificant by comparison, I was deeply dismayed by another death: my darling Fish, whom I often called the only witness to the murder, because his tank had been in the dining room at Academy Hill that April morning. Fishie had been listless for a few days. Then one morning I found him at the bottom of his tank, with big sad eyes. I sat down, stroking the side of the glass so he could see I was there. Hours later, he was gone. The depth of my sorrow surprised me; I cried buckets. Then Bill and I fashioned a coffin from an empty check box lined with foil and tissue and buried Fish near the house. I miss him still and never run the lawn mower over his grave without feeling vaguely guilt-stricken.

But thank God, Bill did well after surgery. Though biopsies showed two positive lymph nodes, the cancer had not metastasized. With characteristic humor and unquenchable spirit, Bill completed a course of chemotherapy and today is in remission. The frightening interlude only bolstered our resolve to live every day to the utmost. Many times during his treatment, Bill thanked me for being in his life, saying, "I don't know if I could have faced it without someone to love and live for." It made me glad we had not waited to marry. We make it a point each day to thank each other—and to thank God, who brought us together.

As for Michael and Melissa—well, those kids (kids no more) are my heroes. They have not allowed the loss of their father to destroy them; instead, they've barely broken stride. And they have done this despite their suffering and in spite of major setbacks. They have done their father—and mother—proud.

Our daughter graduated from East Carolina University in Greenville, North Carolina, in December 2000. She lives with Jeremy in Virginia, where they will be married in October 2003. Our son graduated from the University of Delaware in May 2000 then attended Virginia Tech in Blacksburg on a teaching assistantship. He graduated in May 2002 with a master's in sports nutrition.

Michael is still the stalwart one; that's his nature. His mourning for Nino continues but quietly. Still waters. Melissa's emotions are right where they have always been—on her sleeve. Like me, she fears losing others she loves; she can't say good-bye to Jeremy without clinging to him and begging him to be careful. She is still in counseling, and I pray that in time she'll resolve her fears.

All in all, my family has never been stronger. I'd never recommend our experience as a way to grow, but some blessings come in very deep disguise. Because of what happened, we've learned hard, vital lessons about time and togetherness and the ephemeral nature of it all. Our blessing is the little piece of knowledge that most only know in theory, the knowledge that time and people really do pass. Because we know it, we celebrate life, even its setbacks. We do it together. We do it today.

I guess we're fortunate, in a backhanded sort of way.